TRIUMPHS & TURBULENCE

TRIUMPHS & TURBULENCE

MY AUTOBIOGRAPHY

Chris Boardman

EBURY
PRESS

1 3 5 7 9 10 8 6 4 2

Ebury Press, an imprint of Ebury Publishing
20 Vauxhall Bridge Road
London SW1V 2SA

Ebury Press is part of the Penguin Random House group of companies whose
addresses can be found at global.penguinrandomhouse.com

Penguin
Random House
UK

First published by Ebury Press in 2016

www.eburypublishing.co.uk

A CIP catalogue record for this book is available from the British Library

ISBN 9780091951757 (hardback)
ISBN 9781785031120 (trade paperback)

Typeset in India by Thomson Digital Pvt Ltd, Noida, Delhi
Printed and bound in Great Britain by Clays Ltd, St Ives PLC

For Sally

This is our book, not mine.
But you know that: you wrote as much of it as I did.
With love.

Contents

Prologue: Coming Up for Air

I was in a chamber the size of a cathedral, filled floor to ceiling with the most awe-inspiring natural architecture. Stalactites and stalagmites grew everywhere: some ten metres tall and thicker than a man's torso; others no broader than my little finger and ready to snap at the slightest touch. Flowstone ran down the walls and between these structures like melted chocolate, disappearing into the fine white powder that covered the floor. All this ornate and delicate grandeur had stood silently in the darkness for tens of thousands of years, undiscovered until recently.

It was the most spectacular place I had ever seen and I was probably one of a handful of people on the planet to have seen it; this wasn't the easiest location in the world to visit. I glided between two of the huge columns, careful not to brush them. As I did, my feelings of wonder and privilege suddenly gave way to a more basic concern.

How much air did I have left?

I was about a kilometre from the exit of a flooded cave 30 metres beneath the scrub jungle of the Yucatan Peninsula in Mexico. I could simply have checked my pressure gauge to see what was left in the tank, but my third and final torch had just given out. My dive partner and I were now floating motionless in the most exquisite blackness.

Zdene wasn't having a good day either. All three of his lights had also gone and he had already run out of air. He was now attached to me in the pitch dark via my spare regulator hose, noisily sucking up my precious reserves. Luckily, I still had my hand on the guideline. This 4 mm thick nylon thread was the only physical connection between us and the exit.

Six torch failures, two valves blown and one catastrophic loss of an air supply between us in less than 20 minutes: if I hadn't had a big lump of plastic in my mouth I would have let out a long sigh. Instead, I groped around for Zdene's hand, placed it on the line in front of mine, oriented his thumb towards what I hoped was our way out and gave his arm two strong pushes – the universal signal amongst cave divers for 'Let's get the fuck out of here'.

If we died before making it back to the beautiful Cenote Eden, the sink hole where this dive had started nearly two hours earlier, it would be the fourth time that day, so I was determined we were going to surface alive.

We swam blindly, with the thumb and forefinger of our left hands forming an 'O' shape around the slender line. Every few minutes our gloves would strike the rocks and stumps of old stalag-mites where the guideline had been secured. In the darkness all of these junctions had to be negotiated with delicacy and precision to ensure that we didn't dislodge the line, lose contact with it, or inadvertently turn off the route to safety and into a side passage.

After 30 minutes of silent effort, the inky blackness turned to deepest blue and finally the pale green of Cenote Eden. The emergency training drill was over: we were both still theoretically and actually alive. I hung motionless in the shallows, allowing the excess nitrogen time to slowly seep out of my blood and body tissues. I felt relieved, relaxed, at peace. At the age of 39 I'd found my element: water. But I'd had to cut through a lot of air to reach it.

CHAPTER 1
The Wirral

Stranded between the Dee Estuary and the Mersey, the Wirral peninsula struggles a bit for an identity of its own. The posher part believes it is Cheshire's long-lost cousin, while the northern fringe would desperately like to be recognised as an annex of Liverpool – so much so that the inhabitants have been christened 'plastic Scousers' by the true Liverpudlians.

I grew up in the village of Hoylake, in a quiet cul-de-sac where kids played outside and dads worked on their cars. If people know Hoylake at all it's probably for the Royal Liverpool Golf Club, one of the best links courses in the country. I couldn't have cared less about golf, the focal point of my childhood was Hoylake's other distinguishing feature – its huge, open-air, seawater swimming pool.

My obsession with water predates my memory of it. Long before I could swim I was perfectly comfortable being in water way over my head. My strategy was to stay below the surface and bounce up off the bottom when I needed to breathe. I was addicted to Jacques Cousteau programmes on TV. I wore my first pair of flippers to bed. My birthday present every year was a season ticket to the pool and throughout the summer months, no matter what the weather, I'd be there. When it was freezing and the place was deserted I'd be the lone figure diving under the springboards to look for change on the bottom, where it invariably fell from people's pockets as they bounced up and down. I'd then run across the cold stone floor to the coin-operated showers and use my prize to warm up. I loved it. I wasn't a complicated lad.

And if I wasn't in the baths then I was in the sea, usually in my canoe, surfing in on the waves and enjoying the freedom of an unsupervised 1970s childhood.

On land, family life revolved around my parents' great love: bike racing. On Thursday nights we'd go to Huntington, just outside Chester, where my dad would ride a ten-mile club time trial. Afterwards we'd head to the pub next to the start area, The Rake and Pikel, and there'd usually be chips eaten by the River Dee on the way home.

At weekends we'd be woken at 5 a.m. and crammed full of toast before piling into the hand-painted family Mini Van to head off for an early morning race, my dad's bike strapped to the roof. Afterwards, I'd hang around the kerbside results board and listen proudly for people talking about him and how well he'd done.

Keith Boardman – quiet, unassuming, sardonic sense of humour – had been long-listed for the Great Britain cycling team to go to the Tokyo Olympics in 1964, four years before I was born, but for reasons we've never discussed he decided not to pursue a sporting career. He settled down to life as a Post Office engineer and kept cycling as his pastime. I think perhaps my dad knew just how much pressure he could cope with and that was the moment he chose his path. When I was in the final ride for Olympic gold in Barcelona, he couldn't bear to watch the race; he lay in the bath with a cup of tea and waited to hear the outcome second-hand. I don't think going out to Spain and watching the event in person would ever have crossed his mind.

His talents extended to more than just riding a bike quickly. I don't recall ever seeing a tradesman of any kind in either of the two houses we lived in while I was growing up: painting, plumbing, electrics, shed-building, car maintenance, my dad did it all and usually very successfully with not much more than mole-grips, a hammer and some black plastic tape. If our house had been powered by a nuclear reactor I suspect he'd have donned some oven gloves and got stuck in. On my seventh birthday he presented me with a homemade miniature scuba set: he had fashioned the tanks from a pair of plastic GPO cylinder-shaped cable junctions and some plumber's copper pipe. I was ecstatic and spent many happy hours walking around our cul-de-sac wearing them.

Even well into my twenties, whenever I got stuck with a piece of cycle mechanics or electrical wiring in the house, I'd call Keith, who would always find a way to fix the problem, no matter what it was, using only materials within a two-metre radius of his position. It was a dark day when he retired from the Post Office and his ready supply of PVC tape dried up. He still has the mole-grips.

Even now, having spent most of my adult life around athletes, I can honestly say that my mother, Carol Boardman, is the most ferociously competitive person I have ever met. A cook at a local nursing home, she has always been full of energy, which is fortunate because she is a stealth combatant: one of those individuals who can quietly turn *anything* into a contest. Like my father, she had been a racing cyclist of some promise, finishing just behind the legendary Beryl Burton on one occasion at an event in the Isle of Man. When my sister Lisa and I came along, the demands of racing and home life became too difficult to juggle so she retired, but that didn't stop her trying to get her fix in other ways.

On the ten-minute walk to my Nan's my mother would often force us to skip – it didn't feel as strange then as it sounds now – which inevitably turned into a dog-eat-dog contest: a woman and two children frantically speed-skipping along a suburban pavement with a blue garden gate as the winning post. God knows what it looked like to people driving past. Later, I would sometimes find myself cycling the last few miles home from a club ride in a group with her. It's standard practice for cyclists to take it in turns at the front, pushing through the air while the others sit behind in relative shelter until their turn comes. One Sunday afternoon, as I led our small bunch into the outskirts of Hoylake, I spotted in the corner of my eye a fast-moving dark shape. It was Carol launching a surprise attack, sprinting for the village sign.

Many of my childhood memories involve my mother and the outdoors, walking out over Hoylake sandbank, swimming in the deep gullies, or hunting for fossils on Llandegla Moor in North Wales after a bike race while my dad had his nap. The highlight of the summer holidays was our trip to Yorkshire for the Harrogate cycling festival. We didn't have a lot of money and I don't think hotels or holidays abroad were ever an option. It might only have been the other side of the Pennines but it felt like a magical foreign land.

Each year we'd arrive at The Lido campsite in Knaresborough, unfold the wings of our trailer-tent and that would be our home for the next two glorious weeks. Our parents slept in one wing while Lisa and I had the other, but I preferred to sleep underneath, with the trailer's tarpaulin as a groundsheet and a dinghy for a bed. I can still remember waking to the blue light filtering through the canvas, the smell of the grass and the sounds of sheep and distant birds. Dad would ride his various races while we battered around the park barefoot with the other cyclists' kids, climbing the rocks around the River Nidd and daring each other to jump off cliffs into the brown water. Once we got hold of a life raft and sailed it over a weir. It was a wonderful time, a working-class *Swallows and Amazons*.

Up until the age of eleven, I didn't care what bikes looked like. They were strictly for entertainment and transport, vehicles to tear round childhood on. Then shiny BMX machines began arriving in the shops from America and suddenly bikes became cool, covetable objects in their own right. In the run-up to Christmas 1979 I hinted shamelessly, leaving the mail-order catalogue open on the kitchen table at the appropriate page. My parents, though, wanted me to have the same experiences growing up as they'd had with their friends, and on Christmas morning I ran down to the front room to find a second-hand blue Carlton racer. I was secretly gutted. Or perhaps not so secretly, because 12 months later they bought me a bright red Raleigh with yellow mag-alloy wheels. The Carlton was instantly consigned to the shed and I spent Christmas Day 1980 riding my BMX in the road for two or three minutes at a time before coming back in and cleaning it for an hour. It was my pride and joy.

Water, though, still exerted the stronger pull, and if I needed any kind of push there was Uncle Dave. Dave Lindfield, my mum's younger brother, was everything an uncle is supposed to be: mischievous, childlike, not wholly responsible. Dave and his wife Mo didn't have children of their own then, so Lisa and I often got spoiled by them. When I was ten he bought me the most heavily used item of my childhood, a tiny wetsuit. Encased in neoprene, I could belly flop off the springboards of Hoylake pool with complete impunity.

In 1981, for my 13th birthday, he arranged for me to have an introductory session with the local sub-aqua club, who were on the lookout for new members. It was the most amazing thing I had ever experienced, BREATHING UNDER WATER! I was so smitten that even though the club wouldn't actually train me to dive because of my age, I persuaded my mum and dad to enrol me anyway. So on Thursday nights my mother would take me to Neston pool, where she sat patiently while the instructors did their best to tolerate me. After several weeks of doing the same thing, holding my breath a lot, the novelty began to wear off. I still loved water – being in it and under it – but I was frustrated at not being allowed to go further.

My mother was frustrated too, not that she ever said so, as Thursday was supposed to be Huntington night – time trial, pub and chips by the River Dee night.

*

'Five, four, three, two, one, go. Good luck!'

It was a warm, dry evening with a light breeze blowing when I got my first ever countdown. I'd heard the starter recite his mantra many times before, but never directed at me. During that summer of 1981 I'd begun pestering my parents to let me have a go in one of the Thursday night club races. They were the scene of many people's first competitive experience and it wasn't unusual to see entrants turn up to take the start in cut-off jeans or football shorts.

Mum and Dad were reluctant to give their consent, for a number of very good reasons. I'd already disrupted the rhythm of family life by insisting Mum take me to the pool on Thursdays instead of going to watch Dad race. And I'd already rejected the racing bike they'd bought me. Now, I was proposing to give up the lessons they'd paid for, along with the flashy BMX, and take up time trialling. They saw it as yet another fad and they were right. I was curious, no more than that, and just fancied having a go at a race. Eventually, perhaps because it was an activity they could relate to better than my desire to swim about underwater, they relented. The neglected Carlton was retrieved from the shed.

I charged off down the road like my life depended on it, with no idea about anything as sophisticated as 'pace judgement'. The next ten miles was a series of all-out charges followed by grinding to a near halt as I sucked in air through every orifice in my body, trying to recover. As soon as the nasty burning feeling in my lungs subsided, I repeated the process. This vicious cycle went on for 29 minutes and 43 seconds.

The beauty of the event was that despite posting one of the slowest times of the evening, I wasn't obliged to compare my performance with anyone else's – that time was mine. So I chose what for me was a new way of thinking, to forget everyone else and have a competition with myself. I wanted to see if I could better my mark. The following week I lined up again with a new strategy. It was called 'Don't start a ten-mile race with a sprint' and the result was a time more than a minute faster than I'd managed in my first go. It was a satisfying experience, to have taken my own ideas, tested them and got a positive outcome. It didn't escape my notice, either, that there were now several names below mine on the piece of A4 paper taped to the lamp post by the finish line. I wanted to do it again.

One of the regular timekeepers back then was an elderly man called Alf Jones. Late that summer, at one of the final events of the season, Alf presented me with a challenge as I lined up for the start. It was a light-hearted, spur-of-the-moment offer that would change my life: 'I'll give you 50 pence if you can keep Dave Lloyd from catching you until Aldford Bridge.' Dave Lloyd was an Olympian and had been an accomplished professional, riding for Raleigh on the continent. He'd also won more national time trial champion-ships than I could count. Since he lived on the Wirral himself, he'd turned up at the race for a bit of training and was scheduled to set off one minute behind me. Aldford Bridge was the midpoint of the outward leg, some two and a half miles away.

It was the first time I'd ever had a specific goal that I truly considered to be achievable: a win/lose proposition in which I had a decent chance of winning. I started strongly, pushing hard down the twisting B5130 towards Aldford and the prize. After a mile it started to hurt more than it should. I'd gone off too fast. As the road climbed I knew my destination would soon be in sight and chanced a look back: Dave Lloyd was bearing down on me; it was going to be close. I let go of all thoughts of a ten-mile race, mine had just a thousand yards left to run. As the road narrowed and gently dragged up towards the curve of the bridge, I could hear the swooshing of his tyres on the road behind me. With less than a hundred yards remaining he swept past, leaned hard into the bend and pulled away into the distance.

Having overextended myself, I struggled through the next seven miles and went slower than I had for some weeks. But what I encountered that night, triggered by that personal challenge, was unlike anything I'd experienced before. I had been scared of losing but I'd also been excited at the prospect of success. Alf Jones and his 50 pence – he still gave it to me – had started something rolling.

CHAPTER 2
Births, Marriages and Deaths

Of the three routes to adolescent popularity available at my secondary school – football, fighting and success with the opposite sex – I excelled at none.

I definitely liked the idea of getting a girlfriend, but on the rare occasions when I managed to snag one I had no idea what to do with them. Short of money and imagination, a date with me consisted of wandering around aimlessly and a series of stilted conversations: Kim Smith and Lorraine Evans, I can only apologise. Steve Carney and Neil McDonald were the Casanovas in my circle, although saying that I had a circle is overstating things a bit. I'd often tag along with them to the house parties that some parents were reckless enough to let their teenagers hold. I'd sip my contraband cider in the corner, listen to Ultravox and then make my way home.

On the sporting front, I had absolutely no talent for or interest in football, which got me labelled as dysfunctional by my peers at Hilbre High. The same went for most other school sports. As far back as I could remember, I'd never won so much as a single ribbon in the sack race. As for fighting, there were various gangs in our school, but I didn't belong to any of them. When beatings were being handed out I'd usually be on the receiving end, so I became very good at spotting trouble developing and removing myself from the vicinity.

I didn't do any better in class than I did in the playground: I was totally uninterested in almost everything. I think it was an attitude rooted at least partly in self-defence, a reaction to my undiagnosed dyslexia. The word didn't seem to exist in the seventies and eighties, at least not in the world I was growing up in. People who couldn't spell or write neatly were simply labelled as slow. My condition wasn't extreme but it did make expressing my thoughts in written form painful, so I avoided it, as I tried to avoid school in general. For me it was a place that generated and then reinforced low self-esteem.

I wasn't the only one struggling through secondary school. In the same year at Hilbre was another lad who didn't fit in, who seemed like me to be doing his time until he could get parole. Flouncy is the first word that springs to mind when I think of him as he was back then. I'd see him every now and again during the summer, striding bare-chested and alone along the Hoylake promenade. If you'd transposed him from that seaside setting onto a catwalk he wouldn't have looked at all out of place.

At school he seemed to be in every theatrical production. Regardless of whether or not he had the lead role, he was three times as loud and animated as every other cast member. At the time it was painfully embarrassing to watch, but on reflection the reason he stood out was because he was the only one really acting, like a peacock in the middle of a flock of flea-bitten pigeons.

Standing out at our school made you one of two things, a leader or a target. He wasn't a leader. Still, I like to think that his character-forming experiences at Hilbre High were what helped Daniel Craig develop that marvellous pout.

For me, only two subjects relieved the tedium of the school timetable: woodwork and sociology. The former is an interest I hold to this day and it was pretty typical of my group, but sociology was perhaps a less obvious favourite for a boy in his teens. It was the beginning of another lifelong interest: human psychology.

I can't say I remember my time at school with fondness or made friends that I've kept in touch with. I couldn't wait for it to be over and once it was I never looked back. I didn't even go in to pick up my mediocre exam results.

Built just outside Liverpool in the 1960s while Britain was having its love affair with concrete, Kirkby Stadium was a tatty, well-used establishment. Habitually windy, spitting with rain and five degrees colder than its surroundings, it seemed to have its own microclimate. With its peeling paint and broken fencing it might not have looked like a world-class facility, but without it I would never have been an Olympic champion. It was there, in the spring of 1984, that I was first introduced to track racing.

Having started out in my dad's cycling club, the Birkenhead Victoria CC, I had now jumped ship and joined my mum's. The North Wirral Velo had a growing contingent of members my age and as I found myself spending more time both riding and racing with them, it seemed like the logical move. One of their regular activities was track racing, over the Mersey in Kirkby, and I was encouraged to have a go. I needed a fixed-wheel bike for that and mine was a Keith Boardman special. On a visit to the local tip, my dad spotted an old frame in a skip, took it home, sprayed it Kingfisher blue and built it up.

It was a typically chilly Kirkby evening when I lined up to ride it in my first track race, a handicap event. The riders – all ages and genders – were spaced around the bumpy asphalt circuit according to their ability, as defined by John Mallinson, one of the track league's regular organisers. Each person was to be pushed off by a helper when the whistle blew. My helper was more help than most: Bob Memery was a keen cyclist and family friend. He was also the winner of five British weightlifting titles in the 13-stone class and still incredibly muscular in middle age. He was in high demand as a pusher-off.

When the whistle blew Bob launched me down the straight like an Exocet and it was a good half a lap before I even had to pedal. Thanks to Bob's overdeveloped right arm and John's generous handicap, I won my first ever race on the cracked surface of the Kirkby track. All through that summer and well into the autumn Wednesday night became firmly established as track night.

As is often the case with grassroots events, it was only made possible because of the commitment of a group of characters who, without knowing or seeking recognition for it, became a small but important part of many people's lives. John and Doreen Mallinson did everything from setting the race programme to pushing riders off. Doreen – always called Alf for reasons I never discovered – handed out numbers, smiles and encouragement to everyone. Chief adjudicator was commissaire 'Ginger' Hewitt, working from a set of rules known only to himself: he frowned a lot and sometimes lost his temper, but every week there he was, doing his bit to keep it all going.

On the coaching side – whether people wanted it or not – was Fag-Ash Bert, often seen crouching beside the track making pedalling motions with his fingers to the riders as they sped past. No one had the nerve to ask him why he did it so we never found out what wisdom he was trying to impart. John Geddis, an Olympic medallist himself at the 1956 Games in Melbourne, was always in charge of the PA and took the time to learn all the riders' names, especially the young ones, for his colourful and terribly partisan commentary.

Just a handful of individuals presiding over a low-key activity on the outskirts of Liverpool, helping people take their first steps in the sport. What they didn't realise was that they were the true pioneers of the Olympic success to come, quietly preparing the ground for Britain's cycling revolution.

In August 1984, the regional track championships were held at Kirkby – it was the only track in the region. Although I was 15 and racing as a juvenile, I fought my way to the final of the senior pursuit, where I found myself up against international roadman, Alan Gornall. It was my first big track event and to match the occasion my blue skip special had been replaced by one of Dave Lloyd's old frames, provided by my first ever coach, Eddie Soens.

My dad had overseen my introduction to cycle racing and been the early source of coaching guidance, but by the end of 1983 he felt he'd done all he could. The better I'd become at cycling in those first two and a half years, the more winning had started to mean to me. Although neither I nor anyone around me could see it building, I was already heading towards a classic early-achiever crisis. For someone struggling to fit in at school, even small successes were disproportionately important and my sense of self-worth was becoming heavily reliant on my results. Winning and losing, even at that fledgling stage, was linked to enormous swings between euphoria and despair. In one event towards the end of 1983 I'd climbed off mid-race for no other reason than I thought I was going to lose. My dad, who had sensed that something wasn't right, decided to ask his old coach if he'd consider taking me on.

Often compared to the legendary Liverpool football manager Bill Shankly, Eddie Soens was one of the greatest British cycling coaches of all time and had helped his riders win more UK, world and Olympic titles than any other domestic coach. But it wasn't just cycling: he'd also enjoyed success in a variety of other sports from boxing with world light heavyweight champion John Conteh, to distance-running with double Boston Marathon winner, Geoff Smith.

A short, stocky man with an almost permanent scowl, Eddie spoke in brusque, staccato statements. His no-nonsense demeanour was intimidating and gave him tremendous presence. Praise from Eddie carried a lot of weight. That was my 15-year-old impression. Only years later did I flesh out that view and remember the accompanying twinkle in his eye, the slight twitch at the corner of his mouth as he delivered a lot of those declarations, which showed that under it all he was a warm-hearted man.

Eddie's style was perhaps forged during his time in the army where he had been a regimental sergeant major during some of the most ferocious fighting in Burma. If you can get men to run into gunfire, everything else is probably a walk in the park. His strength gave him absolute credibility, and believing in him made people believe in themselves: if Eddie said you could do it, you had faith that you could. For a kid who was low in self-esteem this was an amazing boost.

So it was Eddie behind me, holding the bike he'd supplied me with, as I lined up on that gloomy late summer evening for my first ever pursuit final, mirrored by the figure of Alan Gornall in the opposite straight. The whistle blew, Eddie pushed me off and I bounced down the track towards the bend, my new bike noticeably lighter than my original machine. The near dark made it a surreal, dreamlike experience, increasing the sense of speed as I powered round the bottom of the track. The noise made by the handful of spectators seemed to be absorbed by the night. I was aware only of the sound of my own breathing, the instructions being shouted by Eddie each time I entered the home straight, and the figure of Fag-Ash Bert crouched at the edge of the track making his pedalling motions. When I crossed the line for the final time, the whistle blew a full two seconds before Alan Gornall reached his own station in the back straight. I had won. There might only have been about 30 people present but it felt like winning a world title.

On the road, I was already starting to win national honours. The previous month I had taken the under-16 10-mile time trial title and then broken the national juvenile record for 25 miles, with a time of 52.09. That performance made me favourite for the junior national 25-mile championship, contested on home turf, just outside Chester, the following week. But I crumbled under the weight of expectation – my own as well as everyone else's – and didn't even make the podium.

In late 1984, I switched clubs again, from the North Wirral Velo to the all-conquering Manchester Wheelers, a club Eddie had strong links with. The following June, Eddie took me to Leicester's Saffron Lane velodrome to try out for the national junior team. The GB head coach Geoff Cooke had organised the event to scout new talent and it was open to anyone who thought they could make the grade. It was the first time I'd ridden on a wooden track and after the relaxed geometry of Kirkby the severity of the bankings was daunting. For now, though, we weren't expected to climb the boards, just cover 3000 m around the bottom as fast as we could, a task I completed six seconds quicker than anyone else.

I was deeply content on the way back up the M6. The National Championships were just a few weeks away and I hadn't just shown that I was faster than any of the competition, I'd done it on the track where the event was going to be held. I thought I was heading for my first junior track title. I wasn't.

It seemed that every time it looked as though I had the measure of the opposition, someone appeared to pip me at the post. In 1982, my nemesis had been local time-trialling ace Lee Proctor. A year later, once I'd managed to claw my way past him, it was Guy Sylvester who had kept me off the top step of the podium. In July 1985, just in time for the National Championships, 17-year-old Colin Sturgess and his family returned to the UK after living in South Africa. Colin proceeded to power his way to the junior pursuit title, relegating me to the silver medal position. Again.

Although I was deeply disappointed, Nationals week wasn't over yet. Despite being new to the track and still a junior, Eddie had made sure I was included in the Manchester Wheelers team pursuit line-up. It was a decision that annoyed the star of the team, Darryl Webster, who had wanted his brothers Martin and Alex to ride alongside him. I'd be replacing Alex. In our qualifying ride my inexperience showed and although we got through to the final it had been ragged. Darryl climbed off and immediately raged at Eddie, pointing towards me, screaming 'He is useless!' Darryl was the rider who had usurped the great Dave Lloyd as the UK's time-trialling supremo and I'd followed his career in *Cycling Weekly* ever since I'd started riding myself – I even had pictures of him on my wall – so his outburst was deeply upsetting and embarrassing.

What happened next was something of a blur. Eddie went to sit on a pile of mats under the bridge that led from the track centre. I had no idea then that it wasn't thoughts of the race that occupied him but his own health. Feeling unwell, he was escorted away from the riders' area and a short time later out of our view, into an ambulance. We were told that he was just being taken to hospital for checks.

Absorbed in my teenage self, my concern was fleeting and my thoughts quickly turned back to the pending final. Determined not to be the weak link, I gave it everything. I closed on the wheel in front to get maximum shelter and matched Darryl turn for turn. We won the national title, my first at senior level. But Eddie hadn't been there to see it.

In the few hours between him leaving the track and the end of the day's racing, Eddie's wife Mima had travelled down to Leicester to be with him. When I phoned the hospital to see how he was, she took the call. Mima was a wonderful, warm and gentle person with a resolutely positive outlook on life. She told me that Eddie had suffered a 'small heart attack' but was OK, then in true Mima style switched the conversation back to me and the day's sporting events: 'I've just left Eddie and he saw the highlights on the TV. He said, "Did you see Chris, wasn't he great?"' High praise from the man whose approval meant as much to me then as my own father's.

Reassured, we made the long trip home and, as tradition dictated, went straight to my Nan's house to show her my winner's sash. While we were there the phone went and my mother answered it, returning to the small backroom a few seconds later pale and in tears. Eddie had suffered a second – this time massive – heart attack and passed away. I was devastated and had no idea how to deal with it. I learned later that those words of praise for me that Mima had conveyed were Eddie's last. I felt guilty, as if I'd somehow wasted the last few days of his life.

We'd known each other less than two years but I'd become highly dependent on Eddie, not just for training advice but for validation. His powerful style had made it all too easy to accept that someone else had the answers; his praise was enough to let me know when I'd done well. All I had to do was follow instructions and trust in his expertise. Without Eddie, I was utterly directionless. I'd achieved a modest amount of success, shown potential, but I had no idea how to move it on.

Despite being only 16, I was selected to represent Great Britain at the 1985 Senior Track World Championships in Italy the following month. After Eddie's death I was glad to get away.

My performance at the championships could best be described as modest, but the trip was not without interest. The British Cycling Federation had brought along a prototype bike to see if it met with the approval of the UCI. It didn't, as things turned out, but it met with mine.

It was unlike any bike I'd ever seen. No frame tubes, just a triangle of carbon fibre. The streamlined forks and wing-shaped handlebars had been machined from a single piece of aluminium. It weighed a ton. It was sitting unattended in the track centre on a training day, so I decided to have a go. Despite its heft and the fact that it was a bit too big for me, once it got going it felt noticeably quicker than the bike I was competing on. It was my first ride on one of Mike Burrows's carbon fibre creations.

In the 1980s, Assos was by far the most prestigious and expensive clothing brand for cyclists: the stitching impeccable and the form-fitting cut light years ahead of any other manufacturer. The Swiss-made garments could be relied on to last for years, by those who could afford them. I couldn't and neither could any of my mates, but when I joined the Manchester Wheelers I was given two full sets of Assos kit. I had other clothing for everyday use but only two pairs of the precious shorts. One of these pairs would do more than keep me comfortable and let me pose on rides with my friends: they would change my life.

I almost met Sally in early December 1984 at the North Wirral Velo annual club dinner, held in The Red Rooms function suite above a café in Arrowe Park. It was a cost-effective affair, a few trestle tables tarted up with some paper table cloths and the obligatory one-man disco with his lonely three-bulb flashing light box. It was the social highlight of our young lives. In charge of handing out the various medals and plastic plaques was Pete Johnson, the club president. Slightly rotund and red-faced with a mischievous grin, he was a real character and the club was his primary passion.

On one of the tables across from ours was the Edwards family. Barrie and his son Andrew were both racing members of the Velo. As Barrie was an adult and Andrew younger than me, we were only on nodding terms. I was vaguely aware they had two daughters, who I'd glimpsed from time to time at local events. His older daughter – not a cyclist – must have been dragged out of bed at the weekends to accompany the family. She could sometimes be seen hanging around the results board, wrapped up in a duffle coat, looking generally unenthusiastic and waiting for her dad to finish racing so she could go home. I'd noticed her but never spoken to her.

Tonight she looked very different from the figure I'd glimpsed in Broxton picnic area: dressed in a simple black outfit with little make up and no jewellery, her dark hair cut short in a Phil Oakey wedge. She was quite beautiful. And she seemed to be looking at me. I had no idea what to do about this, it was an utterly alien experience. I wanted to talk to her but knew if I went over it was sure to turn out to be a terrible mistake. I sat there in turmoil and did nothing. A couple of hours later, as the evening was winding up, I still hadn't made a move. I watched her put on her coat and head towards the door where she turned, looked at me again, smiled once and left, leaving me disgusted with my lack of courage. I hadn't even tried. Pathetic.

I was still brooding on this a week later while I was out with the local gang – a mix of Velo and Port Sunlight Wheelers members. Dave O'Brien, a lad who could always spot a potential angle, announced with a sly grin that he had, in fact, got the contact details for one Sally-Anne Edwards but believed that a negotiation was required before he would hand them over. He didn't want money, he wanted something more precious: the cachet that came with owning a pair of Assos cycling shorts. His inside information for my hard-earned Manchester Wheelers kit – that was the offer. I tried to haggle but he wouldn't budge. Eventually I gave in and the deal was done. An old receipt with a phone number scrawled on the back was handed over.

That evening, scrap of paper in hand, I stood in the hallway where my parents kept the phone, staring at it for a good 20 minutes, before plucking up the courage to lift the receiver and dial.

'Hello?' A female voice.

'Can I speak to Sally please?'

'Who's calling?'

'It's Chris Boardman.'

Rustling, a hand going over the mouthpiece, a muffled, sing-song shout: 'Saaaallllly!' Another 30 seconds passed. Eventually Sally came to the phone and after a short but excruciating exchange of polite conversation, I blurted it out: would she like to go to Chinatown with me and the gang? Amazingly, she said yes.

The following Friday, I went with some of the group to call at No.22 Kelsall Close, a small semi-detached in Oxton. I was resplendent in my Guinness jumper and flat cap, sporting a barely visible moustache as I escorted Sally into the back of Simon Flood's blue transit van for the trip through the Mersey Tunnel to Liverpool. Our first date: a night out with the lads and a Chinese meal. Classy.

It was a damp, foggy night a week later when I rode around to Sally's for what we now refer to as our real first date on Christmas Eve, 1984. It was also the first time I stepped over the threshold at Kelsall Close and met her family.

Our house was quiet, with a small back room where my parents read. The front room was where the TV resided, and when it was on it was considered rude to talk. Sally's house couldn't have been more different. Picture an early pilot of *The Royle Family*: everyone sat together in the lounge, the only downstairs room, the TV was permanently on and there was lots of shouting. Sally's mum, Sandra, sat in her armchair wearing big furry slippers and chain-smoking. Barrie wandered in and out, making jokes and chuckling, while Sally's younger siblings, Nicola and Andrew, squabbled continuously. I felt instantly at home.

A little later on we stepped out into the foggy night. The silence came as a shock. We strolled down the hill past The Swan pub and up into Prenton village where I bought half a chicken from the local chippy. I still don't know why I did that.

Sally was beautiful, confident, quiet and clearly very smart. She excelled at physics, which she was studying in the sixth form, and didn't partake in exercise of any kind. She loved playing Trivial Pursuit, listening to music and reading poetry. I did none of these things. I was ambitious; she was happy to see where life took her. I worried about details; she preferred to focus on the bigger picture. I never worked out why she was interested in me and she's never really told me. If you'd put in our personal details, no dating agency in the world would have matched us up. It was clearly a relationship that couldn't possibly work. Within a matter of weeks, we were officially an item.

Over the next two years, Sally and I spent as much time together as possible. She was finishing off her 'A' levels, while I'd finally escaped school and was pursuing a career – in the loosest sense of the term – working with wood. I attended Cavendish Enterprise Centre on Laird Street in Birkenhead to learn my trade – carpentry – but was enticed away by an offer of paid work making furniture. For someone aspiring to be a cabinet maker, I thought this was a good career move. It turned out to be assembling chipboard panels. After that I did a short stint fitting out an ocean-going yacht, the dream of a one-man band in a farmyard in Thornton Hough.

While I was enjoying having some money in my pocket to fund my social life, the demands of training and riding for the national team were making it difficult to fit everything in. Employers weren't keen on their workforce disappearing for weeks at a time to ride their bicycle. In 1987, I was offered a job by North Wirral Velo club president Pete Johnson, who knew about the problems I was having. Not only would I be able to work with wood, I'd also be allowed as much time off as I needed to pursue my cycling career. I spent the next 18 months at Pete's Furniture Emporium on Church Road, Higher Tranmere, making furniture to order – often badly – and occasionally helping out with house clearances. All for ten pounds a day.

Stacked floor to ceiling with a chaotic mix of cheap furniture, ornaments, curios and boxes of old cutlery, the three floors of Pete's

Emporium were almost impossible to navigate. It was perfectly normal to move around large areas of the premises without setting foot on the floor. Some rooms hadn't been entered since the seventies. Out the back there was a small area with two huge metal tanks. These were filled with hundreds of gallons of caustic soda solution and usually had 20-odd doors soaking in each. The paint was slowly being dissolved off them and in many cases so was the glue that held them together. Each door was periodically turned and eventually jet washed by the master of the yard, Billy, his red face made redder by a speckle of burns from the sodium hydroxide, a roll-up permanently sticking out from under the left corner of his moustache.

To the side was a small workshop where Paul, Pete's only officially declared employee, toiled away finishing furniture. I also worked in this cramped, unventilated space from time to time. The fumes from the large amounts of petrol-based wax we used kept us happy all day: Sally used to be able to smell it on me for hours after I came home.

Big Dave led the house-clearance crew and conveyed the booty back to the shop in one of the two barely functioning vans. Pete had a strict rule never to pay more than £30 for his vehicles, a philosophy that often saw the police returning them to their rightful owners. Every day we would all meet for lunch – usually chips and a fishcake – in the shed in Billy's yard, where Big Dave tried to overdose on salt and tales of the day were exchanged.

Running the whole show was Pete, a cross between Mr Pickwick and Del Boy. He was a generous man who had given me a job not because he needed a furniture maker, but because he wanted to help. I loved him. His character was reflected in the shop itself, where barely a day went by without a miniature drama of some sort. Altogether it would have made an excellent soap opera, although I don't think the script would ever have made it past the lawyers.

While I enjoyed life at Pete's, Sally had taken a more conventional job at the Unilever laboratory in Port Sunlight, testing washing powders for £5,200 a year. She hated it. The only thing she detested more than working there was having to give her parents half of what she earned for her keep, so she quickly resolved to buy her own house. This was bold for a 19-year-old with virtually no money but fairly typical of Sally: strong-willed, courageous and imaginative.

Somehow her project became our project and the house hunt turned into a joint venture. After looking at several basement flats and dilapidated properties on the eastern side of the Wirral, we found a tatty semi behind Birkenhead Technical College. With the help of a deposit from Sally's parents and a dubious letter from Pete Johnson guaranteeing my 'salary' we were able to buy it. We also bought a cat called Bob who despised us from the off and promptly moved across the road. He'd glare at us from his new bay window as we walked past.

It took me a while to get used to living somewhere different. Once I rode the 12 miles from Birkenhead back to Hoylake and was through the front door before the surprised faces of my parents made me realise I'd come to the wrong house. The best bit about having my own home was not getting told off for cleaning my wheels in the front room with the telly on and being able to set up a full woodworking shop, complete with a 12-inch circular bench saw, in the spare bedroom.

By this point, Sally and I were engaged. We hadn't actually discussed marriage: everything had just evolved along what felt like a natural path. There was nothing more natural than the next two events that would rock our lives. It was June, three months after we'd got the keys, when we sat on the bed – a mattress on the floor of our small bedroom – Sally holding a stick with a blue stripe on it indicating that the spare room would soon not be. We were living happily together, doing the shopping, the cleaning, all the things couples do, so I suggested we might as well get married now as later. It wasn't as romantic as it might have been.

I went home and told my parents that I had some good news and some bad news. The good news was that I was getting married and having kids, the bad news was it'd be a close call as to whether it happened in that order. My dad's first response was 'Well, that's the end of your cycling career then, you'll have to get a proper job.' I was distraught, as my parents were very by-the-book about these things, and even though I'd left home I hadn't really left their jurisdiction. But it only took them five minutes to get over the shock and become very supportive.

Sally phoned her mother the same day, but before she could break the news Sandra launched into an account of her trip with friends to see a medium the previous evening. At about the same time we'd been staring at the blue stick, she'd been told she was going to become a grandmother. 'Yes, that'd be me,' Sally replied.

In September 1988 I made my Olympic debut in Seoul, South Korea, where the GB squad helped to make up the numbers in the team pursuit, and a few weeks after returning Sally and I got married. I had mixed feelings about our wedding day. Being so young, we didn't have a clue what we wanted and so we let Sally's mother organise the whole thing. But I've come to realise it was the perfect wedding for us, it reflected our characters to a 'T'.

It started off pretty conventionally with a posh car to the church in Prenton and staged photos of me glancing nervously at my watch and worriedly looking over my shoulder down the aisle. To save money, I wore my Team GB Olympic dress suit. We'd also decided to skip the expense of a formal lunch in favour of buying a washing machine, so while we waited for the evening do and buffet we sat with friends in our front room – Sally still in her wedding dress – eating toast and watching *Blind Date*. My abiding memory of the day is of Eddie Alexander, one of the national team at the time, leading a rousing chorus of 'Pick the fat one!'

That evening in the function suite above The Naughty Edwardian there was nearly a fight. No speeches were made because none of us wanted to. Our wedding night was spent at a local hotel, which was not something I was keen on, but my best man, Jon Walshaw, insisted that was what you did when you got married. I suspect his real motivation was wanting the use of our place with his girlfriend, Carol.

In true obsessive fashion, I got up at 5.30 the next morning and dragged Sally to a hill climb race on the Nick O'Pendle pass in Lancashire. It wasn't an important competition, but it was the only race that would be held on that course ahead of the National Championships the following week.

A few months later, just after Christmas, came our second shock. I rode my fixed-wheel bike the mile and a half from our house to Pete's shop to find Johnny Fryer, Pete's best friend and drinking partner, standing on the pavement outside.

'Hi Chris, Pete's dead,' he announced. John was a man of few words.

I hadn't met many people who lived their life as unhealthily as Pete had. Beer and chips were his daily diet, so it shouldn't have come as such a surprise. But it did. Despite being a bit of a rogue, Pete was a lovely man who'd employed me for my benefit not his. I could take weeks off to go on cycling trips or even just to go training. To this day I'm desperately sad that he wasn't around to see my Olympic win, something he'd contributed to more than many will know. I'd have loved to bring that gold medal back to his shop and hang it around his neck. He'd probably have sold it.

Pete's shop stayed closed, putting me out of work. Sally, now seven months pregnant, was about to give up her post at Unilever and wouldn't be eligible to return as she hadn't been there the required two years. We were now facing married life, having a baby and paying for a new house while living on the dole. Typically, none of this fazed Sally in the slightest. On 11 March 1989, in the maternity wing of Arrowe Park Hospital, Edward Thomas Boardman arrived in the world, named in honour of Eddie Soens and weighing a whopping 10 lb. I was scared to death.

The following weekend I'd accepted an invitation to ride the prestigious Porthole Grand Prix. The Porthole of the title was the restaurant of the sponsor, Gianni Berton, and the event was a tough time trial on the rolling lanes around Lake Windermere. All invitees were asked to dine at his establishment in Bowness the night before the race. I'd ridden the Grand Prix the previous year, but I hadn't eaten at The Porthole because I'd travelled to and from the event on the day with my dad. Remembering just what a long slog that had been, this year I'd arranged to stay over.

Despite Ed being just six days old, Sally had decided to come along, which probably seemed odd to onlookers. It certainly did to the midwife whose advice not to travel Sally ignored. But that's how we'd both grown up, in families where life fitted in around cycling.

Gianni's restaurant was nestled in the centre of Bowness village. Through the window we could see tables set with long-stemmed glasses and candles, it didn't look like the kind of place we would ever eat. Just to the right of the front door, which was fitted with a genuine brass porthole, hung a menu: £6 for soup! My hand almost froze on the doorknob.

We were greeted by Judy, Gianni's wife, who sat us in a quiet corner of the restaurant with Ed next to us asleep in his car seat. Despite having been invited we couldn't be one hundred per cent sure we wouldn't be presented with a bill at the end of the night. Too embarrassed to ask, we ordered starters and told Judy we'd eaten on the way. After an hour, we asked for the bill. Our request was met with a warm smile and dismissive wave of the hand from Judy, before she hugged us both like long-lost family. We filed out through the fantastic smells and past delicious looking plates of food. We went to the local chip shop, got two bags of chips and ate them in the room of our little B&B.

It was the first time we'd been away with a child and I was worried that Ed's snuffling as he woke every few hours for feeds would disturb our fellow guests. It was the end of an exhausting week and it showed in my result the following day. I finished a lowly fifth behind road rider Paul Curran.

I returned to ride the Porthole Grand Prix as often as I could over the next ten years, even as a pro for GAN and Crédit Agricole, not for the prestige of the race but because of Gianni and Judy, two of the most wonderful people we'd ever met. The Porthole Eating House is where many a happy birthday was celebrated, where I had my first and last experience of grappa, where my kids were stuffed with rich food that they invariably threw up later in the caravan. I was never once allowed to pay for a meal.

CHAPTER 3

Barcelona

The ticking sound was coming from my left, cards flipping over one at a time inside a small yellow box. As they turned, the numbers painted on them changed, dropping second by second towards zero. On the final flip the brake mechanism in the start gate would spring open, releasing its hold on my rear wheel, and the most important four and a half minutes of my life would begin.

It was a searing hot summer afternoon in Barcelona and I was clipped into the pedals of my Lotus Type 108 bike. Waiting. The Velodròm d'Horta was packed but apart from the odd cough the crowd was silent. I was seconds away from starting the 4000 m Olympic pursuit final. I was also an unemployed carpenter with a wife, two kids and no money. If I won it would be Great Britain's first gold medal of the 1992 Games – the first for 72 years in the sport of cycling. The world was watching. The Wirral was watching. It was all wrong.

Yes, I'd beaten the world record in training. Yes, I'd set the fastest times in each of the previous rounds. But I still wondered what the hell I was doing here. This was what sports stars did – athletes, people on the telly – not people like me. I was terrifyingly aware of the opportunity the next few minutes represented. It could make history, change our lives forever. As the final few seconds ticked away, I had no idea how I was going to get my legs to go round.

It had taken me more than ten years and a series of crucial events to reach this moment. But if I had to identify one specific starting point on the journey to Barcelona, it would be the car park of Chichester University, where I first met Peter Keen.

In January 1986, the British cycling team, of which I was a very junior member, had begun serious physiology testing. It was not as part of any grand masterplan but because the rest of the world had started measuring stuff and someone in the hierarchy had decided we'd better do the same. I was instructed to get myself down to the south coast to meet a new student in the university's sports science department who'd been engaged to conduct these tests. I was sceptical. The national squad had dabbled in testing before but I hadn't really got much out of it. I had felt more like a lab rat, a source of data for some PhD project, rather than an athlete there to gather information which might improve my performance.

After a 260-mile drive with national coach Doug Dailey in his ultra-modern GB team Ford Sierra, we pulled into the staff car park at Chichester to be met by a tall, blond, fresh-faced young man wearing a Persil-white lab coat and a warm smile. Peter Keen didn't seem to be much older than me. As we chatted on the way to his tiny laboratory – little more than a large cupboard – I began to think that this encounter might be different from those I'd previously had with academics. For a start, Peter was a cyclist: he had competed successfully as a teenager, winning the schoolboy national ten-mile time trial in 1980, four years ahead of me. He had packed in racing to pursue his studies but from the questions he was asking me, I could tell his fascination with the sport, and not just the physiological side of it, was still strong.

On the parquet floor in the centre of the small lab space was a rather tatty looking steel exercise bike. Its white paint was chipped and spotted with rust. A broad nylon strap looped around a cast-iron flywheel to create resistance in the usual way, but the knob that would normally tighten it was taped off to one side. Instead, the strap had been wound around a makeshift pulley before terminating at a handmade wooden cradle stacked with weights. Alongside were several large plastic bags hanging from what looked like a clothes rail on wheels. These apparently would be used to collect my exhaled breath for later analysis.

The whole set-up was an odd assortment of high-tech and low budget. It looked like something Doctor Who might have knocked up had he been trapped in a cash-starved hospital rehab unit and forced to fashion something from the available parts to save the world.

As we adjusted the saddle height and bar position to match that of my road bike, Peter talked me through the tests I'd be doing. The first would be a 'max-minute' test: I'd start at a steady pace and every 60 seconds he would drop a precisely calibrated weight onto the cradle, increasing my workload by 20 watts. This would go on until I could no longer sustain a full minute or I vomited, whichever came first. At this point he would stab me in the thumb to check the lactic acid level in my blood. In the afternoon, I'd do a 'sub-maximal' test, which meant riding at my greatest sustainable effort for ten minutes while he stabbed me periodically to take blood samples. Pete liked stabbing. Over the course of the next five hours, I completed the bank of tests and got the results, along with a thin smile from the tester that let me know he wasn't overly impressed.

On one side of the piece of paper he gave me were my power numbers – maximum, sustainable and per kilo of body weight – along with figures relating to my oxygen use, showing how efficient I was at processing it. These were all pretty standard. But there was also a brief list of identified areas for improvement, along with notes on how these advances might be achieved. This time it seemed the researcher wasn't just interested in the figures: he wanted to see if he could improve athletic performance with new ideas. And there was more. On the reverse side of the paper was something I'd never seen before: training intensities had been categorised into four levels of effort with my personal information overlaid.

Up until then I'd only heard coaches describe effort in vague terms such as 'flat out' or 'dead easy'. Here was something very different. Each level was expressed as a 10 or 20 heartbeat range and accompanied by a brief description of what it should feel like to ride in that zone:

Level 1. 1–2 hours.
A recovery ride, no stress at all. If having a conversation, you will not need to pause for breath. The main limiting factor will be fuel. 110–130 BPM

Level 2. 2–3 hours.
Some concentration needed. If conversing, you will have to pause for breath occasionally. In this zone, feeding and drinking becomes essential over 1:30 H. 150–160 BPM

Level 3. 10–45 minutes.
This is aerobic threshold, the limit of your body's sustainable effort. Mentally very challenging, requiring full concentration to maintain. Conversation will be almost impossible. 170–180 BPM

Level 4. 30 seconds to 4 minutes.
Maximal training. The intensity above threshold power will define the amount of time that can be spent here but typically seconds to a few minutes. Intense concentration is required (-mind-bending stuff!) 180 BPM to destruction.

Pete had created what amounted to a training language for cyclists: a method for people to discuss effort without ambiguity and misinterpretation. To my knowledge, he was the first person in British sport to use evidence-based reasoning rather than history or reputation to make his case. I was impressed – and inspired. It might have said physiologist on the door but Peter Keen was a coach. He just didn't know it yet.

Completing the tests gave me a clear marker, showing me exactly where I was. I'd then been handed a road map, complete with directions on how to get where I wanted go, along with a persuasive argument as to why the path indicated would get me there. I left the lab motivated and excited. Everything was set out, and because of the evidence I'd been shown I truly believed. Pete's application of science to cycling had turned me away from my love/hate relationship with winning and instead given me a fascination with the journey itself.

Two months later, having implemented all his recommendations, I trundled back down to the south coast and repeated the tests. I was four kilograms lighter and 50 watts more powerful. The look on Pete's face was exactly the reaction I was after. After that, the lab tests became a regular feature. I was making trips to Chichester every other month, now under my own steam in my newly acquired rusty Renault 14. I craved the information that came after each session on the testing rig. Our relationship remained a distant one for a while, though. My big improvement between tests had piqued Pete's curiosity, but I still wasn't good enough to capture his full interest.

One of the things I liked about Pete was that although he'd given up racing, he still rode his bike hard and often tried out training ideas on himself first. So he not only knew the theory, he knew how it would feel. That gave me an added layer of confidence in his advice, which isn't to say that he always got it right.

Although he was only 22, Pete's reputation had spread quickly and he was soon advising one of the best athletes of the day: the pursuit star Tony Doyle. For all his brilliance as a physiologist, though, Pete didn't know much about aerodynamics. Tony fitted the classic template for athletes who had historically excelled in the pursuit discipline – big and powerful. I, on the other hand, was small – and not powerful. I had a good power-to-weight ratio – the number of watts I generated per kilogram – but my absolute output was nothing like Tony's. In the second year of our association, before we started to understand the significance of power-to-frontal-area, Pete gently advised me to give up track racing and concentrate on the kind of endurance events more appropriate for someone of my stature. I still remind him of that counsel from time to time.

By 1988, two years after our first encounter, Pete had become a constant presence with the British squad. In the run-up to the Seoul Olympics he became the National Endurance coach. It was the first Olympics for both of us and it was a fantastic experience, but in those days little was expected from Team GB and that's what we duly delivered. Our team of Rob Coull, Simon Lillistone, Glen Sword and myself finished thirteenth. Colin Sturgess was the best performer of the track bunch, placing fourth in the individual pursuit.

On the UK racing scene things were going well for me during this period. I won most time trials that I put my mind to, while road races, which were less predictable, I largely avoided. I was a bit of a coward and enjoyed being the biggest fish in my own small pond. I was comfortable and would probably have stagnated at this point, never getting any further as a sportsman, if it hadn't been for the arrival of a weird Scotsman on a home-made bike who stopped me having it all my own way.

Like most people, I didn't know what to make of this eccentric loner with his odd riding position and his strange machine with its upturned handlebars. But over the 10- and 25-mile distances that I had made my own, and even when I was in my very best condition, Graeme Obree could beat me. He might have been unusual but he certainly commanded respect. I didn't know it at the time, but I was witnessing the first real innovator in British cycling: the Dick Fosbury of his sport and his era. Graeme hadn't just brought new thinking to cycling but an approach that would fundamentally change how we all looked at races against the clock.

Over the next two years, the constant threat of defeat he represented forced me to be better than I was, more than I realised I could be, in order to beat him. Graeme Obree was the catalyst I needed to get me to the next step, to the point where I believed I could compete on the world stage. Without him, I don't think I would ever have won an Olympic title.

Although our performances were incredibly closely matched, with usually only a handful of seconds between us after an hour's racing, our methods were very different. They weren't necessarily different in the ways everybody thought they were, though.

Pete Keen and I were labelled as the ones with the scientific approach, often credited with being the first to free ourselves from the way things had always been done in cycling and instead look purely at 'the demands of the event'. But we weren't, we were more constrained by what we thought bike riders should look like than we realised at the time. It was Graeme who was the first to really turn his gaze outside the sport and recognise that air resistance was the single most important obstacle to be overcome. He had the guts to ignore what the rest of the world thought, shrug off the ridicule and alter his position radically in an attempt to improve his aero efficiency. In doing so he changed pursuit cycling forever.

As Graeme and I competed in the same races and were often pictured in magazines together, there was always an assumption that we knew each other when, in fact, we hardly did. The only time we would really meet was at or around a competition, so we never got past the stage of polite small talk about whatever event it happened to be. We did once find ourselves on a cruise ship in the Caribbean, along with the great Italian Francesco Moser and a few other pros, as guests of a cycling-mad Swiss travel agent, but we never took the opportunity to get to know each other. Perhaps this was because we were rivals and you can never really turn that off.

At events, people were amazed by Graeme's bike, with its washing machine bearings, and his seemingly Heath Robinson approach to performance in general. He clearly enjoyed this and seemed to play up to it. His 'I eat marmalade sandwiches and bashed this bike together on the kitchen table' persona irritated me at the time. We were working so hard to claw our way forward and Graeme seemed to make a mockery of that. Of me. In my arrogance I failed to see what his approach could teach us. He'd supplied proof that there was more out there than we knew about, but in our annoyance, we focused on the eccentric public image and missed what he was actually *doing*.

On the first weekend of June 1990 I managed to win the national 25 mile title 30 seconds ahead of Graeme, before collapsing on a grass verge at the finish with severe stomach pain. It was the fourth such attack I'd had that year – sharp appendicitis-type pain – but despite several trips to hospital the specialists had been able to find no cause for it. Six days later the pain was back and I was taken to Arrowe Park where the surgeon decided to open me up and investigate. What was supposed to be a ten-minute look-see turned into a four-hour operation that left me feeling as if all my insides had been taken out, chopped up and squeezed back in. That turned out to be pretty much what had happened. I had a condition called Meckel's Diverticulum and, left unchecked, the complications might have killed me.

A week later, out of hospital and walking like an old man, I resigned myself to the season being over. I spent the remainder of June moping around the house and the beginning of July moping around Terry Dolan's workshop. Terry is a frame builder from Liverpool, although that description short-changes him so badly it's hard to know where to start to put it right. He's a frame builder, ducker, diver, eternal optimist, philosopher – for those who can understand him – and someone who's never happier than when he's getting the better of 'the man'. He's an evader of security, a serial materialiser in VIP areas without the necessary credentials and the central figure in a long list of stories that couldn't be published in this or any other book. Actually, what he is, really, is an honourable man disguised as a rogue.

On several occasions Terry had helped me out – with frames and bits of equipment – for no other reason than that he could. After my operation we were very short of cash, so Terry let me come and do a bit of work for him to earn a few pounds. When I first went to his workshop, he tried to show me how to build a frame. Step one was mitring the steel tubes so they met at the right angle, then carefully filing them until no daylight could be seen when the parts were pressed together. I focused intently on the task, filing away, checking for fit and, still seeing light through the joint, filing again. By the time I'd finished, the frame I was working on had gone from an XL to an S. He never did show me how to weld.

By the end of July, I felt a lot better. I'd even started to travel to work by bike, so I decided to try my hand in a small race – just an evening ten-mile time trial near Rainford. I think Terry was relieved to see me go. Surprisingly, that Thursday evening I posted a time of 20:42, no slower than when I'd ridden the course fully fit. I decided on the spot to go to the National Track Championships at Leicester's Saffron Lane and see if the trend would transfer to the boards. It had to be a snap decision – the first round of the individual pursuit competition was the following day.

I qualified in third place, won my semi-final comfortably and went on to finish 0.8 seconds behind my friend and national team-mate Simon Lillistone in the final. Silver in the individual pursuit from pretty much a standing start. The selectors took my lack of a proper build-up into account and decided my performance was good enough to warrant the second pursuit spot on the team for the upcoming World Championships in Japan.

On 20 August, we lined up in Maebashi Velodrome – the Green Dome – famous for hosting the professional Keirin races that pull in large crowds and even larger amounts of gambling money. I qualified seventh, posting what would be the fastest final kilometre of the whole meeting. The following day, though, I was out, beaten by America's former Olympic champion Steve Hegg. Despite not getting near the podium, I flew home excited and energised. Pete Keen and I had seen something that changed our whole outlook. My qualifying time had been just two seconds slower than the fastest ride by the winner and world champion, Evgeni Berzin. We had what we believed was a bridgeable gap, a target to aim for, and so we set about planning a campaign to win the World Championships in Stuttgart the following year.

Over the next 12 months Pete and I devoted more time and energy to the project than I would have thought existed. Certainly more than was healthy for a proper family life. Sally became pregnant with our second child and we moved to Hoylake – a tiny terraced house in Walker Street that put us nearer my mum and dad. But she was the one who sorted it all, I just tagged along, my mind on power outputs and split times even when I was physically present.

On the evening of Friday 30 June 1991, Sally went into labour. I ran her up to Arrowe Park Hospital, dropped her off and went back home to bed. That Sunday was the national 25-mile championship near Bristol and I not only wanted to ride it, I wanted to get up there the day before to see the course.

On Saturday morning, I rang the hospital and was told the baby would be some time yet, so I drove the 170 miles to the event with my father and completed my all-important reconnaissance ride. That afternoon my dad phoned home for news – I was having a post-ride soak in the bathroom of our B&B – and came in to inform me that I had a daughter. I was the fourth person to find out. We had decided that if our second child was a girl she would be called Maisie, but alone in hospital that weekend Sally changed her mind and called our new daughter Harriet. With the tiny fragment of remaining common sense I had, I chose not to object.

In the end my obsession was my downfall. Pete Keen and I committed a very predictable mistake, or at least one that was totally foreseeable with hindsight: we'd overdone it. In the 12 months between hatching our plan on the flight home from Maebashi and the 1991 World Championships in Germany, I trained harder than ever in my desire to force the result we wanted. Every exercise session and every race was turned into a test to reassure myself that I was on track. As a result, I arrived in Stuttgart over-trained and jaded. Although I qualified fifth, two places better than the previous year, I got no further than the first knockout round. Worse than that, the time gap between me and the podium had widened. The rest of the world had moved on and at a faster pace than I was chasing them.

Demoralised, my first reaction was that it was all over. I should get a normal job. I had a badly neglected wife, two young children, a mortgage and no proper income. What the hell was I doing forcing everyone to make sacrifices so I could dedicate my life to going around in circles faster than other people? Maybe this was the time to grow up and start behaving responsibly.

I'm not sure how seriously I really wrestled with this new future, or whether I was just mentally trying it on to see how it felt. Either way – and in the face of the available evidence – the topic of winning quickly crept back into my conversations with Pete. The next day he began dropping in the odd comment about what we'd done wrong, what we could have tackled differently, and how that might have changed the outcome. I started to contribute, also identifying things we'd missed. The faint embers of belief were being rekindled and before we realised what we were doing, the past tense in which we'd been talking turned into a conversation about our next campaign.

By the time we got on the plane home a new plan was taking shape. This time the goal was to win not a world but an Olympic title, although I'm not sure that in our hearts we believed anything more than that we weren't ready to give up.

In early 1992, before the new season started, I received a phone call from Rudy Thomann, a French test driver for Lotus cars and an enthusiastic amateur cyclist. He told me they were exploring a relationship with a man named Mike Burrows, a bike inventor who lived close to their headquarters at Hethel in Norfolk. They wanted to make the world's fastest bike and they wanted it to be ridden by a British cyclist at the next Olympic Games. Rudy asked whether I'd be interested in going to the Motoring Institute Research Association wind tunnel outside Birmingham to help test Mike's prototype. I was on the M6 heading south before the phone was back on the hook.

In fact, I'd already ridden this bike, or at least an earlier version of it – the strange, futuristic-looking carbon fibre and aluminium beast that I'd sneaked a go on at the World Championships in Italy in 1985. Then, it had seemed like a design dead-end. The UCI had rewritten their regulations to outlaw it, or anything like it, specifying that a bike frame couldn't be a single continuous shell but had to be constructed of three main tubes of a certain diameter. Five years on, though, the ban on one-piece frames – *monocoques* – had been rescinded. It was a decision that would precipitate a renaissance in bicycle design and throw the UCI's technical commission into turmoil for the next 20 years.

It was a cold morning in February when I arrived at the gatehouse that guarded the entrance to the MIRA Centre. Security was tight; lots of motor manufacturers tested here and they were paranoid about cameras being taken onto the site. Inside, the place was like a huge version of Q's workshop, with men in white coats making notes on their clipboards as they wandered among low-slung vehicles masked with camouflaged bodywork.

Eventually, I arrived at an aircraft hangar on the far side of the complex where the wind tunnel was housed. I was met by Rudy Thomann, his Lotus colleague Richard Hill, and Mike Burrows. I'd never met Mike before but he had a reputation as a mad professor. I could see why. His scarecrow hair stuck out from under his bobble hat and he talked non-stop without punctuation – or, as far as I could make out, drawing breath – for the next six hours.

The objective of the session was to compare the aerodynamics of Mike's 'Windcheetah' with one of the bikes the GB team was currently using. In addition, if time allowed, we'd take a look at how riding position affected things. My role in all of this was basically to sit on the bike, which was attached by wires to two force plates, metal slabs that operated like ultra-sophisticated scales, measuring in six directions rather than just vertically.

It didn't sound like a particularly tough job for me, until it dawned on me where the wind tunnel was going to be getting its wind from: outside on a freezing February day. I'd assumed the whole set-up would be inside a heated building and the experience would be no more testing than sitting in front of an oversized hairdryer. In fact, with the winter air being sucked in at high speed the wind chill made the temperature a steady minus ten.

It quickly became apparent that half a millimetre of Lycra was inadequate thermal protection for what amounted to a six-hour ride in Antarctica. Every time I got off the bike and staggered into the control room to crouch over the tiny electric heater, the scientists frowned at me because my shivering was being picked up by the force plates and reducing the accuracy of the results. My hypothermia was an inconvenience for them.

The primary role of the MIRA tunnel, what it had originally been designed for, was to measure the aerodynamics of trucks. Using it to measure the aerodynamic performance of a bike was about as accurate as weighing individual peas on a set of bathroom scales. But the lack of precision didn't matter and neither did my trembling – the magnitude of the differences between the machines we were testing was plain to see. From the very first run it was clear the Lotus project could offer us an advantage. When we started to look at riding position things got even more interesting.

The man leading the session was Lotus aerodynamicist Richard Hill, a bearded academic in his thirties. My main impression of him at the time was that he was a little arrogant, condescending. Only much later did I appreciate that he possessed the perfect mix of expertise and ignorance that can bring about giant leaps of innovation. Richard, who knew a lot about aerodynamics but less than nothing about cycling, asked me to assume several very different positions: stretching my arms out, elbows together, fists up in the air, fists down. His sole focus was reducing drag, bending me into a shape to make the air flow as smoothly over me as possible. He neither knew nor really cared about what might be comfortable or biomechanically efficient.

All through the process Rudy was whispering to him, 'You can't ask him to do that!' and 'He won't be able to ride in that position!' Rudy knew this because he knew cycling. 'Why not?' asked Richard. Rudy had no specific answer other than that this wasn't what cyclists did. I agreed with Rudy: it certainly wasn't stuff that cyclists normally did, but since I wasn't signing a contract to replicate what we did here in the real world and I was curious to see what the differences would be, I was happy to play along. With the aid of cardboard and gaffer tape to simulate changed bar shapes and helmet visors – Richard thought my polystyrene helmet could be vastly improved on – we continued to experiment. By the end of the day we had settled on a position that was both rideable and a massive 20 per cent more efficient than the one I'd come in with. Coupled with the revolutionary bike design, the gains were extraordinary. I left both very excited and without feeling in my extremities.

Over the next few months I trained hard to adapt to this lower, stretched-out riding position. Pete devised some special training exercises and my time trial bike was changed to accommodate the new dimensions. All serious work was done in this orientation. During the spring we tested two more prototypes: one based on Mike's design, the other Lotus's own. The trials were conducted on the outdoor track at Kirkby. These were the most advanced and expensive bikes the world had ever seen; Olympic success might rest on the outcome of the tests. But before we could try them out we had to chase off the local kids and clear all the bricks out of the way. The Lotus guys were a long way from MIRA.

Mike's second-generation design was sleeker than his 1985 original. Finished in black and adorned with Lotus stickers it looked even better. But Lotus's own take on the concept was something else again. Its heritage was clear to see, but in the few months since the first wind tunnel test the frame had clearly been on a computer-aided crash diet, revealing a whole new set of curves. The Lotus Type 108, as it was called, was a thing of beauty.

It wasn't just the body that had received an overhaul. To create the exquisitely aerodynamic one-piece handlebar and fork blade, many layers of carbon cloth had been bonded and compressed to make a solid, T-shaped block. Hundreds of man-hours had then gone into filing every millimetre to shape. Even the axle was an integral part of the structure, so that the front wheel simply slid onto it. At either end of the cross-member – it hardly warranted the name handlebar – were two bullet shapes for me to grip when starting. They were so small I could just about wrap three fingers around them. The whole set-up looked incredibly slender and didn't appear strong enough to support a starting effort. Looking down to see the front wheel held only on one side made it doubly disconcerting. In truth, it no longer looked like a bike.

A little worried about the possible reaction of the UCI to this latest radical design, British Cycling sent another national squad rider, Bryan Steel, to an early season world cup race in order to set a precedent for the bike's use in competition. It attracted a lot of attention, but since Bryan finished outside the top four it didn't ring any alarm bells at the world governing body. Mission accomplished, it was legal.

Away from the Lotus workshop, the year was going well. I was winning races and posting personal best numbers in Pete's physiology tests. With six weeks to go until the Olympics I entered my last road event, the Circuit des Mines in Northern France. After that, I'd be switching almost exclusively to track work.

I didn't do much road racing and certainly not abroad, so it was a great feeling to win the opening time trial and take the first international yellow leader's jersey of my career. It was followed the next day by my first crash in an international yellow leader's jersey. With strong crosswinds stringing the race out into one long line, I overlapped the wheel of the rider in front and went down heavily, fracturing my collarbone. In denial, I rode the remaining 60 miles of the stage with my right arm resting on the handlebar. On crossing the finish line, I was put in an ambulance and taken to hospital where I spent the night breathing in the antiseptic smell, listening to the clock, staring at the wall and believing my Olympic chances were over.

Although it was by accident rather than design, I was actually giving my medal chances a major boost. The crash prevented me repeating the mistake of the previous year and overtraining. So when I arrived at the gates of the Olympic Stadium, my dream destination, I wasn't just armed with the best technology in the world, I was fresh and in the form of my young life.

The journey to Barcelona had only been possible because of the structure Pete Keen had introduced into my life: an effective learning process, all wrapped up in a formula the intrinsic beauty of which was its sheer simplicity. It was as easily applied to long-term strategy as it was to devising a five-minute training exercise: evidence, idea, plan, execute, debrief, new idea, new plan and so on. It was the non-judgemental nature of this process that made it easy to become fascinated with improvement rather than race results, to focus on being better rather than always trying to be the best. For a fragile young man it was a fantastic way to deal with doubts, stress and failure.

But it wasn't going to work at the Olympics. This was not a test: it was THE test. I couldn't give a toss whether we learned anything. I had to deliver a winning performance: right here, right now. And I wasn't dealing with this reality very well. The sheer scale of it would probably have finished me off if it hadn't been for John Syer, a quiet individual with a gentle disposition, who gave me the tools I needed to cope.

A former volleyball player, John was a psychologist with a fascinating history. When we first met in the mid-1980s, he had a broad spectrum of business clients from Ford and Jaguar to BP and even GCHQ. His personal passion, though, remained sport and Tottenham Hotspur had been his most high-profile success.

Team captain Steve Perryman credited John with turning the Spurs squad from a group of talented individuals into a motivated and communicating force, one that won two FA Cups and a UEFA Cup in a four-year spell.

After that experience, John wrote a book, *Sporting Body Sporting Mind*, which has become a classic sports psychology work. British Cycling's Jim Hendry read it and invited him to work with our squad. It was a forward-thinking move in the late eighties, particularly in cycling where people still thought a psychologist was someone you went to see when you had 'problems in the head'. Despite the general prejudice at the time, though, our little team pursuit group was open-minded and readily bought into the concept of mental training, giving every session our full effort. John was a valuable sounding board, a neutral party with no vested interests. Riders knew they could discuss any issues with him in confidence. It's the role that psychiatrist Steve Peters would play for the GB team a decade later. If it helped us as a team it didn't show in the race results, but on an individual level John would prove to be the right person for me. We began to work closely together, having sessions on our own as well as with the squad.

Pete Keen made sure that John was part of the team in Barcelona by engaging him to help manage the endurance team. With all meaningful training completed before we travelled, the week leading up to my first race was spent riding around the athletes' village, doing some short efforts on the track and generally killing time. Eventually the day of qualification arrived.

Although I was highly stressed, I knew that the first round at least offered me some wiggle room; as long as I finished in the top 16 I'd be through. However, that first ride would also decide the seeding for the next – the fastest rider would be up against the slowest and so on down to eighth versus ninth – so it would still be best to qualify strongly.

Three weeks earlier during our final training camp in the south of France, we'd staged a full dress rehearsal. We practised everything I'd use on the big day, from warm-up strategy and clothing to race schedule and gearing. It was during that run-through that I'd unofficially broken the world record, so I knew my form was good. But being a natural pessimist it still came as a shock when I posted the fastest qualifying time. I progressed through the rounds in this fashion, surprised at every success, and eventually found myself in the final.

Between events I just waited, taking long showers and sleeping to pass the hours, struggling to cope with the scale of it all. At our daily team meeting on the eve of the gold medal race I asked John if he'd mind just hanging around with me in the run-up to the final, and thank God I did. An hour before the start, the pair of us were ensconced in the small, dimly lit mechanics' room beneath the track, sheltering from the incredible heat of the open arena above us. I sat in the relative cool of that stone-tiled space, on the edge of a massage table, swinging my legs, waiting. I was in a right state, which must have been obvious to John. He did what psychologists have done since the job was invented, asking me 'How do you feel?'

'I feel absolutely terrible. I'd rather be anywhere than here right now, I just want it all to be over.'

John's reply was not what I was expecting. 'That's alright, you have to feel like that.'

'What?'

'Oh yes,' he said, a calm, earnest look on his face. 'Elation and despair are two sides of the same coin and generally in equal and opposite proportions to each other.'

'Hang on. You're supposed to be making me feel better here!'

'Oh no,' he was unrelenting, 'if you want the big highs, you have to risk the big lows, that's just how it is. So rather than try to not feel like that, why don't we talk about how to manage it instead? Tell me what it is that makes you feel so uncomfortable.'

I started to tick off all the things my mind was throwing at me: 'What if I can't get out of the starting gate, what if I hit one of the sandbags at the bottom of the track, what if I go out too fast and die off, what if I puncture, what if the guy on the other side of the track is faster than me ...' I went on in this vein for maybe the best part of a minute before running out of steam and mumbling, 'Well I can only do my best.' At this, John looked at me, gave a small smile and an almost imperceptible nod, which is the other thing all psychologists do. In that instant he had got me to form what I can only describe as an 'anchoring thought'.

It didn't anchor me for long. Once I'd swapped the sanctuary of the mechanics' room for the start gate, and John's calming voice had been replaced by the ticking of the little yellow clock, the stress flooded back, threatening to swamp me. Flailing about, my mind returned to that notion from our last exchange and grasped hold of it again just in time. 'Fuck it,' I thought. 'I can only be the best I can be. And when I've crossed the line I'll look at the scoreboard and see what it got me.'

Suddenly, I was calm. I wasn't trying to win an Olympic gold medal any more; I was trying to do something that was completely within my control. John Syer had freed me by showing me the difference between dreams and objectives. The dream – an Olympic title – was really important, the single reason for all the hard work and sacrifice. But like a dream, it was something that I couldn't control. John made me confront the fact that any of the what-ifs I'd listed could well happen; it was entirely possible that my opponent, Jens Lehmann of Germany, might simply be faster than me. There was nothing I could do about that. But I *could* choose what position to ride in, what equipment to use, how to pace my ride. Those elements were totally within my control and concentrating on them was all I could do to try and realise the dream.

As if to test my newfound outlook, when the clock struck zero the gate jammed and ruined my start. Didn't matter. Nothing I could do about it. I rolled around for a lap, my bike was set back into the gate and I visualised a perfect restart. This time the gate sprang open on cue but I wobbled as I got underway. I barely noticed. I was focused on what was ahead of me, not what was behind.

Entering the banking of the second bend, I sat down and settled into the tucked position. I eased off the pedals slightly and waited for Pete to come into sight with the small board that would tell me whether I was up or down on the schedule we'd set: red numbers on white for down, white numbers on black for up. I saw a white 0.5: I was half a second ahead. So far so good. The next lap, another half second. I had to be careful now, there was still a long way to go.

A few laps later, I entered the straight to see Lehmann disappearing around the far banking in front of me. I stopped looking at

Pete's boards and started focusing on my opponent. That I might catch him and end the race early was a prospect that hadn't occurred to me – it had never been done in an Olympic final – but in that instant all I knew was that I had a visual target.

We'd studied Lehmann's performances and he never went faster towards the end of a race, always fading. I was going to win. 'No you're not,' said a voice in my head, 'that's what sports stars do, you're just a bloke from Hoylake.' But common sense began to drown the voice out. The proof was in front of me, I was catching him. A minute later I eased past Lehmann's back wheel: the gun fired, the race was over. I had won the Olympic 4000 m individual pursuit title.

I'd daydreamed about this moment many times. It would be like *Rocky II* when he finally triumphed over Apollo Creed: there'd be lots of jumping up and down, crying and general elation. It did feel unreal but not in the way I'd imagined. I punched the air and that kind of thing as I'd seen it done on the telly, but inside I couldn't come to terms with the fact it was over – and I'd won. Years of work, focusing only on the next step and the next, then in an instant it was all done: someone was pushing me forward and there was a medal being placed around my neck. Standing on the podium holding my flowers in the air, I felt relieved, stunned, shocked. The other thing I did that you see in sports coverage was try to find my wife in the crowd – that was as close to Rocky as I got.

Sally wasn't even supposed to be in Barcelona. The plan was for her to be at home looking after Edward and Harriet, but after seeing the qualifying session on TV, she had decided she didn't like that strategy and made an executive decision to fly to Spain the next day. In the classified section of one of her grandmother's magazines, she found an advert for reasonably priced accommodation in Barcelona. Sally phoned up and explained her rather curious circumstances. The deal was still available – not surprising, as it turned out to be a mattress on the floor of someone's spare room. Having secured somewhere to stay, she set about finding a flight. The only tickets available for the following day were business class – or so she still maintains. She drew our savings out of the bank and booked.

Once she got to Barcelona, Sally realised she had no way of actually getting into the stadium, so she caught a bus to the venue and haggled with a tout. Inside, the strangeness continued as she found herself sitting next to the parents of another GB rider, Glen Sword, who had also travelled out from Merseyside. The newspapers made quite a meal of all this: '*First GB Gold Medallist's Wife Forced To Buy Ticket From Tout.*' The British Olympic Association were highly embarrassed by the situation, which had not really been of their making. As a working class family living on the breadline, it hadn't occurred to us to ask for help or expect special treatment. It was all well beyond the borders of our little world.

As I stepped off the plane from Barcelona three days later, I began to wonder whether our world still existed. It seemed to have been replaced by a wholly different and frankly daunting one. The press were out in force at Manchester Airport: everyone wanted shots of me, Sally and the kids holding the medal. Harriet wasn't old enough to understand what all the commotion was about while Ed seemed bemused by the fuss but happy enough. Their father was less comfortable than either of them, but I knew I was just an hour or so away from home and normality. Outside the terminal, there was a shiny Lotus Carlton waiting to whisk us back to our tiny house where we could close the door and watch the telly.

As we drove into Hoylake, it dawned on me that things weren't going to be quite that simple. I'd been holed up inside the athletes' village for three weeks. Apart from the press scrums at the velodrome and the airport, I'd been totally protected from the real world and had no concept of how the whole event had been perceived. Driving down what should have been the familiar streets of our small village came as a shock. Virtually every shop window was festooned with some form of Olympic display: balloons, flags and hand-knitted cycling effigies. Of me. As we turned into Walker Street the celebratory atmosphere intensified. There was bunting hanging from windows and the entire road was rammed with crowds: people waiting to give me cards, home-baked cycling-themed cakes and baskets of muffins, everyone wanting photographs and signatures.

I didn't like it. This was my home, my village, and these were the people I'd known all my life. I didn't want to be on a pedestal, have people staring when I walked past. I wanted to be anonymous, normal. It was hours before it all died down, and when it did I stepped out into the now quiet street to celebrate with an age-old tradition. I went to the Dolphin.

A converted corner terraced house, the Dolphin had been a chip shop for as long as I could remember and was run by the Choi family – lovely people who had no idea what portion control meant. That night it was the owner Ming on duty. Very shy, he just grinned as he handed over the wrapped bundle and with no eye contact gave a small wave refusing payment. Free chips. That's when I knew I'd really arrived.

This only happened the once, though. I think Ming's rule was one medal, one portion of chips. They had high standards at the Dolphin.

CHAPTER 4

The First Hour: Build Up

For all the Olympic success, I was still unemployed. In the run-up to the games, I hadn't been available for work because training had been a full-time job. Now, dealing with the aftermath was.

As soon as we got back from Barcelona, the flood of phone calls and letters began. Many of them were offers of money in return for doing not much more than simply being that bloke who'd won the Olympic gold medal ('Oh, and could you please bring it with you when you come?'). For a couple who had been scratching around to pay the mortgage and feed the kids, the idea that I could suddenly nip out for the afternoon and come back with three thousand pounds' worth of Asda vouchers took some comprehending.

One company offered me a thousand pounds to turn up for half an hour at one their leisure complexes. A THOUSAND POUNDS, just to TURN UP! I was so stunned, I forgot to ask what kind of leisure complex it was, so it was with a bit of a jolt one afternoon the following week that I pulled into the car park of a bingo hall.

I was the surprise celebrity bingo caller. Smuggled in through the stage door, I found myself in a smoke-filled room, the occupants of which wouldn't have recognised me if they could have seen me. Completely out of my element, I decided to make the most of it and try to inject some humour into the situation.

'Legs …' Pause '… 42!' I cried.

Great joke, Del Boy-like, I thought. Silence. Before I'd reached my punchline, 150 women had deftly scored out the number 11 on their cards, invalidating them. I wasn't asked back.

A run of TV appearances followed. I got my *Blue Peter* badge, although only after some hurried taping-over of the manufacturer's logo on the bike they'd supplied for me to make my studio entrance on. I managed to survive *Noel's House Party* without meeting Mr Blobby. The fees were very welcome, but it didn't really add up to a career.

I wasn't entirely sure what would. We'd spent years focused on a dream and, not wanting to tempt fate, hadn't dared to give any thought to what we'd do if it came true. Now Sally and I were over-loaded with new experiences, bombarded with them on an almost hourly basis. All these unfamiliar and very public activities created a media incarnation far bigger and more intimidating than the real me, which would have been fine if I'd been able to clock off at five every evening and head home to my normal life.

Before Barcelona I used to enjoy going shopping, the simple pleasure of wandering around the supermarket filling the trolley. Now people said hello with brittle, nervous smiles. Someone even asked Sally 'Why are you in Sainsbury's?', incredulous that we'd be doing something so mundane. Worst of all, friends and family had been infected. A subtle awkwardness had appeared. It seemed they didn't quite know what to say, perhaps thinking the usual topics of conversation were now not big enough, not worthy of discussion with the guy off the TV. I was stuck between two worlds and didn't feel as if I belonged in either.

Sally and I knew nothing about managers and agents, including what the difference was between them, so for the first few weeks Sally was dealing with it all. We had no computer or mobile phone – not that unusual in the early nineties – just a landline and an old fax machine. As the various activities were taking us out of the house so much, staying on top of everything was becoming impossible. The children spent lots of time with their grandparents and at the new nursery that had opened at the bottom of our road. In between, Ed learned to pose for the papers, a series of almost identical shots of him on his little bike, gold medal around his neck and hands in the air. Harriet was usually spared on account of her age.

After a heavy schedule of celebratory dinners and civic receptions, it was a relief to escape back to the track and the National Championships in Leicester, where Sally decided we needed to buy our first mobile phone. She came back from the shopping precinct with a second-hand Motorola flip model, slightly smaller than a brick, with a cracked screen and a battery that lasted a full 30 minutes as long as you didn't use it.

Still carrying the momentum of my Olympic form, I won the national pursuit title early in the championships. A prize that a few weeks earlier would have been the biggest thing in my life now seemed almost quaint. My main focus of that championship week was an attempt to regain the world amateur 5 km record. I'd taken it from Denmark's Hans-Henrik Ørsted in the summer of 1991 with a time of 5:47.7, only for America's John Frey to beat that by just over two seconds a few months later in Colorado Springs. On the now famous Lotus 108 and despite the blustery conditions, I stormed round the Leicester track to stop the clock at 5:38.1, setting not just a new amateur mark but breaking Gregor Braun's professional world record for the distance in the process.

I didn't know it then but that would be the last time I ever rode the Lotus superbike in competition. The race also, finally, brought an end to my season. We needed a break, some space to take stock and consider our options. With our close friends Anne O'Hare and Pete Woodworth, we booked a caravan just outside Bassenthwaite in the Lake District and set off with a folder full of faxes to sift through. The weather was perfect: pouring rain. We got a lot of talking done.

One of the faxes was from Harry Middleton, a veteran of the northwest cycling scene, who'd known my parents since the early 1960s. As well as words of congratulation, he also offered me an introduction to his business connections, people he thought might be of help in my new circumstances. A trusted, worldly-wise, long-time family friend sounded like a great place to start, so in late August I arranged to meet him for a chat.

As well as owning a bike shop in Ormskirk that bore his name, Harry had an impressive business background. More importantly, he was a mild-mannered and lovely man, the kind of character people make an effort to stay in touch with. As a consequence he had quite a list of acquaintances to mobilise on my behalf. The first of these was Bill Warren, Operations Director of Kodak's processing division in the UK. He was keen to get involved and quickly sold his colleagues on the value of linking the film giant with Olympic success and the photogenic sport of cycling. An offer of sponsorship quickly followed and with it the need to make some very big decisions.

First of all, I could have politely declined Kodak's offer and just turned professional. That was the most logical next move for a rider in my position. But doing it properly would mean swapping the track for the road and joining a continental team. As far as I could see – apart from the fact they were both performed on bikes – European road racing and what I did were completely different sports. It looked hard, dangerous and would entail spending many months abroad. I found nothing about it attractive.

All I needed was a decent income that would allow me to stay at home and pursue my own sporting agenda. Individual sponsorship by Kodak would, on the face of it, enable me to do exactly that. In reality, Bill's offer as it stood would have given me the worst of both worlds. Under the rules of the day, receiving any direct financial help meant that I would be classed as a professional and excluded from the Olympics. Great. Accepting the money I needed to help me defend my title would instantly disqualify me from defending my title.

There was another factor in the decision-making process that I didn't acknowledge, perhaps even to myself. Barcelona had brought me to the outer edge of my comfort zone and I was scared to take the next step. I'd reached a level of success and notoriety I'd never dreamed of and I wasn't keen on doing anything that might jeopardise it. What I really wanted was to have my cake and eat it: to carry on pursuing the type of challenges I enjoyed as an amateur and make some significant financial progress at the same time.

Thanks to the fine print of the Olympic charter, that's what I was eventually able to do. I might not have wanted to be a card-carrying continental pro, but I had always enjoyed being part of a team, having other riders to travel, race and train with. Sally suggested that, rather than have them sponsor me directly, we should ask Kodak to back an amateur racing team that I could be part of. Harry talked to Bill Warren who liked the idea and so we began to hatch a plan.

That an athlete could be paid unspecified 'expenses' to ride for a sponsored club yet not be classed as a professional was an anomaly that had been exploited for years. In the days before lottery funding it was the only way to remain competitive. I didn't know at the time, but the artificial pro/am divide was a dilemma the International Olympic Committee was also wrestling with and by the time the Atlanta Games came around in 1996 the distinction would be dissolved.

I approached Barbara O'Brien, the secretary of my former club, North Wirral Velo, and asked if they would allow us to use the Velo as a sponsorship vehicle. There wouldn't be a great deal in it for them beyond some free jerseys and the chance to see the club name on a few national trophies. They agreed and the NWV Kodak racing team was formed. I'd found a way to create the environment

I wanted to operate in, if not the enhanced bank balance I'd have ideally liked.

The new racing section of the club ran as a separate entity and included my GB track colleagues Simon Lillistone, Paul Jennings and Matt Illingworth, alongside former Manchester Wheelers club mates Scott O'Brian and Pete Longbottom. Harry fell into the natural role of manager of this group and during 1993 the strong stable of riders we'd assembled would go on to win most major UK titles.

While all this was going on, Peter Keen and I were working on other ways to keep the Barcelona ball rolling. I needed another big target, something with the word 'world' in front of it. We already had a good idea what that would be.

Back in 1989, we'd identified what we believed to be an attainable target: the world amateur hour record set by Italy's Ercole Baldini on the legendary boards of the Vigorelli Stadium in 1956. His mark of 46.394km was so astounding that more than three decades later it had still not been beaten.

We'd decided to mount our challenge at Leicester's Saffron Lane, the only wooden track in the country. It had been a disaster. The attempt had been made during the last track race of the season, the Autumn Gold meet. Piggybacking on an existing event ensured the ready availability of officials, but it also meant that track time was scarce and the only slot we could get was late at night, after the final race of the day.

Clear skies and very light winds were forecast for the evening in question. Perfect we'd thought, but like many amateur enthusiasts before us we'd missed several fundamental factors that would have a huge impact on the outcome. We'd only considered climatic conditions in terms of wind and rain, or the lack of them, not giving any thought to either the high pressure that was creating those conditions or the evening temperature drop that would come with the lack of insulating clouds.

As we waited in the track centre for the night's racing to finish, it began to cool from the sunny mid-twenties we'd enjoyed during the day to low single figures. These factors combined meant that I'd need to produce at least 30 watts more power to ride at 10 p.m. than if I'd been able to start at lunchtime. It was something any aerodynamicist would have been able to tell us, if we'd known enough to ask.

So I set off in optimistic ignorance and it was like riding through cold treacle. Before half distance I'd had enough and abandoned. Assuming it was all my fault, I was very disappointed and a little embarrassed. We put the experience behind us and moved on, with only a handful of people ever knowing that the attempt had taken place.

Still, the record stayed in the back of our minds, even as we focused all our energy on the Olympics and the 4000 m pursuit. In fact, the subject cropped up again by the beach in Barcelona at one in the morning after my gold medal ride. Unable to sleep and still trying to take it all in, Pete and I had sat on the sea wall in the athletes' village, gazing out at the darkness engulfing the Mediterranean. Our conversation moved away from what had just happened towards the future and while we were tossing around ideas Pete mentioned it.

*

Emboldened by our Olympic success, he was no longer talking about the amateur record but the 51.151 km set in Mexico
in 1984 by the great Italian professional, Francesco Moser. I had
been 15 years old when Moser set that record, it was the stuff of
cycling legend. I remembered being with Eddie Soens and my dad
as they discussed it in reverent tones. Eight years later, here I was,
contemplating an attempt to better it.

Actually, to start with, it was Pete who was contemplating an
attempt to better it. After Barcelona he headed back to his lab – at
Brighton University now – and started to crunch the numbers.
I was hard at work failing to know anything about football on
A Question of Sport and agonising over my list of *Desert Island
Discs* in anticipation of an invitation that never arrived. After a few
weeks, I got the word to join Pete on the south coast to look at
the results.

Scribbling furiously on a board, Pete outlined what I'd need
to do to break the record and why he was convinced it was possible. Even then, after the Lotus experience and seeing first hand the
impact aerodynamics could have, we still talked solely in terms of
power required and never linked it to drag, never fully considered
looking for ways to reduce the power needed in the first place. That
particular streamlined penny took about a decade to drop.

Although the brief trip to Brighton had convinced me that the
hour record was a worthy goal for 1993, there were still a lot of
unanswered questions. Where would we make the attempt? What
bike should we use and when would be the best time to do it? It
was clear we needed to do some homework. National Coach Doug
Dailey suggested that the indoor track in Bordeaux might be better

than anything available in the UK for conducting trials. It was an excellent, practical idea, just the kind of outside help we needed more of. The man we turned to in search of it was Pete Woodworth – modest, slightly reluctant, but full of good will.

I'd known Pete for years as a fellow member of the North Wirral Velo, but while he was often involved in the club's social activities he was always on the periphery, never a fully fledged member of the gang. Quiet and largely sensible, he was viewed as the reliable grown-up among us. Back in 1991, sick of living hand to mouth, I had been trying to secure some sponsorship. Pete was a manager at Asda and often got accosted by people like me seeking financial support, so I'd asked him what kind of approach would get his attention. He did more than offer advice: he actively helped Sally and me pull together a CV with which to attract potential backers. From that moment, he became a confidant, someone I could run ideas past knowing that I'd get a sound and considered response. He'd been a valuable member of the caravan cabinet up in the Lake District when we'd sifted through all my post-Olympic offers.

When Peter Keen was exploring the possibility of marketing a glucose polymer sports drink he'd been researching for several years, I introduced him to Pete Woodworth as someone who could help him work through the numbers. From there, the two Petes found other common interests and it was at Pete Keen's insistence that his namesake became involved in the hour project.

In order to answer some of the big questions, we'd decided to take Doug Dailey's advice and head out to Bordeaux to test various bikes and see if I really could sustain the effort required to set a new record. Working from the small office above his bike shop, Harry Middleton liaised with the British Cycling Federation and through them arranged for us to get access to the Stadium Vélodrome de Bordeaux Lac.

In early May 1993, we crammed all the test bikes into the back of Harry's Nissan Patrol and set off for the French wine capital. Up front were the two Petes, Harry and me, four Brits without a word of French between us. It was a long drive down to Bordeaux, made longer by having to stop to change a blown out tyre. It was late when we crossed the Pont d'Aquitaine over the Garonne river and pulled into a seedy truckers' hotel that Harry had booked to save money. It had dark blue carpet on the walls and 15-watt bulbs. Luckily, we would only be there for two nights.

The next morning we arrived at the Stadium de Bordeaux Lac and after a cordial exchange of arm-waving and blank stares with the security staff, we gained access to the deserted velodrome. Pete Keen's plan for the two-day session was simple: first we would assemble bikes from all the manufacturers we believed were worth using: then I would ride each of them at exactly the same pace while my heart rate was logged along with my perception of how much effort I'd had to put in. It was incredibly crude, but we had yet to lay our hands on a power meter so it would have to do. On day two the trials would be repeated in reverse order with a whittled down number of bikes. I'd also do a 30-minute trial at record pace as the acid test.

Among the bikes we were looking at was a radical boomerang-shaped Zipp 2001 frame. There was also a curvaceous Corima 034 and two steel machines of different designs made by

Terry Dolan. Each had been chosen for no more scientific reason than that they looked as though they might do the job.

There was no Lotus 108. A few weeks earlier I'd had a disastrous meeting with Lotus. We were there to discuss our continuing relationship and the possibility of attempting the hour record on a Lotus bike, but we got nowhere. At one point, a senior executive intimated that I should be grateful for being allowed to use their machine. I spat the dummy and we left with no agreement in place. Despite the soured relationship, I'd still have used a Lotus had it proved to be the best tool for the job, but repeated attempts to secure one for comparison with the other bikes were blocked. If I was going to set a new world record it would be on a new machine.

By day two of our testing session the word seemed to have got around and a few men in suits wafted in and out, muttering and frowning. There was also a lone journalist, apparently intrigued that an amateur was contemplating tackling one of cycling's great records. He spoke English, so while I trundled around the track and Pete Keen blew his whistle, Pete Woodworth engaged him in conversation and learned a great deal. The stadium had recently been acquired from the local council by the same group that owned the Tour de France. It was one of the reasons that stage 18 of that year's race was scheduled to finish on the road adjacent to the velodrome in July. It also transpired that the makers of one of our test machines, Corima, were vying for the position of equipment supplier to the Tour.

Testing complete, we stopped for lunch on the outskirts of Bordeaux before the long haul back – steak and chips, the only words we could get the waiter to understand. Up until that point we'd been considering the outdoor 7-11 Velodrome in Colorado Springs as the most likely venue for the actual attempt, mainly due to the advantages of riding at altitude. But Pete Woodworth recounted his conversation with the journalist and put forward three points in favour of Bordeaux: our testing had satisfied us that its hardwood boards were fast enough; the indoor environment meant we could specify an exact time to start our attempt rather than wait for a weather window; and making the attempt on 23 July, the day the Tour de France came to town, would maximise exposure.

Over steak-frites in a French motorway service station restaurant the plan for the attempt on the hour came together. It now had a bike – the Corima had been chosen due to Harry's connections as much as its performance – a venue and a date. At the end of May 1993, having just broken the national record for 25 miles, I announced the details to the press. Now we were publicly committed and Pete Keen set to work on a training schedule to bring me to peak form for the event.

There was one last question that needed answering: could I cope with the heat of a July day in south-west France? Our first failed attempt at an hour record in Leicester four years earlier had not been wasted on Pete. Now more aware of the impact climatic conditions could have, he checked the likely July temperature for Bordeaux and devised a trial to replicate it. A few weeks later, driven by Sally's brother Andy in the new Vauxhall Calibra a local car dealer had given me in a sponsorship deal, I headed down to Brighton for a battery of lab tests. The key one was to be a simulated hour record attempt in a room heated to 24 degrees. That might not sound high but in a cramped lab with no cooling airflow it was stifling.

In fact, the temperature rose a fair bit higher than we'd intended. Now that the attempt was in the public domain, a TV crew was following me to make a series of pieces for Granada's regional news programme. Pete's advance calculations hadn't allowed for the extra heat generated by their lighting. By the end, my core temperature was touching 40 degrees. We knew this because I had agreed to the indignity of having a body-probe installed – I still maintain that riding flat-out for an hour with that apparatus in place is the reason I received an honorary degree for services to sports science. But despite the probe and the heat, I completed the trial at the projected power and Pete declared himself satisfied. All systems were still go.

CHAPTER 5

The First Hour: Countdown

During the late summer of 1992 Harry had introduced me to another of his friends, Alan Dunn, whom he'd known since the 1960s when they'd lived and raced together in France. Realising that they weren't going to make it as professional cyclists, they had eventually returned to the UK and gone their separate ways. Alan's path, which was worth a book in its own right, had culminated in the position of Logistics Manager for the Rolling Stones.

Despite being immersed in a very different world and spending huge amounts of time on the road with the band, Alan still followed the sport as much as he could and kept in touch with his cycling friends. So when Harry contacted him with a vague request to see if there was any way to link up his universe with ours, he too answered the call.

I first met Alan in front of the Saffron Lane sports centre during the National Track Championships. Not knowing what he looked like, I wasn't sure about being able to pick him out from the hundreds of people arriving in the car park for the event, but

I thought heading towards the only Ferrari F40 I could see was a fairly safe bet.

A large man extracted himself from the driver's seat and walked slowly over to say hello.

'Hi.' Massive pause. 'I'm ...' Massive pause. '... Alan.'

That's how Alan spoke, even on the phone. I was never sure if he'd forgotten who I was, who he was, or if he'd just mentally bumped into something else more interesting to think about. Despite the occasional silence, though, we hit it off straight away. I got into the habit of meeting up with Alan for dinner whenever I was in London, which was increasingly often as commercial work began to come my way. It turned out that he'd actually witnessed the setting of the record I was hoping to break. In January 1984, the Rolling Stones had been in Mexico City shooting promotional videos. When they heard about Francesco Moser's hour attempt, he and Mick Jagger had gone to the Olympic Velodrome to watch. Mick didn't show up in Bordeaux – that would have been the support act of all support acts – but through Alan, he did end up making a contribution to the success of the project.

Sally's dad, Barrie, did make the trip to Bordeaux, although in many ways I wish he hadn't. It would have meant Sandra, Sally's mum, was still alive.

In 1991, Sandra had started to have accidents. Nothing serious, just a small fall at work and a few things dropped at home, but as a nurse she knew better than to ignore even faint signs of something wrong. She went to her GP who referred her to a specialist. In December 1991 Sandra was diagnosed with motor neurone disease and over the next 17 months the terrible condition advanced. On 2 May 1993 she died, leaving Barrie, who'd cared for her day and night through the worst of it, looking ten years older.

A cyclist since his early teens, Barrie's life revolved around twin hubs: family and bikes. Every weekend, he was either riding himself in a local time trial, or taking his son Andrew to compete in a schoolboy event. Every day, in all but the very worst of weather, he'd cycle the ten miles each way to the Vauxhall car plant in Ellesmere Port where he maintained the paint shop.

How he held down such an important job I'll never know, as in every other area of life Barrie and tools spelled disaster. This was a man who would take scissors to the back lawn when it needed trimming and take off the end of his finger in the process. He once planed three inches off the front door to stop it jamming on the carpet, when half an inch would have done. It still stuck: he'd taken all the length off the top. Always joking and fabricating wild tales about his time as a fighter pilot, or the day he was run over by a tomato sauce truck, Barrie was great company and dealt with all but the most dire of life's adversities though humour. Masked in mirth, his bad moods were hard to spot but usually manifested themselves as a tendency to take up contrary positions in whatever conversation was going on. If you saw it coming, it was possible to get him to champion even the most bizarre of causes.

'That Hitler, what a terrible bloke.'

'Well, are you sure about that? I hear he was a vegetarian who could mend a puncture ...'

But it was Sandra who had steered the Edwards ship and without her he was lost. During this period cycling became more precious to him than ever. It was a cord that linked him to people, gave him a reason to congregate with others and a common topic of discussion. When Barrie turned out to cheer me on in Bordeaux it would be his first holiday without Sandra in twenty-three years.

In early June 1993, I flew out to Bordeaux with Pete Woodworth for two weeks of intensive training on the track. With a full-time job of his own to worry about, he wasn't thrilled to be making a second trip to France, but we'd come to rely on his calm, clear-headed input. To help us with pacing for the record attempt, he had written a simple computer programme that would update my average speed on each lap and display it on a screen at the side of the track. Pete Keen persuaded him to come out 'to test the electronics'. The fact was, we just couldn't do without him.

We landed amid the biggest thunderstorm I had ever experienced. The plane lurched violently as we descended and lightning struck an airport light tower, blowing out the bulbs. Over the next five days I became convinced that the weather had been trying to warn us. Pete Keen had flown out separately and it was late when we met up in the arrivals hall with him and Phil O'Connor, a *Cycling Weekly* photographer who'd come to document the trip. The four of us hauled all the kit and bikes to the Avis desk to pick up the hire car Harry had booked. It was a Fiat Punto. Forty-five minutes of faffing about later, we put the gear in the back of a Renault Espace and set off for the house Alan Dunn had helped find for us.

The house turned out to be an hour's drive away from the track. It was midnight when we reached our destination: an old, dark building with no one out front to meet us and not a sign of life in the surrounding streets. Phil, who had both a mobile phone and a smattering of French, called around to track down keys. It was the early hours of the morning before we managed to get into the place and our problems weren't over. Damp ran down the walls, every surface was covered with a film of grease and the horsehair mattresses had unidentified microscopic inhabitants. Pete Keen was horrified.

At first light, after not much sleep, three of us headed for the track bleary-eyed, while Phil kindly took the car and went in search of lodgings fit for human habitation. A lacklustre morning session didn't improve our mood. Neither did Phil when he reported back – Bordeaux was hosting an international wine festival and the only alternative accommodation he could find was nearly 100 km away on the coast. For the next two days we tried to put a brave face on it and commuted four hours a day there and back from Soulac-sur-Mer to the velodrome.

There was a sliver of good news on day three when I rode a 20-minute session on the first Corima prototype and unofficially broke Moser's 10 km mark by 22 seconds. It was a much needed confidence boost after the stressful start, but the good feeling was soon squashed. On day four we arrived at the stadium to be met in the foyer by a small group of official-looking people who informed us we were no longer allowed to use the track. The reason for the sudden change wasn't clear to us but the consequences were.

It was a disaster. The clock was ticking, the costs were mounting, we had already announced our intentions to the world and now it all seemed to be unravelling. I began to think maybe we had been foolish, that we were out of our depth here, thinking we had a chance at wresting such a lofty prize from a cycling legend. The lockout was the last straw. I phoned Harry, explained the situation and asked him to fly out to fix it. The pressure of trying to break the record was enough without all this added stress, and Pete Keen and I were really starting to feel it.

But what was really making us anxious, what had cast a shadow over the whole exercise, was a problem neither we nor Harry could fix. Back home, at the national 25-mile time trial championships on 13 June, Graeme Obree had declared his intention of tackling the hour record himself: a week before the date we'd set for my attempt. 'We just need to find a track,' said his manager, Vic Haynes.

Yeah, just a track. They didn't need to find their own project – we'd done that for them. I was seriously annoyed: in taking on Moser's Hour, we'd dared to think big, put months of work into researching the feasibility of the attempt, travelled across Europe, done physiology tests, found the track and committed money I didn't really have to make it happen. Graeme had a growing public image as the man who ate jam butties and drank beer before 'just going out there and doing it'. But this time he was only able to just go out there and do it because other people, the people whose bandwagon he was jumping on, had put in the hard yards for him. It didn't seem fair.

My indignation wasn't really founded on ideas of fair play, though, it was emotionally driven. I felt threatened. Graeme's athletic credentials were beyond question; if he managed to pull it off, to set a new record distance, then the margin between success and failure for me would become very slender. And having already announced a time and a place, I was helpless to do anything but watch it play out. Put simply, we'd been outmanoeuvred.

The day after the lockout, in emotional turmoil, I trained on the road, the only available option open to us, before heading to the airport to meet Harry. With the best of intentions, his opening gambit was to look on the bright side and try to put a positive spin on the situation. Unfortunately for him we were now totally out of *bonhomie* and Pete Keen exploded. I felt for Harry, especially as I was the one who'd put him in this position. I hadn't really been listening when we'd first met and he had told me what he was offering: 'I'd just like to help out ... No, I don't want paying.' I'd pushed him into a managerial role he had never wanted because I needed someone I trusted to take all the pressure off me. He'd shouldered the burden and now he was getting an earful for his trouble.

After a long discussion it was decided that Pete Keen and I would cut our losses and fly home, leaving Harry and Pete Wood-worth – who'd found himself volunteered once again – to see what could be salvaged. A meeting was scheduled for the following day at the velodrome for all interested parties: us, Corima, the local council, the French Cycling Federation and the organisers of the Tour de France. Late that evening, realising that he and Harry were going to be at a serious linguistic disadvantage, Pete went to the reception desk of our small hotel and asked if they knew anyone who could act as translator at short notice. Luckily, they did.

The meeting was due to start at 10 a.m. but when Harry, Pete and their new colleague Muriel arrived in the conference room at 9.30 it was already full of babbling people. Pete asked Muriel to stay and listen while he slid out. Twenty minutes later, she emerged to explain what she thought was going on. It turned out that there were more agendas in play in that small room than at the average EU summit.

The Tour organisers were annoyed that someone was trying to capitalise on their event coming to town and worried we might steal their thunder on what would likely be a quiet, transitional stage. The French Cycling Federation, who had their headquarters at the velodrome, were offended because no one had officially informed them that this prestigious record attempt was taking place in their back yard. Corima had a foot in both camps. It would clearly be good for business to have me set a new world record on one of their machines. But since they were also bidding to land a major contract with the Tour de France, under no circumstances did they want to do anything that might upset the race organisers. The only group unequivocally on our side were the representatives of the local council. They could see nothing but good in having a high profile event staged in their city.

Pete Woodworth took all the information on board and over the next couple of hours tried to find a way through the competing interests towards a solution. The national federation officials were encouraged to see past their initial indignation to the benefits of having a world record set on their home track; it could only add to the international prestige of the velodrome. They came around to the idea and sided with the council. Together they convinced the

Tour de France executives that the record attempt could be made to work in their favour too. As long as it was staged at the right time of day on 23 July it could be an added attraction to the race rather than competing with it. It might spice up a dull stage and pull in extra media coverage. Corima, who had started out very upset with Pete for jeopardising their commercial chances, never got off the fence, but they were relieved when it all finally seemed to be settled.

It was a watershed moment, for me and for the enterprise as a whole. Pete took over formally as project manager for the hour record and Harry focused on running the Kodak team back in the UK.

Between these stressful forays to France I was still racing at home, although every event was ridden in service of the greater goal. Using a fixed-wheel bike, the position carefully mimicking that of my hour machine, I set a new national 25-mile mark of 45:57. Riding in the same position on a geared road bike, I broke the record for the Isle of Man mountain time trial. With the Kodak team, I took my second victory in the Pro-Am Tour of Lancashire, organised by mild-mannered clubman and future UCI President Brian Cookson.

As if setting up a racing team, dealing with a new, post-Olympic life and taking on the biggest record in the sport weren't enough to be going on with, Sally told me she was pregnant again. For the previous two announcements of impending births I'd failed miserably as a partner, showing my own shock and worry rather than simply being supportive. At my third attempt I was, sadly, true to form. I was struggling to cope with all the new responsibilities and demands yet at the same time seemed unable to stop myself taking on more. It was as if there were two of me: the larger part of my character just wanting to run away with the family and live on the Isle of Skye, subsistence farming; the smaller, yet somehow more powerful voice saying, 'Yes, yes, you're right – but you're going to do this anyway.'

The evening before I was due to head to France for the record attempt, Sally, my mother, Ed, Harriet and I walked across the fields over the railway lines in Hoylake. They played on the grass, I lay on my back and stared blankly up at the sky. I felt utterly removed from what was going on around me, like a spectator in my own life. If someone had driven up in a car at that moment, thrown open the door and said, 'Come on, lets escape,' I'd have climbed in without hesitation.

In the absence of a mystery vehicle arriving to save me from myself, I had one of Mick Jagger's tour vans. Quite late in the process we'd decided to change tack. Instead of training at home and travelling to Bordeaux just a few days in advance of the attempt, I was going to head out for a full fortnight's preparation at the track with Pete Keen, who'd asked for extra time off from his lecturing duties.

At one of my dinners with Alan Dunn, I'd explained how the extended stay meant more equipment to carry and he'd offered us the use of a Transit van belonging to Jagger's company, Marathon Music. Pete Keen and my Velo teammate Paul Jennings, who was coming along to help out, volunteered to drive it over to France.

*

The weather was perfect and the landing was soft on my flight to Bordeaux, but I was too caught up in worry about what was to come to read the clear skies as any kind of good omen. I was met by Pete Woodworth, who'd already been on site for a few days to ensure that everything was in place and working smoothly. With him was Muriel – our life-saving eavesdropper was now a full member of the team.

On our previous, problem-filled trip, Phil O'Connor had done what all lost cycling pilgrims do when they're in trouble, he'd popped into the local bike shop to ask for help. The owner of this one, Jacques Suire, had been incredibly helpful and all but adopted us. After a series of calls, Monsieur Suire had arranged for us to stay at the Centre d'Accueil et de Promotion: a little used hotel facility for conferences and exhibitions. It was basic but perfectly adequate for our needs and just 3 km from the track.

It was a haggard Pete Keen who arrived at our new base later that night after what had been an eventful journey. At Dover, he and Paul had been pulled over by customs officials and asked for the van's documents. They had none. They were asked if the vehicle belonged to them.

'You're not going to believe this,' Paul beamed as he leaned across from the passenger seat, 'but it's actually Mick Jagger's.' How he thought that would help, I'm not entirely sure. Luckily, one of the customs officers was a cyclist and knew about the record attempt. The cavity search team was stood down. One ferry crossing later, they were in France and on their way. Billowing more smoke than the Trotters' three-wheeler, it became clear the van was nearing the end of what had been a hard life. About

200 km from Bordeaux it began to sound worryingly asthmatic and Pete had to nurse the ailing machine along at a maximum speed of 60 kph for the last few hours. After pulling to a halt in the hotel car park, he didn't so much kill the engine as turn off the life-support. It was the last journey the burgundy Transit ever made.

That night, while unloading, Paul found a pair of old Y-fronts under the seats and, thinking quickly, wrote the initials M.J. on the waistband before throwing them back in the van. Later he 'discovered' the underwear and for several days, had us all convinced they belonged to the rock star. OK, he had me convinced. The unlikelihood of Mick Jagger initialling his Y-fronts didn't occur to me, much less the chances of him wearing M&S own-brand. I was preoccupied.

The one piece of kit Pete and Paul hadn't brought with them was the bike. That had arrived the day after we did, direct from Corima. They had spent the weeks since our last trip making final adjustments, most importantly reworking the tri-bar set-up to accommodate the extreme position I'd adopted for the event. We had no way to measure how aerodynamic it was but it was certainly elegant.

On 16 July, while finishing up the day's session at the track, we got word from the Vikingskipet Velodrome in Norway that Graeme Obree had failed in his attempt on the record by more than 400 m. To that point we'd been forced to base all our work on beating a mark we knew might suddenly be revised upwards. His attempt had been a cloud hanging over us and we were hugely relieved at the news. That night I even had a beer.

The next day I thought I'd misheard when someone told me Obree had made a second attempt and this time he'd gone 445 metres further than Moser – a turnaround of nearly a kilometre in less than 24 hours. The new world record hour distance was 51.596 km. I was bitterly disappointed. A year earlier we'd dreamed of surpassing the mark of an Italian legend, now I'd have to pull my tripes out to beat a bloke from Scotland on a homemade bike. The prize had undeniably lost some of its lustre. Not only that, but I was going to have to work harder and ride further to claim it. Still, the pace we'd settled on for our attempt was 53 kph – enough to take the record by over 1400 metres. We were rattled but still confident.

On 23 July 1993, with nearly a hundred of the world's press, 20 or so friends and a handful of local enthusiasts there to bear witness, I stepped out on to the boards of the Bordeaux velodrome. It was hot, much hotter than we'd planned for, a problem not helped by the velodrome management who'd turned on all of the arc lights for the TV cameras. In fact, conditions in general weren't ideal. As well as the heat, humidity was close to 80 per cent.

Five minutes earlier, Pete Keen had doused my clothing with a rapidly evaporating mixture of 50 per cent water and 50 per cent ethyl alcohol – a trick we'd developed for Barcelona to keep me cool. This wasn't a 4000 m Olympic pursuit so the benefit wouldn't last the distance, but it would at least help with the high temperatures for the first few minutes of the effort. We just needed to ensure no one smoked near me.

Our new French friend, Jacques Suire, had turned out to be not just a friendly local bike-shop owner but also a UCI *commissaire*.

He was holding the Corima as I settled into the saddle, raised my head and looked down the straight into the first bend. It was the highest pressure moment I had yet experienced on a bike, harder even than the Olympic final where losing would still have earned me a silver medal. Here, failure would send me home with nothing. Less than nothing, I'd be in debt.

The small crowd was silent which made me oddly self-conscious. I could see Sally's dad Barrie, Kodak team sponsor Bill Warren, Harry Middleton and several members of the Velo. In there with them were people who'd never seen a bike race before, let alone something as unusual as this. Two representatives from Reebok, another sponsor, had turned up a few days earlier and were clearly out of their element. One had asked me how long the record attempt would take.

'When you're ready,' someone said.

No countdown, no gun, just silence. As if you could ever be ready for this. I fleetingly registered this unique and perverse aspect of a record attempt. Despite knowing what is about to happen, that this will be the most unpleasant experience of your life, the decision as to exactly when the suffering starts is up to you. I remember the voice in my head. 'You've got to go. Go on. Any moment now. You've got to go. Move.' At two minutes past ten in the morning, I moved and the spell was broken.

An instant later, I am out of the saddle, straining, pulling up with all my strength to get the big gear turning. Into the back straight, leaning forward, pumping the bars, trying to get as high a cadence as I can before the G-force of the second bend pushes me back into the saddle.

There's no pain at all, I'm full of adrenalin and fear. What I need to settle me down is to come out of the second bend into the home straight and see Pete Keen's little board showing white numbers on a black background, the side of the board we use to show 'up on schedule' information. But there's no number, just a horizontal dash. No loss, no gain. OK, how do I take that? Is the glass half-full or half-empty? I'm not reassured but I know I should do nothing about it.

This is the most dangerous part of a record attempt, when the body is flooded with natural painkillers and the invoice for all the effort has not yet fallen due. In the anxiety of the moment it's all too easy to overextend yourself, a trap many hour contenders have fallen into. In his 1972 attempt Eddy Merckx set off at an incredible pace, covering the first kilometre in under 1:10, faster than many of the world's best pursuiters during a 4000 m race. He paid dearly for that and I'm convinced he'd have travelled well over 50 km if he'd just stayed calm for the first few.

It's like being at the controls of a racing motorboat that has a hole in the prow and water pouring through it. The faster you drive the boat, the quicker the water comes in. There is a speed at which the rate of ingress and your ability to bail water are perfectly matched. This is aerobic threshold and it's what the hour record is all about: as long as I can balance the amount of lactic acid my effort is producing with my body's ability to process it, I'll be OK.

Barely five minutes in, the cooling effects of the alcohol spray have worn off and the hot, humid conditions of Bordeaux begin to take their toll. Sweat is already running into my eyes, dripping from my nose and splashing onto the top tube. Encased in a close-fitting black aerodynamic shell, my head might as well be inside a pressure cooker. It's funny: 'overcooking it' is a term we often use for going too hard – now it's threatening to become literal.

I've done several long training sessions in the last two weeks so I know the danger, I'm extremely cautious. But being cautious is also a danger. The velodrome scoreboard is showing my time against Obree's at every major split. I'm not supposed to be looking at it – it's a distraction from our schedule – but I glance up and see that I'm one second behind him for the first 5 km. At least I have history on my side. In every time trial we've ridden together, he's started quickly and faded slightly towards the end

At 10 km, I'm struggling to stay on 53 km pace but the scoreboard says I've got my nose in front of Graeme by two seconds. It's nothing, I know I have to start squeezing my speed up. But this heat. It's not legs, lungs or heart dictating the pace now, it's the heat.

I push on. Half distance – a huge psychological barrier. But physically I'm really starting to suffer. My eyes are blurring with sweat and the strain of holding this extreme position, effectively forcing myself to look 'upwards' against 2Gs of force in each banking. I'm struggling to hold the black line at the bottom of the track. I'm getting seriously concerned about passing out.

Pete Keen ditches the 53 km schedule now – along with his boards: he's run out of numbers big enough to show how far off the pace I am. He steps back through several well-rehearsed trackside positions to settle on one representing a speed of 52.3 kph, the slowest he has. It's a speed that seems to hold me on the thin line between maximum effort and unconsciousness.

Each time I come into the home straight I can see my average speed dropping on the trackside monitor and Pete stepping back from his mark. Pete abandons schedules. He shouts to me that his position either side of the finish line will now indicate how far up or down I am on Graeme Obree. He takes up a position in positive territory.

Struggling desperately with the temperature now. I dare to push harder, gaining confidence the closer I come to the end. Twenty minutes to go, 15 minutes. From 15 minutes to 10 takes at least six months. Muscles are starting to cramp, lower back screaming, sound fading in and out, I'm a punch drunk boxer on the ropes. Then 10 to go, the final barrier. Now I believe I can make it. I'm going to beat Obree's distance with seconds to spare, just got to hang on.

Five minutes. Head pounding, right eye closed with sweat. No longer able to see the average speed as I zip past the screen.

Three minutes. I let go of pacing and start to push for home. Let the water start pouring into the boat – the beach is in sight. I just need to reach it before I sink.

Suddenly I'm speeding past blurry people jumping up and down. I'm past Obree's distance and into new territory, a place no one has been before. And I've still got nearly a minute to run, to add to the distance to make it as hard as possible for the next brave idiot. Now I'm being flagged down, people are walking on to the track. It's over.

I ground to a halt in an unnecessarily frenzied press scrum in which my helmet disappeared never to be seen again. I'd done 52 km 674 metres – two and a half laps of the track further than anyone had ever cycled in one hour. I'd imagined a sense of elation, of satisfaction and joy at having achieved something special, but the overwhelming sensation was one of relief. Film crews, sponsors, friends, everyone had invested in this attempt, in me, and I hadn't let them down.

Our new best friends, the organisers of the Tour de France, seemed as delighted as anyone. They invited us across the road to attend the finish of that day's stage and presented the whole hour record entourage with VIP passes. Paul Jennings and Dave O'Brien, who'd come out to act as mechanic, brandished theirs like Wayne and Garth from *Wayne's World*, determined to see just how far they could get. It seemed the passes really were access-all-areas, as they waltzed by the final security guard and found themselves standing on the finishing straight looking at an oncoming mass of sprinting riders.

I was asked to pose on the podium with the yellow jersey wearer, Spain's Miguel Indurain, who was heading for his third straight Tour de France victory. 'Why not?' I thought. 'I'll never have the chance to do this again.'

CHAPTER 6

Turning Pro

For the second summer in a row I'd achieved a dream and woken up the following morning with no idea of what came next. As with the Olympics, Sally and I hadn't dared to plan beyond the hour attempt in case it didn't come off. Now that it had, Pete Woodworth persuaded us to stay on in Bordeaux for a few days after the madness had died down and the Tour circus had moved on.

Pete had fallen naturally into the role of Head of Strategy and although he knew of my reluctance to turn professional was adamant it was the way to go. It was the reason he'd been keen to tie my hour ride so closely to the Tour de France.

'If you stay as you are, what happens?' he asked me over a coffee in one of the pavement cafés in the old town. 'You stand still and wait for someone to knock you off the top step. If you turn pro, on your own terms, then you have a chance to move forward, to be more. And if it doesn't work out then you can come back to exactly where you are now, nothing lost.'

In the end the decision wasn't the result of a light bulb moment. There were no cries of 'Let's do it!' or exchanges of high-fives. I simply didn't have an answer to Pete's reasoning.

Several team managers had already contacted him to express an interest in signing me but only one was being truly proactive. GAN boss Roger Legeay had taken a day out from his duties on the Tour de France to watch me set the hour record and he'd been calling daily since, trying to secure a meeting. This was a man whose outfit had won the race three years earlier with an English-speaking rider, Greg LeMond. Greg, who I admired as an innovator as well as a great athlete, was still on the team. GAN were due to ride the Tour of Britain in August and Pete arranged for us to meet Roger in Cardiff at the team hotel.

My only experience of continental cycling was watching it on the telly, a medium that always makes things seem bigger and more important. I pictured professional team managers plotting their annual campaigns in darkened rooms with huge maps of Europe in front of them, pushing tiny figures of riders around the continent to implement their master plans. The figure who greeted us at his hotel room door looked like somebody's favourite French uncle.

Roger welcomed us warmly, ushered us in and resumed his seat. He looked over the top of his half-moon spectacles and asked me what I wanted to do as a rider. I hadn't been expecting this, the grand tactician deferring to me, but since he'd asked I thought I might as well jump in with both feet and tell him.

I ran through the racing calendar, reeling off a list of races in which I thought I could perform well. To my astonishment he wrote everything down. While I babbled on Roger barely said a word, he just looked at me and listened, nodding every now and again. So I kept going. When I got to the month of July and stated that my main goal was to win the prologue of the 1994 Tour de France, an event I saw as a logical target for me, Roger's hand came up. With a faint smile he said, as if to an enthusiastic ten-year-old, 'Normally, first year professionals don't ride the Tour. We will see.' I think he liked the fact that I was aiming high but thought me naive to aspire to such grandiose ambitions in year one. I hadn't even told him about the plan to take two world titles the following month.

No deal was struck but it was a good start – I liked Roger – and we agreed to meet again a few weeks later at the world track championships in Norway.

After what had been the most stressful year of my bike-riding life, I arrived in Hamar for the World Championships mentally and physically spent. In the semi-final of the pursuit, I was well beaten by a storming Graeme Obree who produced another great ride in the final to become world champion. It was an amazing achievement for someone who had only recently made a comeback after having retired the previous year.

The following day, Pete Woodworth and I drove into Hamar to visit Roger at his hotel. This time I had more than just a few aspirational thoughts about winning races in my head. Having had time to digest that first meeting in Cardiff, Pete Keen and I had formulated our ambitions into what we hoped was an attractive proposition for him. Highly detailed, including intermediate targets, main goals for the year and even scheduled periods of down time, the proposal was the sporting version of a fully worked up business plan. We called it a performance plan.

All of the activities listed in the document were subservient to the year's big objective: to win the opening stage of the 1994 Tour de France. But it didn't stop there. The document also listed the inaugural World Time Trial Championship and the individual pursuit title as targets. Both of these were to be contested in Sicily just three weeks after the Tour. In order to recover and have time for some specific training on the track, I was proposing to withdraw from my debut Tour de France after ten days.

For my first year as a professional we had just outlined a scheme to win a stage of the world's greatest bike race, taking the yellow jersey in the process, followed by a couple of world titles. This didn't seem unrealistic to us. I'm sure Roger didn't believe half of our aggressive battle plan but, somewhere between amused and impressed, he agreed. It probably didn't fully register with him, but in my eyes he'd just signed up to the fine print of my schedule for the next year – and I wouldn't want to deviate from it without very good reason.

When the talk turned to money I excused myself and went for a walk, something Pete had been eager for me to do. I had no real idea about my worth as a pro and would have been happy with about £50,000. I knew that Pete saw things differently: he didn't want to base the asking price on sporting potential alone, but factor in the media value we'd generated already. An hour later, I met him in the hotel lobby for a progress report. A base figure of £90,000 was being proposed. In addition, should I achieve the ambitious goals we'd set out, there was a hefty bonus arrangement that would see me not only receive a cash sum for each performance but an equivalent hike in my base salary for the following year. I was delighted. It would be the first stable income Sally and I had ever had.

All that, though, was for next season and this one wasn't quite over. Due to my hour record success, I had been invited to several prestigious end-of-year time trials and Roger was keen that I should ride them in GAN colours. Pete's proposed solution was an interim contract to see us to the end of 1993 while he and Roger hammered out the final details of the main deal. As well as a source of extra cash, it would be a useful introduction to the pro world before breaking for the winter, a chance for the enthusiastic 'ten-year-old' to spend a day in the big school before moving up.

I signed the letter of intent Pete had with him and walked out of the hotel a professional bike rider. I was both delighted and scared by the magnitude of the commitment I'd just made. Devising high pressure situations for myself and then dreaming about how to get out of them was becoming a habit.

My first event as a professional was the Grand Prix Eddy Merckx, an invitation time trial held on the outskirts of Brussels. It was a crisp September morning when Pete Woodworth and I walked out of Charleroi airport to be met by the GAN team *soigneur*, Michel Decock.

As far as I know, the term *soigneur* is unique to cycling. Although the role revolves around massaging the tired legs of athletes, it's much more than that. Imagine Jeeves with a physiotherapy degree and you'll be on the right lines. Short, stocky and bearded, Michel made up for his lack of English with a warm and welcoming smile. He had worked with Roger for many years – had been his *soigneur* when he was a rider – and was part of the team's DNA. He would be my friend and companion for the duration of my time as a pro. Eight years later, it would be Michel who dropped me off at the same spot to fly home from my last professional race.

Bike loaded into the boot of the team car, we set off for a small Best Western hotel adjacent to the famous Atomium on the edge of the Parc d'Osseghem. Nearing the end of the season, the team's stock of equipment and clothing was running low. It was also unusual for a new rider to come on board so late in the year, so there was no team kit or bike set aside for me. I was allowed to use my own TT machine, an aluminium Terry Dolan model that he'd resprayed for me in GAN colours. For clothing, I had to make do with one of Greg LeMond's spare skinsuits.

The race was 66 km: two laps of a wide, fast, course through the park and the Brussels suburbs. It might have been no big deal for the team – part of an end of season wind-down, ridden largely for contract money – but for me, it was akin to a world championship. Amateurs rarely got an opportunity to test themselves against those in the paid ranks so I had no idea how I would fare.

It was spitting with rain as I waited on the start ramp, with a clock – exactly like the one in Barcelona – ticking down to my left. On both sides photographers snapped away and behind was a GAN team car with my name emblazoned across the front. It felt as though I'd parachuted into one of the TV scenes of my youth. I was as nervous as I'd been for the Olympic final.

The starter's hand hovered in front of my face, fingers being withdrawn in time with the five-second countdown. As his last digit disappeared, I bolted out of the start gate and threw myself around the first couple of bends, almost running out of road. Soon, though, all the colour and noise was wiped away to be replaced with the realities of riding against the clock: the zing of tyres on tarmac, the rumble of traffic and the sound of my own breathing. I'd burst out of the unfamiliar into a world I probably knew better than any pro cyclist.

In 1993 there were no wireless earpieces for riders and no in-car TVs relaying live images of the event to team managers. All the race vehicles had were CB radios on which the *commissaires* issued timing and other information. Anything worth passing on was screamed out of the car window. The single checkpoint on the course was at the finish line, so the only useful update on how I was doing would come at the end of the first lap. Twenty seconds or so after I zipped past the half-distance mark Roger started to shout from the car that I was leading.

Over the second lap I increased my advantage on the next fastest man, my new teammate Pascal Lance, with the Dutch star Jelle Nijdam, who'd won the race the year before, finishing third. It was my debut as a pro, the first opportunity to measure myself against the big boys, and I'd won. The trophy, a dinner plate-sized bronze Eddy Merckx logo complete with rainbow bands, is one of the few mementos I've kept from my time as a pro. Now broken in two parts from some forgotten accident, it sits on the bookcase in my office.

*

Roger, still finalising negotiations with Pete, seemed happy enough but wasn't overtly ecstatic. I later learned that having driven back to Paris that night to the team's HQ, he walked into the local bar with a straight face and paused before shouting 'Champagne!'

CHAPTER 7

Pro Life

Among the many events I had been invited to as an Olympic gold medal winner was a dinner hosted by British Airways, who were launching a new direct route from Manchester to Barcelona. My fee for attending was four club class tickets to anywhere they flew in the world.

During the evening there was a business card draw with a first prize of two of the same unrestricted tickets. Not knowing that it wasn't the done thing to enter competitions at gatherings you'd been paid to attend, Sally and I dropped in a card each. An hour later when mine was drawn out I had just enough of a conscience to tell the master of ceremonies to draw it again, which he did and took out Sally's card. Sod it, I thought, and accepted.

In December 1993 we used the tickets for our first proper holiday since we were 17, taking the children and my parents to the ski resort of Mammoth Mountain in California. We'd never flown as a family before, let alone in club class, and I half expected one of the flight crew to come and tell us we were in the wrong cabin and had to move. It was especially odd seeing our two toddlers with their own seats. Harriet, though, seemed pretty relaxed about it: she fell asleep and wet hers.

We'd never been to a ski resort either, but it was exactly what I needed to escape from the two-wheeled world. On the first morning we all awoke with headaches and it was only when the top blew off the jar of Nescafé we'd brought with us, spraying granules around the kitchen of our apartment, that the penny dropped. We were at 9,000 feet. The extreme environment was probably a contributing factor in George Douglas Boardman's unexpected arrival shortly after we got home. He was six weeks early and spent the first seven days of his life in the neonatal intensive care unit at Arrowe Park.

All of our children's names were chosen for their own specific reasons but the influences weren't always obvious or particularly profound. George was the lead character in one of Sally's favourite films, *It's A Wonderful Life*, which she'd watched on the return flight. The other main role was an angel called Clarence, so I think George dodged a bullet there. His second name, Douglas, had a source closer to home: family friend and national cycling coach, Doug Dailey.

Born in Liverpool, Doug was a member of my dad's first club, the Melling Wheelers, where he'd been a strong road cyclist, winning the national title twice. I had first really got to know him at Kirkby Sports Centre where he was the manager. He often came out training with us on the North West Centre of Excellence rides that left from there every other Saturday through the winter. In 1986 he left his job in Kirkby to become the national cycling coach, and during his time in charge he took me to my first international time trial, the Grand Prix de France, drove me down to Chichester for my initial meeting with Peter Keen and managed the GB team at the 1992 Olympics.

In 1997 he handed over the performance reins to Peter Keen and after a short break resumed work with the national squad as head of logistics. From Barcelona to London, Doug was always there. I doubt there is one of Britain's Olympic or Tour de France stars of the last decade who doesn't have a Doug story to tell. He was even responsible for talent-spotting a young Chris Froome at the 2006 Commonwealth Games and flagging him up to Dave Brailsford as one to watch.

In all the time I've known him, Doug has made a point of leading by example. I've never seen him eat anything unhealthy, his strongest curse is 'bloody hellfire', and he does 50 star jumps before breakfast. I'm not sure if that last bit is true but I'd like it to be. By anybody's standards, Doug Dailey is the epitome of the sporting role model. After London 2012, his eighth Olympics with Team GB in one role or another, he retired. Doug now lives on the outskirts of Ruthin in North Wales with his partner Norma, who is still slipping illicit sugar and fat into his diet.

On 24 January 1994, nine days after George's arrival, I travelled to France for GAN's annual training camp, held just outside the ancient hilltop town of Monflanquin in the Lot-et-Garonne region.

The village, with its narrow cobbled streets, dated back to the thirteenth century and had an effortless charm. Surrounded by miles of quiet lanes that wound through rolling hills – dusted with frost when I arrived – it was the perfect place for training. I'd been looking forward to meeting Greg LeMond, but the GAN team leader was not attending this pre-season gathering, so of the 18 riders there I was the only English speaker.

The team's approach to training wasn't overly complicated: five- to six-hour group rides every day. The long distances discouraged anything other than a steady pace and the size of the group meant seeing the front as few as four times in a ride. For someone used to doing a fifth of the volume at three times the intensity, it was a shock. I wasn't there to train, though, I was there to integrate, understand the workings of a professional squad and get to know my teammates. That was easier said than done. And it wasn't easily said – I spoke almost no French. Six hours on a bike every day for a week listening to everyone laughing and joking around me was tough. I'd had some lessons through the winter but hadn't made much progress. 'Passe-moi le sel et le poivre s'il vous plaît' was one of the few phrases that had stuck, so although I was lonely I never had to endure under-seasoned food.

At the end of the week Gilbert Duclos-Lassalle, one of the team's elder statesmen, hosted a gathering in his lodge where riders were obliged to drink the local prune liqueur. The only food on offer was a huge mound of cold duck confit in the centre of the table. It was a wholly predictable recipe for disaster.

Team climber Jean-Philippe Dojwa made the most amazing transformation. The shy, retiring individual we'd seen in camp until then disappeared to be replaced by a prune-fuelled party animal. The metamorphosis lasted about 15 minutes before he threw up in the bread basket, which unfortunately was wicker. During those 15 minutes, though, he'd revealed himself as a fluent English speaker. In fact, after a week of shrugs and linguistic solitary confinement, I found most of the team now seemed to speak my language, an ability that had evaporated by breakfast the next day.

After a week back at home I flew to Montpellier for my first continental stage race: the Tour of the Mediterranean. The field of almost 200 riders was double anything I'd been in as an amateur. My room-mate for the trip was 22-year-old Nicolas Aubier, from Roger Legeay's home town of Le Mans. He was a quiet lad but could speak a few words of English, which is probably why he got stuck with me. Nicolas was alongside me when we lined up for stage 1a: a short team time trial to place the leader's jersey before the race hit the road in earnest later in the day. For GAN, it turned out to be more of a stampede, an uncoordinated charge in roughly the same direction, rather than a squad effort. I put the crude approach down to the fact that this was a minor event early in the season.

That afternoon we congregated in Beziers town centre for stage 1b. The 99 km route consisted almost entirely of narrow, undulating roads which would take us along the Mediterranean coast to Lattes. As soon as the flag dropped, the strongest teams decided that the stiff crosswinds blowing in off the sea made it the ideal time to go on the offensive. Road racing is all about slipstreaming, letting the rider in front punch a hole in the air for you. It saves an enormous amount of energy, sometimes halving the amount of effort needed to travel at the same speed as the unprotected man you're riding behind.

When the wind blows from the side, though, things get tricky – and diagonal. With a large bunch of riders all trying to shelter just behind and slightly to the side of the man in front of them, the width of the road soon becomes the limiting factor in the size of any one group, or echelon. So the bunch splits into a series of echelons and if you aren't in the first one you can quickly find yourself out of the running. That's why the strongest and most skilful riders try to use crosswinds to isolate their rivals.

As the pace shot up, the air filled with the sound of screeching brakes and the smell of burning rubber as riders played chicken with each other, fighting over every scrap of shelter, desperately trying to make sure they weren't the ones left behind. Despite the 60 kph speeds, some cavalier individuals were even bunny-hopping up kerbs to extend the echelon one place wider than the road surface would allow. The more experienced riders cut their losses early and swung out, encouraging others to go with them and form secondary lines – temporary alliances to share the burden of trying to keep pace with the leaders. The fighting, braking, skidding and sprinting to catch up was relentless and 20 minutes into the stage there were diagonal lines of riders as far as the eye could see. I had a great view of them all because I was at the back. It was a baptism of wind. For a rider with only UK road racing under his belt, and whose forte was riding alone against the clock on dual carriageways, it was also terrifying. An all out punch-up would have been preferable as far as I was concerned, and possibly less dangerous.

The next morning, having lost both time and a little skin on the road to Lattes, I started stage two filled with dread at the prospect of another day of the same. Comfort arrived in the figure of Robert Millar. When I was 16 I'd had a poster of him on my bedroom wall: the Scottish legend in his Tour de France polka dot King of the Mountains jersey. Now we were in the same race, although to this point I'd only caught glimpses of him. Seeing me riding along stiff-armed and terrified, he pulled alongside to offer some support.

'It's not like this all the time,' he told me. 'It's just first-race syndrome. Lots of new pros not used to the big bunches and desperate to prove themselves. It'll calm down soon.' It hadn't occurred to me that this wasn't the norm and that others might be wetting themselves too. I found his words immensely reassuring.

Robert was right: as the general classification became established, the race settled into a rhythm and I even managed to slip into a breakaway on the final stage. At the start of the week, I'd been convinced my peloton partners were all crazy, willing to risk their lives to get into a move or be in the first 20 around an important corner. Then I realised the more depressing truth. They weren't mad – the relatively small number of crashes amid all the mayhem was testament to that – they were simply much, much better at this than I was.

After the race had finished, we travelled inland to the mountainous Var region, the team's base for the next few weeks of racing. With almost no flat or straight roads, the area is peppered with sleepy hamlets, each dominated by its arrangement of gnarled olive trees standing watch over boules-playing pensioners. I would return to the same family hotel in the ancient village of Seillans several times during my career, always in February; late enough for the mimosa to have begun to flower but retaining enough of a chill to ensure the evening air was streaked with wood smoke, the smell of which will always remind me of the place.

Our tranquil sojourn in the low mountains was broken up by regular sorties to single day races, both in France and just over the border in Italy. The last of these was the toughest of the year-long French Cup series, the Tour de Haut Var. In the few races I'd ridden so far, I'd had neither the skill nor the courage to hold my place in the peloton and had been near the back every time things got serious. If the pressure stayed on I was usually able to claw my way forward just in time to see the move of the day slip away. This looked like being the pattern for the Tour de Haut Var too.

At half distance, a vicious assault on the climb up to the hilltop city of Mende strung out the field and from that point on the race never slowed. Over the next couple of hours I passed body after suffering body, yet whenever I looked behind I seemed still to be among the last few. As we passed through Draguignan to complete our final hilly lap before the finish, I became fully aware of how hard the event had been – and not just for me. There were now only 20 of us left in what had become the lead group, not because of any attacking move but through simple attrition. Alongside me was former world champion Gianni Bugno. Maybe I wasn't doing too badly.

I eventually crossed the line an exhausted sixteenth and with mixed emotions. Up until this race I had been out of my element;

linguistically isolated, frequently scared to death and taking a daily battering on the bike. Now here I was feeling happy with having clung on for a top 20 finish. Is this what I'd been reduced to? For someone used to winning it had been a tough opening month. I'd got through it, but I still couldn't see how I was going to survive long-term in the world of European road racing, or even whether I wanted to.

The performance plan we'd agreed upon the previous winter had the opening time trial of Paris–Nice as my first real objective of the year. But when the route came out there was no opening time trial. Clearly the race organisers hadn't been aware of my carefully worked out schedule, or my need for a morale-boosting early-season win. Based on my performances so far, Roger decided I'd be best served by going to the Vuelta a Murcia instead, news he delivered in apologetic tones. Not being an aficionado of pro cycling, it took me a while to work out why.

Murcia, I discovered from asking around, was the poor relation of Paris–Nice: a second division bike race stocked with a ragtag mix of riders, some of them heading for retirement, others coming back from injury or starting their seasons late. But it did have a prologue: at 6.7 km, flat and non-technical, it was practically a pursuit – as close to home territory as I was ever going to get. I edged out the Dutch time trial specialist Erik Breukink to win the stage and with it the first leader's jersey of my professional career.

Wearing yellow turns even a lowly neo-pro into temporary peloton royalty. Instead of having to fight to hang on to the back of the lead group, I was escorted to the front, or at least my jersey was.

With the mountains looming, I didn't think the experience would last long, but for the moment I was able to ride unmolested up at the head of the field.

I was amazed at just how much easier it was in this part of the peloton, and for the first time I could really understand why it had been so hard just 100 metres in arrears. Those at the front decided when life would be made hard. The result of their actions – slowing down or speeding up – took a few seconds to ripple backwards through the peloton and that lag had a profound effect. While the leading riders eased and recovered between efforts, those behind were still working hard to catch up. By the time the chasers were able to freewheel, the front runners were ready to go again. The rear half of the peloton was constantly reacting, never quite in sync with those dictating the pace, and the result was a never-ending fight just to stand still.

With the help of our makeshift team I held on to the jersey through stage one, but the following day I was unable to go with the lead riders on the final climb. For the rest of the race, even without the jersey, I still benefited from an enhanced reputation, a subtle respect that saw others think twice before trying to push me out of line when the going got hard. The last stage was another short time trial, which I won from the overall race victor, Melchor Mauri of Banesto. In the final rankings I was well down the field in an event contested by the peloton's weak and injured. Even so, the Vuelta a Murcia was where my personal fortunes started to turn. I headed home happy.

In fact, being able to head home was an important part of the deal I'd struck with Roger. For most British riders, signing with a continental team meant moving to France, Spain or Italy. But then most riders would be following a familiar pattern: work hard, gain results, turn pro, win races, earn money, get married, have kids. For a very select few, that career arc might culminate in an attempt on the world hour record. I had the marriage, the kids and the hour record already. My home life was well established and so were my working methods. Yes, a move to France would have meant nicer weather, better roads, a ready supply of training partners and easier travel to races. But it wouldn't have been home. I had no desire to move to Europe, I was happy to commute and keep the two sides of my life separate.

The cycling portion of it – considered, planned, structured – couldn't have contrasted more with our domestic situation. In the Boardman household, circumstances were and still are allowed to evolve organically. Whatever develops is then expertly managed by Sally. I'm aware that this description makes my wife sound like either a saint or a hippie, but the reality of Mrs B is much more complex. Sally has no time for: cleaning, U2, people who agree with her, wasabi, Halloween, magicians, being told what to do, sports, pre-planned social arrangements, writing, large plates of food or clowns. She likes: cinnamon, renovating old houses, pub quizzes, mountains, QI, non-smoky whisky, karaoke, Bonfire Night, Disneyland, Flying Saucers (the sweets, not the spaceships), factual books, fabrics, snow, babies and tasting other people's dinners.

While I was immersed in the very narrow world of performance cycling, an activity she only ever had a peripheral interest in, Sally looked after a baby, two toddlers, paid the bills, did the tax returns and generally presided over the important parts of our life. In 1994, in her role as head of Boardman UK, she decided it was time for us to leave our little terraced house in Walker Street and find a 'proper' family home. After scouring the listings in the local estate agents and several visits to properties with potential, she narrowed it down to a shortlist of one. It was her favourite number of choices to present me with when marital etiquette dictated a joint decision.

Our move was scheduled for the end of the season, so I tackled my first pro campaign using the system we'd developed to cope with our cramped living quarters. My bikes, tools and other equipment were all kept in a shed in my parents' small back garden. My King-cycle rig, the sophisticated home-trainer we used for physiology testing, was stored at Pete Woodworth's place. Pounding away on stationary bikes in kitchens and mopping up the sweat afterwards might look laughable from the lottery-funded heights of today's training programmes. But anyone peering through the steamed-up windows would actually have been watching cutting-edge science in action. Each workout was a custom Pete Keen creation, with training loads measured to the watt. Every exercise was logged, the results meticulously analysed, discussed and then used to adjust the design of the next session. We were a learning machine.

My two stage wins in Murcia had been good enough for Roger to include me in the line-up for the prestigious Criterium du Dauphiné Libéré, a race that featured a prologue, a longer time trial and two big climbing days – all the elements of a Tour de France telescoped into eight high-pressure stages. Usually held in early June, it was a race the Tour favourites often used to sharpen their form. For everyone else it was a test, a chance to prove to their managers that they were also worth a place on the team for the world's greatest race.

With an eye towards the long and often mountainous days, most riders prepared by seeking out hilly terrain and pushing their volume of training ever higher. I went the other way, focusing almost entirely on short power efforts. The Dauphiné prologue was 6.7 km long, half a kilometre shorter than the one coming up in the Tour five weeks later, and it was the only stage I was interested in. There'd be no raised hand or amused smile from Roger if I could win impressively here, just a Gallic shrug of acceptance that some riders were meant to go to the big race in their first pro-season.

The route of the 1994 Dauphiné opener drew a triangle around the Alpine spa town of Évian-les-Bains. Starting on the shores of Lac Leman, it quickly turned inland, up a two kilometre climb before plunging back to the lake shore for a one kilometre dash along the Rue de Lac to the finish. It was much hillier than the Tour's Lille circuit would be in July but it was close enough for my purposes. I recced the course to work out my strategy and decided on a steady rather than an explosive start, similar to the way I'd tackled UK hill climbs as an amateur. The danger here was going out too hard and blowing up on the ascent. I asked the team mechanics for an extra large gear on my TT machine, so that I would be able to pedal instead of just freewheel on the three kilometre downhill section back to the lake shore.

As I'd expected, I lost time to the climbers on the first half of the course, but being able to power my way down from the top of the hill allowed me to recover my losses. I hit the flat at top speed and took the win by one second from my teammate Jean-Philippe Dojwa. It was my second yellow jersey of the year, and this time not in the lacklustre setting of the Vuelta a Murcia but at the head of a field building up for the biggest event of the season.

Three days later I won the 38 km time trial stage. The race was now halfway through and I was still in yellow. Judging from the quizzical looks I was getting, many of the riders and team managers were bemused by my continued presence at the head of such a prestigious stage race – none of them more than I was – but they weren't overly worried because the high mountains were still to come.

From the start Greg LeMond had been genuinely excited for me. The Dauphiné was our first race together; in fact it was the first time we'd met. Greg had been struggling with health issues that were hard to identify and even harder to shake off. Whatever they were, it was beginning to look as though his brilliant career was drawing to a close. Having won the Tour three times he was now fighting just to make the team. I'd been slightly starstruck and apprehensive about how he'd take to me. I needn't have worried; whatever his own problems he had delighted in my success. Greg was full of warmth and had an insatiable curiosity that made it impossible not to like him instantly. And, of course, we had a love of innovation and technology in common.

Greg had famously won the 1989 Tour de France with triathlon bars fitted to his time trial bike. He'd been an early adopter of the SRM system, a sort of black-box device that precisely measured power output, pulse, speed, cadence and temperature. When he found out that I used the same German-made gadget, he plied me with question after question about my training. This level of interest in the thoughts of a neo-pro from someone who'd achieved all he had was enormously flattering. He even gave me some tips on how to move through a densely packed peloton that proved invaluable as I fought to hold on to the yellow jersey for as long as I could.

With three stages left we entered the Alps proper. At the crest of the penultimate climb, before the summit finish at Echirolles, there were just 30 riders left in the lead group and amazingly I was one of them. Never having been in this position before, I had no idea what to do. Judging by Roger's face as he pulled alongside in the team car, it hadn't been in his script either. We looked at each other through the open window, silently framing the same question: 'You don't think we could actually win this, do you?' It was a wonderful moment and the thought lingered for almost an hour until the foot of the final climb, at which point I ran out of fuel and blew spectacularly. I rode the last 10 km alone, counting down every metre to the finish line on the computer mounted on my handlebars.

Losing the yellow jersey was more of a relief than a disappointment. The pressure was off: I'd exceeded both my own and everyone else's expectations by an order of magnitude, and my place in GAN's Tour de France team was secure. Now there were only two stages between me and a welcome trip home.

One of the odd habits that persist among the logistics staff on just about every pro team is booking post-race flights ridiculously close to the end of an event. Perhaps they're running a secret competition of their own, with points awarded for the shortest time between podium and check-in. Whatever the reason, most races in my career seemed to be followed by a second race to the airport, with a crazed *soigneur* at the wheel breaking the speed limit and me in the backseat wondering whether I was going to die or just miss my flight.

I'm a worrier in any case, and my chief worry on the final stage of the Dauphiné was getting it over with in time to be home on the Wirral that evening. Stage seven was a 157 km loop around Chambéry, and from the moment the flag dropped it was clear that no one wanted to animate the race. The overall winner had pretty much been decided – ONCE's Laurent Dufaux had a handy lead – and as far as stage honours went it looked as though everyone was happy to wait for the final sprint. As we crawled along I began to get increasingly stressed about missing my plane. In an effort to speed things up I attacked and to my surprise I was allowed to slip away with half a dozen others.

That was too many for ONCE who began to work at the front to reel us in. Knowing that it was the size of the move making the team of the race leader nervous, the experienced members of the break started to attack in ones and twos to see if they'd be allowed some glory that didn't threaten the overall result. I wasn't interested in that: I'd had my two stage wins, I just wanted a good average speed. So rather than join in, I hung off the back, waiting until everyone had made their attempts and failed.

At the foot of a small drag, just as the last escapee was clawed back by the peloton, I made my own bid for freedom and it worked. It was my first successfully executed tactical move; I'd taken the measure of my opponents, watched for an opportunity and countered successfully. My sense of satisfaction wore off when I realised I'd committed myself to an 80 km solo ride to the line that included several hard climbs on the finishing circuit. Having mopped up the other riders, and knowing they could now control the outcome of the race, ONCE chose not to chase and left me out there. Because it had been a hard week and no one else was inclined to take it on either, I picked up my first ever road stage win.

It was common then for even major races to feature novelty prizes, something that would offer finish-line photographers an alternative to the standard podium shots. The most bizarre one I ever saw was a cow. That year's Dauphiné was sponsored by a Swiss confectionery brand, and the winner of each stage had to sit on a huge set of scales while their body weight in chocolate was piled onto the other side. With three wins, I'd accumulated 210 kg of the stuff, which was gleefully loaded by the team staff into the camper van. I took a couple of bars with me for the kids – OK, for me – and dashed off to catch the plane.

It was a dash, too. I was late. Having won the stage, I'd had to go to doping control, attend the presentation and then give interviews. I'd have been able to get away from the finish much earlier

One year old with a bucket and ice cream, what more could a boy want?

The gang by the River Nidd during Harrogate cycling festival, where I spent a lot of time wandering around in just underpants

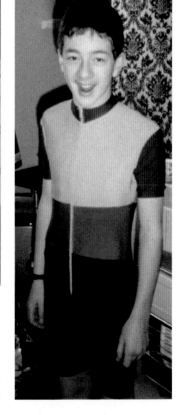

My first skinsuit. Yes, I thought it looked good

With my mother, Carol, in my dancing shoes at one of the many club dinners

With my dad, Keith, post Olympics

Our wedding, October 1988. We're wearing our official Team GB Olympic suits to save money. Left to right: Simon Lillistone, Eddie Alexander, me, Sally, Glen Sword, Louise Jones

Battling the wind in the National
Hill Climb Championships, 1989

Barcelona, 1992.
An unemployed
carpenter seconds away
from Olympic gold

(opposite) The moment I
realised it didn't just happen
to 'people on TV'

(right) Finding Sally in the crowd.
She was begrudgingly forgiven for
spending the last of our savings
on a plane ticket

Returning home to Walker Street it dawned on me: you can't turn this off

With Ed, Sally and Harriet posing for more cheesy post-Olympic photos featuring more fashion faux-pas

The amazing Graeme Obree, the real innovator

A full hour record dress rehearsal in Peter Keen's lab to see if I could cope with the predicted Bordeaux heat (Pete's in the background). The wire going down my shorts is measuring my core temperature…

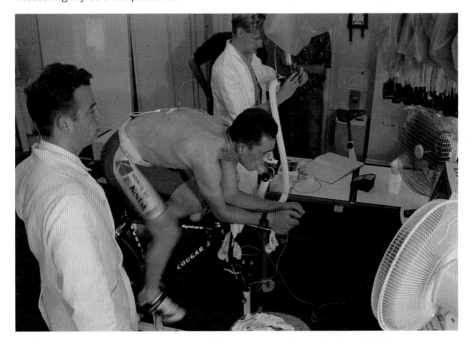

Visibly shrunken after the successful Bordeaux hour attempt. Pete Woodworth is on the right

1997 and weight obsessed in what would be a fruitless attempt to keep up with the climbers

if I'd just sat quietly in the slow-moving bunch all day. As for the chocolate, I never saw another gram of it.

My next race was the Tour of Switzerland in late June. It was my last outing before the Tour de France, and my first on the bike I'd use for the Tour prologue.

Lotus hadn't sat still since we'd gone our separate ways in 1992. Having divorced themselves from Mike Burrows, they'd set about designing a road version of the Barcelona track bike and by mid-1994 the Lotus 110 was ready. They just needed someone to ride it. In theory, any half-decent cyclist should have fitted the bill. After all, as they'd made clear in our post-Olympic negotiations, the bike was the more important component. In practice, things had been less straightforward. I knew they'd already tried to prove their point on the track by sponsoring Bryan Steel, a member of the national team. He was a classy rider, but lending him a Lotus hadn't turned him into a world champion.

My history with the company made me both the most logical and least likely candidate to pilot the new road machine; our successful partnership was a matter of public record, the acrimony of our split made even talking about resuming it a non-starter. But the Tour was impossible for Lotus to resist. As launching platforms for new products went, only the Tour de France could match an Olympics. Even better from a British manufacturer's point of view, this one was heading to the UK in its opening week. So instead of approaching me they went to Roger and offered to sponsor the team. If Lotus became GAN's official bike supplier, I'd be obliged to ride one whether I wanted to or not.

GAN already had a bike sponsor – LeMond, Greg's company. But when he saw the new frame, even Roger – who wasn't a technologically-minded person – could tell it was something special. It was light years ahead of the team's round-tubed, aluminium time trial machines, which were barely more than road bikes with clip-on bars. I don't know what passed between them, but Roger got permission from Greg to try out other equipment and bought three Lotus frames. Considering the back-door route they'd chosen to get me on one of their machines, I wasn't inclined to make it easy for them, but neither was I going to cut off my nose to spite my face. I would let performance be the sole deciding factor.

So it was that Rudy Thomann and Richard Hill turned up at the team hotel in Lugano with their all-new frame. They were cutting it fine: two weeks before the start of the Tour de France and only 24 hours until the time trial stage of this, my last warm-up race.

The S-shaped Lotus 110 looked as much like a sculpture as a piece of sports equipment. Even without wind tunnel data, I'd have staked my salary on it having half the drag of the team's current TT machine. It was clearly designed by an aerodynamics expert, but just as clearly by one who didn't ride a bike. At the time, almost all manufacturers of time trial bikes used a smaller wheel at the front than at the back. Combined with a tiny head tube, this created a slope from saddle to handlebars that lowered the rider into an aerodynamic tuck. Lotus had opted instead for a full-size front wheel, which wouldn't have mattered so much if the bars had sat low, directly on the crown of the fork, as they had on their original track machine. But they didn't, the

110 utilised a standard handlebar/stem arrangement which put the tri-bars a whopping eight inches higher than on the Barcelona version.

In fact, all of the geometry was that of an upright road bike, something it couldn't be used as because there was nowhere on the entire frame to bolt a water-bottle cage. Clearly a lot of money and knowledge had gone into creating this beautiful object, but for the want of a 30-minute chat with an actual time trialist it would never be a commercial success.

Despite all its faults and the long list of compromises that would be needed to overcome them, the frame looked fast enough to be worth persevering with. I asked the team mechanics to build it up using an articulated Look Ergo stem to get it even close to low enough at the front. On the morning of the Tour of Switzerland time trial stage, a straightforward 30 km run along the shores of Lake Lugano, I went for a test ride to see if it was going to justify all the hassle. The advantage of having large wheels and a slack head-angle was that it handled really well for a TT bike. And although it was heavy, the faster I went the more I believed the Lotus had something to offer.

That afternoon's time trial would be the last chance to try anything new in competition before the Tour itself, so with a couple of hours to go until the start I agreed to use the bike. Over 30 km I was 45 seconds faster than Italy's Gianluca Pierobon in second place. For me, the decision was made. For Greg, founder of LeMond Bicycles, there was an obvious conflict of interest. But he was so taken with the sleek lines of the Lotus that he also opted to use one of the frames Roger had bought for the upcoming prologue in France.

After Switzerland, I took the Lotus home, rode it daily, fettled the position and rode it some more. I had a special pair of bars made to get around the height problem at the front. By the time I set off for the Tour I was familiar with every aspect of how it handled.

CHAPTER 8
The Tour

Announcing lofty intentions a year in advance to your boss is a gamble: win and you're a genius-cum-prophet whose opinions are suddenly held in high esteem; fail and you're an arrogant little shit. I was about to find out which label I'd be awarded.

As well as the pressure I'd created for myself, the Tour organisers had helpfully chipped in to raise the stakes. Three days after the opening prologue time trial in Lille, the 1994 race would be marking the opening of the Channel Tunnel by putting the riders onto trains and heading to the UK for two stages. My debut Tour de France offered me the chance not just to be the first British rider to wear the yellow jersey since Tommy Simpson in 1962, but to go one better by being the first ever to wear it on home roads.

A lot had to go right for that to happen. For a start, I had to do my bit and make good on my pledge to Roger to win the prologue. Then I had to keep the race lead for another three stages. The big danger would be the third of them: the team time trial.

Whatever small margin I might manage to eke out over my rivals on a course of 7.2 km would have to be protected by the whole team over 66.5 km.

On Wednesday 29 June, three days before the race began, I left the UK to join my eight Tour teammates for some training in Calais, which is where the time trial would begin. Having invested so much energy and attention to detail in making sure that I had everything shipshape for the big race, it was a shock to walk out of the hotel, shoes in hand and ready to ride, to find most of my team-mates adjusting saddles and triathlon bars. This was the eve of the Tour de France and they were only now thinking about positions. It was another half an hour before the mass tinkering was complete and we set off along the race route.

After 30 km Roger shouted from the following car that we should start riding hard, so like a large breakaway in a race – which is how they approached the exercise – everyone took their turn at the front. The problem with that, of course, is that breakaways are made up of riders from rival teams and we were supposed to be on the same side.

Before our session, I'd wanted to discuss what we were going to do, the length of each man's turn, how we were going to communicate and the best way to utilise the different abilities within the team. The others wanted to 'just smash it'. So they hit the front one by one, none of them looking around to see how their teammates might be doing, nobody adjusting their pace to make it easier for the rider who'd just peeled off from the lead position to rejoin at the back. Unable to keep up, the weaker riders kept missing turns, breaking the relaying chain, and the resulting sprint/stall cycle was exhausting.

I imagined all our errors would immediately be picked apart in the debrief: the approach for the Tour de France would surely be more sophisticated than that of five months earlier in the Tour of the Med. It wasn't. There was no discussion about what had just happened or what could be done differently. The only post-ride team activity was lunch. I was frustrated: it looked like the main thing we'd learned from the three-hour outing was that riding fast makes your legs hurt. I couldn't see how we were going to avoid a repeat performance on the big day.

It wasn't that the GAN riders and staff were lazy or complacent: they just didn't know what they didn't know. In most cases they'd spent the whole of their professional lives in the closed world of professional cycling, where the past was the template for the future and the best way to do things was the way they'd always been done. As a result, progress happened at an evolutionary pace, with the odd giant meteor-type event to shake things up.

The last person who had forced change in the peloton, more than any other rider for a generation, was here now: Greg LeMond. He was the biggest modern day innovator in the sport. Greg wasn't impressed by our collective effort either but didn't seem to have the motivation to press for change. Perhaps it was because he'd already been in this situation too many times before and was out of fight. Perhaps he just had too much to worry about in terms of his own health. Either way, if GAN riders and staff weren't inclined to adopt the outward-looking philosophy of their own Tour-winning team leader, they certainly weren't going to take advice from the likes of me.

We were now just 48 hours away from the prologue, my goal of the year, so as we relocated to Lille for the *Grand Départ* I switched all of my attention to that. Much of what Pete Keen had prescribed for these last few days was doing nothing, which as any motivated athlete will tell you is the hardest thing of all to do. There was one activity I could focus my restless mind on and that was to familiarise myself with the course, but that was something I knew would have to wait until just before race day.

In the meantime, there was my introduction to the Tour's annual pre-race circus, beginning with the bizarre rider medical. As far as I could tell, it served no purpose other than to let the press take photographs of skinny cyclists standing on scales with mock worried looks on their faces, or teammates listening to each other's hearts with stethoscopes.

The other big set-piece waste of a rider's time was the team presentation, held two days before the start and hosted by the amazing memory man of cycling, Daniel Mangeas. Daniel had been at my very first race of the year back in February. Signing on at the small roadside podium, my head had snapped up in surprise when I heard him recounting a list of my amateur results to the small crowd: no notes or aids, just a stream of perfectly recalled facts and figures.

He seemed to be present at both the start and finish line of every event I rode in France, always doing the same thing: conveying in a rush of controlled excitement a constant flow of information about whichever competitor happened to be in front of him. It didn't matter how lowly the rider, Daniel had their career and often family information stored in his head. It was actually quite unnerving. His gravelly voice with its non-stop delivery was the inescapable soundtrack of the Tour. I wondered if he stopped when he went home. Or even whether he had one.

Medical and team presentation done, I could finally focus on my last piece of preparation, the recce. Tour prologues are almost always in city centres, along routes that don't really exist in daily life. They start in pedestrianised squares, head the wrong way up one-way streets and reshape roads and corners with barriers, cones and straw bales. So it's only possible to truly get to grips with a prologue course when the circuit is fully set up and closed to traffic – and usually that only happens the day before the event.

In cycling, as in motorsport, there's little point in technical practice at anything other than race pace. The difference is that in cycling the rider is both pilot and power plant. So the proximity of practice and race day presented a physical and tactical dilemma: how could I go fast enough to learn the Lille course properly without damaging my engine? The solution we devised was for me to slipstream one of the team cars. Serge Beucherie, Roger's second in command, drove around the flat, wide boulevards of the roughly U-shaped circuit at 55 kph, with me tucked in behind. As we approached the important corners, Serge swung the car to the inside and braked hard, leaving me a clear passage into the bends. I could see and feel the line in the same way I would in competition, yet hardly expended any energy.

I did several laps in this fashion, not so much memorising the 7.2 km route as physically absorbing every detail of it. Back at the hotel I replayed my ride again and again in my mind, until even lying in bed I could feel the body movement required to get around a given corner without braking. To Sally's disgust, I can still remember every bend, gradient, grid placement, white line pattern and surface change of the Tour prologue courses I rode, as opposed to our anniversary or the birthdays of any of our kids.

Race day. I got to the circuit two hours before my start time and was momentarily stunned by the transformation the Place du Général de Gaulle had undergone since my training runs 24 hours earlier. The start ramp was surrounded by team cars, crazy vehicles from the publicity caravan, a tented village for VIPs and thousands of noisy spectators trying to get a glimpse of their favourite riders. I stepped into the GAN camping car and took my place at the back, an area I'd claimed as my own earlier in the year. My numbers, folded as small as I thought I could get away with inside the rules, had already been meticulously stuck onto my skinsuit, which I laid out on the narrow bench seat. Next to it, I placed a brand new set of mitts and a carefully cleaned aero helmet. It was a practice bordering on OCD, always the same.

My warm-up routine, a 20-minute set-piece mimicking the Olympic build-up of two years earlier, would begin exactly 30 minutes before my scheduled start time. All there was to do until then was wait.

Although I'd never been much of a reader, when I turned pro and was surrounded by a group of people whose language I didn't speak I became a voracious consumer of novels. These were either good sci-fi or detective stories, never anything factual. They were a fantastic means of being mentally somewhere else.

To the incredulity of the staff, I often had my head in a book a few minutes before the start of the biggest races, when people were bustling all around me. If any of them had noted what page I was reading, they'd have seen that my outward appearance of calm was a sham. I'd stare at the same text for half an hour, my attention constantly slipping off the page and back to the present. In this setting, the time-killing exercise wasn't the reading but the distraction of trying to.

All these activities had become part of a well-practised ritual that remained the same regardless of geographical location or scale of event. It was a familiar framework with which to face the unknown. At the 1991 World Championships in Stuttgart I'd learned about over-training. In Leicester, pursuit racing had helped me master the art of pacing over short distances. At the MIRA wind tunnel we'd gained aerodynamic understanding, and in Barcelona John Syer had taught me how to cope with the pressure of a major event. Now it was time to put all that together for the biggest time trial on the planet, the unofficial prologue world championships.

Sitting in the chair next to the start ramp, awaiting my slot and mentally rehearsing the ride one last time, I barely noticed the press snapping away. Then it was my turn.

The long beep sounded and I dropped down the shallow ramp, the first of the six bends rushing toward me. Banking right onto the wide Boulevard de la Liberté, I quickly sprinted up to speed and tucked into pursuit position, already in the biggest gear I had. My legs were spinning faster than I'd anticipated, perhaps 120 rpm. Had I started too fast? I disciplined myself to hold back. I couldn't let the size of the occasion, the noise of the crowd, or the cries of encouragement from the following car persuade me to push on too early. How far to go? How hard was I working? Was this sustainable? Maybe. The subconscious calculations constantly running in the background.

The second obstacle, an easy 90-degree sweeping left on to the Boulevard Vauban came and went, followed less than a minute later by the fast left on to Boulevard Montebello. Nearly three kilometres in already. System check: working hard, fatigue building but at an acceptable rate, under control. The large roundabout that signified the halfway mark had, like the rest of the circuit, been transformed by the presence of spectators, lining the barriers on the inside of the bend and making it impossible to see the exit. But I already had all the images I needed in my mind's eye, already knew the speed and line I'd take.

I pedalled full gas into the wide curve, hugging the right-hand barriers, waited as long as I dared, then leaned left into the apex. From that pivot point, I started the inexorable drift out towards the kerb, sensing the angles, judging when I could start pushing again without my pedals clipping the road surface. I'd lost only 2–3 kph and was quickly back in the tuck and up to speed.

I was feeling the effort now, starting to rock as my muscles burned. Sideways energy is wasted energy. Another right, past the Place du Maréchal, two kilometres left to go, a little over two minutes of pain. I was approaching the emotional zone, the part of the race where I'd throw everything I had left into the charge for home, but it had to be timed right.

A minute 30 left. One more corner to go, back onto the Boulevard de la Liberté, the finishing straight. This final right was slightly sharper than 90 degrees and was the trickiest of the lot. I reckoned it could – just – be taken at full tilt, but I wasn't one hundred per cent sure. Of the five practice runs I'd had at this blind bend, I'd bottled it and braked three times. If I bottled it now my body was too fatigued to recover the lost speed. Holding my nerve here might make all the difference.

Up ahead I could see a team car. I was catching Festina's Luc Leblanc who'd set off a minute before me. I focused on its tail lights, committed to the last bend without braking, and had to use every millimetre of the wide road to stay upright. The risk had paid off, I'd taken a chunk out of the distance between me and Leblanc and I could sense how much faster than him I was going. A minute 15 left.

In the hot, airless streets, I could feel the pull of Leblanc's team-car 100 m ahead. A moment later it swung out of the way but I'd already had the benefit of a precious few seconds' tow. A minute to go. He was just ahead now, providing a welcome distraction as the effort threatened to overwhelm me. I broke from my plan and started spending the last of my energy early, sprinting to get into his slipstream.

Thirty seconds to go. I catapulted past Leblanc, no time to thank him for giving me a target, and switched my attention to the finish banner looming in front of me. With no shelter and all distraction gone, I was fading fast but it didn't matter, I was already passing over the Fiat logo painted on the road right before the banner. One final lunge and it was done, I was over the line and into the scrum. Michel Laurent, the team's logistics manager, had his arm around me, half holding me up, half steering me towards a chair.

There were still a handful of riders left to come in. Normally the few minutes of waiting for the rest of the field to finish is agonising, but this time I didn't care. It was the closest I'd ever got to a perfect time trial. I'd even got a rare catch to help me maintain speed at exactly the right moment. Regardless of what the others did, I could do no more: 7.2 km in 7 minutes 49 seconds.

I sat surrounded by cameras as one by one the favourites failed to beat my time. Michel was certain it would stand. Someone was saying it was the fastest prologue ever. As the final rider, defending Tour champion Miguel Indurain, came into view it was clear he wasn't even going to get close. The team were celebrating before he hit the line to make it official. I'd won my first ever stage of the Tour de France and with it the most coveted leader's jersey in the world. The previous July, after the hour record in Bordeaux, I'd stood on this podium posing for photographs with the great Indurain. Now I had it to myself.

The rest of the day was a stream of relentless noise and questions like nothing I had experienced before. And on top of the questions, instructions: photographers telling me to hold the champagne glass up, kiss Sally, hold baby George. My initial reaction – the inability to grasp it all – was very much the way I'd felt in Barcelona after my gold medal ride. It was too much and happening too fast to take in. The difference here was that there seemed to be no escape, no protected athletes' village to retreat into. When I walked into the lift at the team hotel a Channel 4 camera crew walked in behind me.

The other advantage of an Olympic medal is that there's no having to get up and defend it the following day from other athletes who want it take it off you. Opening my eyes the next morning confirmed that at least I hadn't lost it overnight. There was the jersey draped across the bedside chair. I lay there for a moment, breaking the news again quietly to myself: I was the leader of the Tour de France. Wow.

At the start, next to the new train station connecting Lille with London, I posed with the other jersey wearers for photographs on the front row of the peloton. I was at the head of 188 of the best professional bike riders in the world, and although handshakes and small talk were being exchanged it was clear the bonhomie wasn't heartfelt. There was an undercurrent of tension. Everyone was acting – more relaxed, confident, cheerful than they probably felt – but I had full-blown stage fright. It was a waking version of the classic anxiety dream: standing in the wings on the opening night of a West End play with no idea of my lines, yet somehow I had the lead role and knew I had to go on anyway. I'd spent years becoming familiar with every aspect of winning time trials, but winning this one had put me in a position I felt hopelessly unqualified for.

For more than half of the opening stage there was a nervous stale-mate, everyone poised with their fingers on metaphorical triggers, waiting for someone else to fire the first shot. Eventually, after an intermediate sprint, the uneasy truce was broken and an escape group of three riders slipped away. One of them was Jean-Paul van Poppel, a multiple stage winner in previous Tours. The other teams looked at us. The chief responsibility to control the race always falls on the team of the yellow jersey, but there were plenty of other people with an interest in pulling the break back – all the squads with sprinters on them, for a start. The situation called for a cool head. When the break-away's lead approached two minutes, I cracked and urged the team to give chase. I wouldn't have made a good poker player.

A little later, Novemail's riders joined in and between us we caught the breakaway with 8 km to go. As we flew into the outskirts of Armentières and under the kilometre flag all together, the sprint-ers' teams took charge. On the finishing straight, with the line in sight, I started to relax, pleased to have got through my first day without incident and still in yellow. A split second later there was a terrible and familiar crunching sound: bicycle parts hitting tarmac. Back in 30th position, I careered to the left, narrowly dodging the fallers and the bits of bike skidding across the road.

Belgium's Wilfried Nelissen, one of the big favourites for the stage win, had ridden head-down and full tilt into a policeman, who incredibly had been standing in the road taking a photograph. Both officer and rider were badly injured and they weren't the only ones. Laurent Jalabert had landed on his face as his frame snapped in two beneath him. I can still see the images of Jalabert sitting dazed and covered in blood on the road.

All this I learned later from TV reports. Then, my first reac-tion was a slightly shaken relief at not having been brought down myself, and the thought that I needed to find Sally to reassure her that I was OK. I imagined her horrified, tears in her eyes, fighting to get through the crowds to see if her husband was one of the casualties. She was in the VIP area drinking champagne.

The crash eventually led to changes in the design of finish lines that are still visible today: regularly spaced scallops in the home straight barriers for policemen to stand in. Presumably, the *gendarmerie* also introduced a strict no-photo policy for officers on duty. More immediately, the incident seemed to have a sobering effect on the peloton and stage two was a low key affair. Festina's Jean-Paul van Poppel took the win, but again, no one took any time from me. I was now just one day from home, one day to survive in yellow before I could lead the race into the UK.

That day, though, was the team time trial. The closest rider to me was Miguel Indurain, 15 seconds back, with the rest of the top ten spaced between 19 and 30 seconds. They were decent gaps for a 7.2 km prologue, but easily erased over the 66.5 km of a lumpy team time trial course, so there were plenty of riders who felt they had a chance of stealing the yellow jersey and taking it through the Channel Tunnel.

Our team rolled down the start ramp in Calais as badly prepared to defend the lead as our pre-race rehearsal had suggested we would be. After 10 km my handlebars came loose. That wasn't a disaster in itself, but the way we dealt with it was. While I dropped back to the support car for an Allen key to carry out some high-speed mechanics, most of the team just charged on oblivious, intent on implementing plan smash-it. By the 22 km mark, we'd lost 36 seconds to the GB-MG Team. Their leader, Johan Museeuw, had started the day seventh, 23 seconds behind me, and was now the leader on the road.

As the strong westerly winds blowing in off the Channel began to buffet us, Francis Moreau was dropped. He was soon followed by Thierry Gouvenou and Jean-Claude Colotti. We were barely past half distance and we were down to six men. With 17 km to go, Eddy Seigneur, one of our strongest riders, powered up the final hill, distancing an ailing Greg LeMond. Greg courageously fought his way back on over the top, which was just as well because Jean-Philippe Dojwa was dropped on the descent. Our time for the stage would be taken on the fifth rider across the line, we couldn't afford to lose anyone else. So at 10 km to go, when Eddy Seigneur inexplicably rode into the crowd rather than take the right hand bend with the rest of us, we lost more precious seconds waiting for him. In the end, we finished a disappointing eighth, one minute and 17 seconds behind the GB-MG team. We were virtually in sight of England's shores and I'd lost the jersey to Johan Museeuw.

Instead of being ushered towards the podium, I was directed with the rest of the team – the other four who hadn't been dropped – in the direction of the camping car to get changed for the journey across the Channel. The transformation from being the focus of the race to a member of the pack was abrupt. The leader's yellow skinsuit was stuffed in the bottom of my day bag, no longer needed. Everyone was flat and no one wanted to talk about what had happened. Roger was putting a brave face on it, as he always did, but I wasn't ready to look forward: I was still frustrated by the needlessly premature end to my ego trip. I continued to brood as we drove the team cars onto the shiny new Eurotunnel train and headed for Dover.

Our island nation didn't seem entirely sure what to do with the Tour when it arrived for the first time in 20 years. Stage four started in the grounds of Dover Castle. A military brass band in full ceremonial dress played on the ramparts in direct competition with a troupe of American cheerleaders strutting their stuff. Meanwhile, the yellow jersey arrived by parachute to be presented to the race leader by a rather rotund and out of place MP. The stunt fell flat, as Johan Museeuw wasn't inclined to change out of the yellow jersey he was already wearing.

Sean Yates and I, the only British riders in the race, were ushered to the front for photographs. I felt a little embarrassed, having failed to be the one in the race lead for the day. It was a relief to roll out through the castle gates and away from small talk, interviews and shouts for autographs.

The race snaked across southern England with me somewhere near the tail. The crowds were huge, pressing in on either side of the road and making it difficult to move up. It wasn't until we reached the barriers of the finishing circuit in Brighton that I finally succeeded in getting to the front. The general classification squads had been riding tempo all stage to keep the time gap to the day's breakaway under control. I arrived just as they were in the process of handing over responsibility to the sprinters' teams for the run-in. I took the opportunity to attack and was surprised to find myself allowed to get away. I shouldn't have been.

Spain's Francisco Cabello and Emmanuel Magnien of France had been out front for most of the day, with Italy's Flavio Vanzella just behind them. With eight kilometres to go the leaders still had a healthy advantage of 1:30, and I'd just launched myself into the gap between them and the bunch. No man's land. At the top of the final climb, with the crowd roaring in my ears, I was joined by another Italian, Enrico Zaina, and we began to work together. But Cabello couldn't be caught. Having dropped Magnien he rode the final five kilometres alone to take the win. Vanzella hung on for third – taking the yellow jersey from his teammate Museeuw in the process – and I took the sprint for fourth. I'd at least shown myself at the front for the crowds. Some sort of honour had been satisfied, although it didn't feel particularly satisfying.

There was no showing off for the home fans the following day. For one thing, I was knackered, and in any case the sprinters' teams took control on stage five to ensure a bunch finish in Portsmouth. By the standards of the time, the Tour's two-day visit to the UK was widely agreed to have been a great success, with an estimated two million spectators watching the race speed by. But when they turned away from the roadside there was nowhere for them to go. No British Cycling machine geared up to guide them into cycling themselves, no mass participation events for them to enter with friends from the pub and no Sky Rides for families. There was just a queue of traffic and a lot of litter. Being in the vanguard of something is not as rewarding an experience for the participants as it is for those who come after. A seed had definitely been sown, but it would take another 13 years for it to germinate.

*

Attacking on the run in to Brighton had been an emotional move born out of frustration and that minor placing came at a heavy price. If I was tired the following day in Portsmouth, I was wiped out by the time we got back to France. Stage six from Cherbourg to Rennes was 270 km, the longest of the race, and I laboured through it. Greg LeMond, though, was in real trouble. Struggling from the off, he finally conceded and abandoned the Tour, citing deep fatigue. He made a few appearances over the remainder of the season, but it was that moment on the road to Rennes that he really called it a day. To leave the Tour in the broom wagon was an inglorious end to what had been an amazing career.

At the other end of the emotional spectrum, Sean Yates, after ten Tours spent almost entirely in the service of others, was having his well-earned moment in the spotlight. Sean had infiltrated the day's breakaway and built up an advantage sufficient to take the yellow jersey. Thirty-two years since the first British leader of the Tour de France, we'd had numbers two and three in the space of a week, even if neither of us had managed it on home roads. Between us, Sean and I had the UK surrounded.

Although all my pre-Tour planning had focused on the prologue, I'd also marked the stage nine time trial from Périgueux to Bergerac as one I might be capable of winning. By the time it arrived I'd lowered my sights. I was now struggling every day not to get dropped. I still rode as hard as I could but was only able to finish fifth, losing a whopping 5 minutes 27 seconds to Miguel Indurain. It was a relief to hit the halfway point of the Tour, the moment in the plan, agreed seven months earlier, that I'd be leaving the race in order to prepare for the world championships in Sicily.

Roger, though, was caught between honour and emotion. He knew what he'd agreed to, that our strategy made sense, but now we were here he wanted me to keep going and worry about the Worlds later. He pleaded with me to continue until the rest day, where we'd 'see how you feel then'. Annoyed at being made to feel uncomfortable when I wasn't the one who was changing the deal, I let myself be persuaded to start stage 11. But it was soon clear, at least to me, that I was utterly spent, emotionally as well as physically. The prospect of finishing the first big mountain stage of the race was not appealing.

I was lying seventh overall and I knew if I went on I was going to get a pasting on the climb to Hautacam. I wanted to stop before that happened. I struggled to hold wheels, as much because I had now lost the desire to fight as through fatigue, and languished at the rear of the field. I dropped back to the car to tell Roger I was going to stop and he continued to try to persuade me to fight on to the end of the day. I was angry. At the time I told myself it was with him, for breaking our contract, for making me feel bad, but in reality it wasn't Roger I was annoyed at. At half distance, I took the unilateral decision to climb off the bike and into the team car at the feed zone. Roger was right: it didn't feel good.

A race *commissaire* stopped alongside me as I got to Michel Decock's car and insisted I remove my race numbers. This was the end of a brilliant Tour debut and yet it tasted like failure. The logical execution of a long-agreed plan had been recast as something shameful, a cowardly way to exit the race. Ah well, shame was one of the few emotions I hadn't experienced on this Tour: might as well add it to the collection. The inside of Michel's car was quiet after the noise of the race, and when I got back to the hotel it was just a hotel. Normal. Well, apart from the TV crew waiting outside. After days of intense pressure, clamour, attention, it was a jarring way to finish.

It would be the end of the season before I understood just how much the 1994 Tour had changed things for me, specifically those first 7.2 km on the streets of Lille. It was then that performance-plan potential became reality, and benign scepticism turned to acceptance of our methods. The Keen/Boardman approach worked in the professional world. At least it had so far.

CHAPTER 9
The Worlds

Six days after leaving the Tour and still deeply tired, I was back on the bike and back in France, in Lyon. There were still two world titles to worry about if I wanted to make good on my hotel room prediction to Roger of 12 months earlier.

In 1994, both Road and Track World Championships were to be held on the island of Sicily. The location and the timing, August, all but guaranteed that they'd be the hottest for years. First would be the track competition, staged outdoors on the bumpy concrete of the Velodromo Paolo Borsellino in Palermo. Less than a week later, 210 km away to the east, the inaugural individual time trial would be run off around the streets of Catania. The circuit, according to a British Cycling reconnaissance trip, would be a rolling, sinuous affair, all on poorly surfaced roads.

To ensure I was properly acclimatised, especially for the near hour-long time trial effort, hot weather training was going to be essential. Lyon had the perfect combination of high temperatures and low quality riding surfaces. I'd competed there at the velodrome of the Parc de la Tête d'Or in the 1989 world championships and the concrete bowl was possibly the slowest track I'd ever ridden, like cycling in a sandpit. When I saw pictures of the Sicilian venue it sprang immediately to mind.

A small team of us flew out to set up camp: the two Petes, my training partner Simon Lillistone and Ann McAllister, a family friend and fluent French speaker. Since I'd barely seen them for the best part of a month, Sally also flew out with Ed, Harriet and George. The summer days fell into a comfortable pattern: riding around the hilly roads of Lyon with Simon, napping, training on the track and swimming in the quiet hotel pool with the kids.

It took most of that two-week trip to fully recover from the fatigue left over from the Tour, but by the time we got back to the UK to perform the unpack and repack for Sicily I was ready for the final phase of the season.

Sally's presence at major events was becoming the norm, although she usually stayed in a separate hotel, allowing me to focus solely on my job. It was especially necessary in this case as she had seven-month-old George with her, who wasn't keen on the idea of sleeping for eight hours at a time, particularly not with night-time temperatures in the mid thirties. In fact at no time during our stay in Sicily did the temperature drop below 34 degrees, often rising above 40 in mid afternoon, which was when I would be riding the time trial.

On the first evening of her stay Sally enquired about meals at her hotel and was told, 'We aren't doing food today, maybe not this week.' The receptionist delivered this message as if it was standard hotel practice. 'Where can I get some?' Sally asked. 'Nowhere, no restaurants in Catania are open,' was the reply, followed by a shrug and a single word: 'Mafia'. Taking pity on her, the hotel staff provided bread, cheese and tomatoes, a diet she lived on for the next two days until everything opened again.

Dotted around were other clues to the invisible forces at work on the island. There were the armed sentries in their bulletproof shelters posted at each corner of the judge's house behind the hotel. Then there were the wreaths along the roadside that I naively thought marked the sites of traffic accidents.

Hot and rough, in every sense, looked like it was going to be the overriding theme of the championships. But after Lyon, the heat at least was tolerable and the rutted Sicilian track was like riding on silk. Now that the exhaustion had faded, I was beginning to feel the benefit of all the hard work I'd done at the Tour. Everything was going to plan, which wasn't the case for poor Graeme Obree.

He had been preparing for the defence of his pursuit title in Ayrshire, where it had been a balmy 16 degrees. But the weather wasn't his biggest problem. It seemed the UCI had come to a decision about Graeme's unorthodox tucked position on the bike. They didn't like it and had decided that it wasn't to be allowed. In the days leading up to the pursuit competition, small groups of officials kept gathering by the GB pen at the track while we were training, huddling next to Graeme's bike and muttering. What happened next has been well documented – there's even been a film made about it all – and as I was utterly wrapped up in myself at the time, I learned a lot of what happened retrospectively.

In essence, cycling's world governing body spent the week crafting new rules to produce the result they were after: Graeme's capitulation or his expulsion. The trouble was that every time they tightened the regulations in one area they created gaps elsewhere, gaps that he was very good at spotting. But they were determined. In the end, Graeme gave up trying to win what was an unwinnable war and rode the bike he'd used to take the world title the year before. He was duly disqualified.

Meanwhile, I dispatched my old Olympic rival Jens Lehmann to reach the final where I faced my new professional teammate, Francis Moreau. Francis, who exemplified the GAN team's philosophy of 'just smash it', had a reputation for going out hard and blowing spectacularly, a strategy he stuck to for the final, allowing me to take my first world pursuit title.

Part one of the Italian job was complete. The next morning our attention switched to the time trial, although we stayed on the track for our training sessions. The state of the road course was so bad that the GB coaches decided to delay the three-hour journey to Catania. When we did finally arrive to recce the route it was everything that we'd been led to believe: undulating, lots of turns and poor surfaces pretty much all the way. Hot and rough.

Graeme had added complications. He'd had a matter of days in which to completely reinvent his riding position and try to get used to the heat. We gave him a set of conventional handlebars which he proceeded to modify and fix to his track bike. He intended to use a single-speed, fixed-wheel machine for the hilly, twisting event.

My modifications were simpler but no less important. Although the race would only last around 50 minutes, I'd be sweating so much that I wanted to take a water bottle. On a normal bike that wouldn't have been a problem, but the Lotus 110 wasn't a normal bike. Back in the UK, I'd designed a simple, T-shaped bar that could be fixed to the underside of the saddle with a bottle cage bolted to it, although the angles meant that the cage had to be upside down. Terry Dolan made one for me and it worked well – until I tested it out on the course. The roads were so bumpy that the bottle had a tendency to bounce out. The solution we devised was to hold it in place with a cut-off toe strap that I could reach back and flip off. There was no way to reattach it, though, so I'd only get one drink. In an attempt to keep the contents cold, we put the filled bottle in the hotel freezer overnight, transferring it to a cool box on the day of the race and fitting it to the bike just moments before the start. We reasoned that enough of the contents would thaw by the time I needed to take a drink – about halfway through.

In my hour ride the year before, humidity had been the big problem. Here, the heat was dry and that made all the difference. It was unpleasant, but I was able to cope. Graeme suffered from heat stress and had to abandon. The sun was so ferocious that by the time I flicked the strap off my bottle the water was not only melted but already lukewarm. It was enough: a warm Tour de France followed by a hot weather training camp had conditioned my body to cope with the extreme conditions.

The GB team management had agreed to let Roger drive the car behind me and the regular time checks he gave me let me know that I was building a comfortable and growing lead. I turned into the kilometre-long finishing straight knowing I'd won, able to celebrate even before the line.

The victory in Catania took my year one professional tally to two world titles and a stage win in the Tour de France. The first few struggling months when I had genuinely thought I wouldn't make it as a pro seemed like ancient history. Sally and I flew home the day after the race – my birthday – stopping in London for dinner with Alan Dunn in what had become our favourite haunt: Sticky Fingers. The owner, Bill Wyman, and his wife Suzanne joined us. This kind of thing was starting to feel normal.

In early September I asked my dad, who'd never been abroad to watch me race, to bring Ed out to the Grand Prix Eddy Merckx in Brussels. I knew he wouldn't have come if I'd asked him on his own. I wanted to show off, let him see his son in action on the world stage amongst some of the sport's giants. It didn't turn out to be quite the take-your-dad-to-work experience I was hoping for.

The long season was taking its toll and I struggled through the race, battling with that year's Vuelta winner, Tony Rominger. We were neck and neck until 15 km to go when I blew, running out of energy so dramatically that I lost four minutes and as many places over the final few kilometres. In the following car, Ed had fallen asleep in the passenger footwell and woken up crying with a cricked neck. My dad, convinced that he'd jinxed the result, never came to another continental race.

Both form and passion were waning fast. There were just a few races left to ride, the last of them a made-for-TV track special: Boardman vs Obree at the Bercy Arena in Paris. The timing of this exhibition pursuit match was dictated down to the second by the live television coverage, so it was a bit of a blow to the schedule when the countdown hit zero and a chunk of Graeme's bike fell off.

While officials ran around trying to work out what to do, the director cut to a close-up of the damage. Graeme's bike was still in the start gate but his cranks were lying on the track. Also visible, although unconnected to the race-ending catastrophic failure, was a spanner that he was using as a spar to stop his saddle slipping down. The name given to his machine, Old Faithful, suddenly seemed rather ironic. I'm not sure what French television filled the rest of the time slot with, but the battle of the track titans was never restaged.

With the season out of the way, it was time for the long-awaited house move from Hoylake to Meols. Seventy-two Bertram Drive was a five-bedroom Victorian semi-detached and as far removed from our terraced house in Walker Street as it was possible to be: a true family home complete with fruit trees and a resident squirrel, Harvey, who would come into the kitchen to see if there was anything on offer.

There was even, briefly, a heron. It left after a few days having eaten every living thing in the garden pond. For a couple who'd grown up in houses with back yards that would fit into the pond, it was magical. We watched contentedly through our kitchen window as Ed explored his new habitat, laughing heartily as he rolled over and over on the grass, straight into the icy fish-free water.

We finished the year with our second family holiday abroad. Alan Dunn had invited us to Miami where the Rolling Stones would be playing over Thanksgiving on their Voodoo Lounge

Tour. Accompanying us on the trip was our part-time nanny, Moira Gillespie. We first met 'Moi' in September 1992 when she came down from her hometown of Dunoon to work in the new nursery at the end of our road. She started coming to us at weekends and gradually became part of the family.

Her first job had been looking after the children of American service personnel at the US naval base at Holy Loch. It was there that she acquired the phrase 'Love you bunches', which she mischievously used with our young and impressionable kids. It stuck, got shortened to 'bunchies', and is still in use today. It will probably be passed down through generations of Boardmans to come, a legacy of which I'm sure Moira would be very proud.

Being a private person I need a lot of space. We never have house guests and I'm not comfortable having anyone other than our kids in our home. Moi, with her dry sense of humour and roll-your-sleeves-up attitude to life, was – and still is – the one exception to this rule.

We were met at Miami airport by Alan and some of the Stones' security team. Momentarily distracted by handshakes and the setting down of suitcases, I turned around to usher Ed forward and he wasn't there. I scanned the arrivals hall, able to see for 100 metres in all directions. Nothing. No way could a five-year-old wander that far in the seconds he'd been out of my sight. Not unless he'd been taken. Like many parents before me, I instantly assumed the worst and raised the alarm. Burly security guys started the search while I, to my horror and shame, became a useless jelly. A minute later, Ed was located. He'd lost us in the crowd, headed immediately for a check-in desk, given them his name and been whisked behind the counter. The whole thing only lasted about two minutes but scares me to this day.

Our suite of rooms at the Ritz Carlton was the plushest we'd ever seen, an impressive setting for the news that Sally delivered after I found an unexpected item in our baggage. She was pregnant. It was my fourth go at this, another chance to be the supportive husband, make up for being such a self-centred individual in every other area. I had a little hissy fit.

We didn't see much of the band, although we had access to the floor of the hotel they'd taken over. I did bump into Keith Richards at breakfast one morning and expressed my surprise to Alan that he was up so early. Not early, late – he was still going from the day before.

We took the kids to the concert at Joe Robbie Stadium, watched Ronnie Wood perform an impromptu set by the pool and visited Disney World. It was a great trip, a different universe from the one I usually inhabited. Not that I really felt part of the sporting fraternity either. Back at home that winter I made my second appearance on *A Question of Sport*. The frozen smile on the face of my team captain Bill Beaumont as I entered the green room, and the sniggers from his opposite number Ian Botham, told me that they remembered my first.

On that post-Olympic debut I'd been asked to identify a football club from a picture of the stadium. I'd said the first thing that came into my head, which since I could see a supermarket in the shot next to the ground was 'Sainsbury's'. This time the questions were tailored to my (lack of) knowledge.

'Who was the only rider to win the world individual pursuit title on four occasions?' asked David Coleman.

'Hans-Henrik Ørsted,' I replied, rather proud of myself. It was Hugh Porter, who I don't think has ever forgiven me.

CHAPTER 10

Crash

Crashes usually come in one of two flavours: 'Oh, shit, here it comes' or 'Why am I in hospital?'

To the outside world my 1994 season looked like a great start to a professional career. It looked that way to me, too. But it was also my fourth straight year of pushing too hard, not touching the brakes, always looking beyond the next bend. From trackside at the Maebashi Stadium in Japan in 1990, when I'd first realised that becoming world champion might be possible, through to standing on the podium in Sicily, I'd been dangerously driven: yearly goals, training targets, maximum sustainable power. Never relaxed, always outside my comfort zone, terrified I'd taken on more than I could deliver. Then, when I did deliver, breathing no more than a sigh of relief that I hadn't let everyone down before fixing my eyes on the next target.

I was heading for a huge fall. If only it had been clear at the time.

In October 1994 I met up with the two Petes for our annual review: a detailed debrief on the season just gone, followed by a look at what opportunities were available in the one to come. From there we built our next performance plan to present to Roger. The main focus of the 1994 season had been to win the Tour prologue. For 1995, it was a bend I was already looking beyond. We pencilled in a repeat victory in July and focused our serious attention on the defence of my world titles. The 1995 World Championships would be the last edition in which track and road were held together, this time in Colombia; Bogotá for the track events and Duitama for the road. We saw the high-altitude locations as a distinct advantage, a challenge that required physiological understanding and targeted research: Pete Keen's specialist subjects. The plan we devised to repeat 1994's Tour/Worlds success was a masterpiece of strategic thinking.

Roger, now a big fan of performance planning, agreed both to the proposed schedule and to act as scout-cum-logistics director. Pete Keen and I thought that Colorado, which we both knew from the 1986 World Championships, would be the perfect place to prepare. Roger flew out and began organising everything we would need for our pre-Colombia training camp. He booked a hotel at altitude in the Rockies and secured use of the Colorado Springs velodrome for training, something the GB team had failed to manage. He even recced the local roads for suitable training routes. Everything was in place well in advance, ready for a smooth post-Tour transfer.

Since my big targets were all in the second half of the year, we had decided on a late start, with the Dauphiné Libéré in June signalling the effective opening of my campaign. No point in piling on the pressure for early-season victories and risk burning out later on, we thought. A psychologist might have advised us otherwise. With no victories to boost my morale and settle my nerves, I entered the summer as highly strung as ever. The way I saw it, my salary now effectively depended on eight minutes in July.

My Tour warm-up went well, with another prologue win in the Dauphiné. On the mountainous final weekend I even hung in with the climbers – for the one and only time in my career – to finish second overall, prompting press questions about my being a potential future Tour winner. The result should have helped my nerves, but I knew the week-long race wasn't the Tour. Worse, my second place was the biggest result the team had managed all year. Since Greg LeMond's retirement, GAN's commitment as sponsor was looking shaky. The management's desire, even desperation, for some success was almost palpable, and by July I could feel them willing me to do something to secure the team's future. Everyone had quietly sneaked their eggs into my basket and it was heavy. By the time I arrived in Saint-Brieuc four days before the Tour start to familiarise myself with the tricky prologue course, I was wound up like a spring.

With multiple bends, cobbles, a fast run down to the Gouët river and a climb to the finish, the 7.3 km circuit had a bit of everything. I rode it several times, memorising every dip, drag and bend, keen to ensure that I had the right gear selection for the different aspects of the course. Not unusually, our training runs were done during the day, but to satisfy the demands of French TV for a prime time Tour opener, the prologue was scheduled for the first time ever to start after six in the evening. That seemed to be roughly the time every day that the heavens opened over the Brittany coast.

Race day: 1 July 1995. Weather forecast: thunderstorms expected by early evening. The forecasters were right, clouds bubbled up throughout the afternoon and before I'd even left the hotel for the start there was a downpour underway. Rather than being disappointed I was relieved, which in itself should have told me something was wrong. On such a twisty, technical course, there was clearly nothing I could do now. I had been absolved of the responsibility to deliver the team's results by an act of God. The victory would go to one of the small number of riders who'd been lucky enough to complete the circuit in the dry. I arrived at the start area happy and relaxed.

As I sat in the camping car, listening to the rain on the roof, my teammate Didier Rous pulled himself, dripping, through the door and made a beeline for me: 'I was only about 30 seconds away from Durand!'

Jacky Durand, not noted as a time trialist, had been one of the early starters, finishing before the rain began. His time of nine minutes exactly had stood for over an hour, as rider after rider either failed to master the conditions or didn't try. Didier, though, was buzzing with belief on my behalf: 'If I was that close, you can still do it, definitely!'

It was a view enthusiastically supported by everyone in the camping car and greedily I let myself be carried along with it. I desperately wanted to wear the yellow jersey again and heard what I wanted to hear. I switched back into race mode. I asked Cyril, the mechanic, for wheels with road tyres on, fatter and with more grip than my usual TT slicks. But the team only had a couple of complete pairs and they were out on the course. He could offer me a front wheel, but no rear disc. My choice at the back was either to stick with an 18 mm slick, or sacrifice the aerodynamic advantage of a disc and fit a road wheel. I chose the disc.

I warmed up in a waterproof jacket and kept it on until the last possible moment on the start ramp. As Serge Beucherie reached to take it off me, he offered some last-minute advice about the course and the conditions, desperate to convey the belief that it was still doable. I didn't need it. By this point, the yellow mist had descended and all sense had gone.

I charged down the ramp and onto the rain-soaked streets. I settled into position and drove into the first gentle curves, the spray off the front wheel hitting my legs. A kilometre later I swung hard left onto the Rue de l'Europe, wet tyres skipping sideways over the shiny cobbles that decorated many of the town's road junctions. The next obstacle was a 280 degree loop onto the Pont de Toupin. I took it in the same reckless style. Even mid-race, a small part of my mind was looking backwards, wondering how I'd got around those corners. Alarm bells were ringing but I wasn't listening.

Two and a half minutes in, a third of the way through. Another right and I was onto the Boulevard de la Mer, the start of the descent, the cobbled patches and tight bends behind me. There was just this fast run down to the river and a single serious corner between me and yellow. Behind, I could hear Roger's tinny excitement through the speaker mounted to the front of his car: 'Just two seconds from Durand! Is finished now, you can go flat out!' Those where his exact words and they were the last I heard before it happened.

Sprinting onto the descent and up to full speed, I took the first easy right, drifting almost into the left-side ditch before I was through. The rain was still falling, the streetlights starbursts on the water streaking my visor. I was pedalling in surges now, going so fast that I'd run out of gears. I got over to the right just in time for the next left-hand curve and again I had to use all the road.

This time, though, the succeeding bend was in the same direction: another, slightly tighter left for which I was now totally out of position. Suddenly I was aware of just how fast I was travelling – about 80 kph. My subconscious mind projected possible courses of action, examined the trajectory changes and braking patterns that might help me rectify my error and came up blank. All I could do was lean in, as gently as possible, and hope. But I already knew it wasn't going to work.

Despite being in one of the most northerly parts of France, Saint-Brieuc still gets very hot weather, hot enough sometimes to melt the tar on the roads. When this happens, particularly on corners, the lateral pressure applied by countless car tyres massages the malleable surface into tiny furrows, pushing the embedded gravel away from the surface and deep into the tar. Once they cool and set, these barely noticeable troughs are perfect for holding water, producing a road surface as smooth as glass. This is what had happened on the Boulevard de la Mer. Below the sheen of water, the meagre few millimetres of my tyre rubber that had until then been valiantly clinging to the tarmac encountered one of these sun-smoothed patches and finally gave up the battle for traction.

The anticipation of a crash is always worse than the thing itself. It usually happens so fast that you examine it retrospectively, but not here. This one took about five seconds from start to finish, a lifetime for a brain already speeding on adrenalin. I hit the surface of the road on my left side and was skidding in a semi-seated position, feet still clipped into the pedals. On the lubricated surface, I'd barely slowed at all from my racing speed. 'It's OK,' I thought, 'I'm down and sliding. No major damage.' Even then I still hadn't stopped looking for options. And then I saw the barriers coming towards me.

It didn't hurt. There was just a thud, a dullness and a pressure in my ankle. Then there was a tap on my head from behind. It was the front bumper of the team car. Unable to stop in the rain, it had hit both me and the barrier, puncturing the front tyre. I didn't find out until later that the impact had reverberated through my skull and broken my nose.

Perhaps this is what people mean when they talk about temporary madness, because I still wouldn't concede defeat. Somehow – and I only know this from watching the TV pictures of the incident – I got up, climbed onto the proffered spare bike and rolled down the hill, trying to click my non-functioning left foot into the pedal. But it just wouldn't go in. At last, a voice deep inside my head started to make itself heard: 'DO NOT TRY TO DO THAT AGAIN!' I gave in and sat down on the soaking road.

My memories of what happened next are blurry, fragmented and probably out of sequence. Officials surrounding us, concerned for the next rider who'd be coming around the corner in a little over a minute. Roger carrying me to the car, which he had to drive with a flat. Being loaded into an ambulance, someone saying 'The organisers will let him start tomorrow if he's OK.' X-rays showing ghost-like images of two sticks: the bones in my lower left leg, each clearly broken near the end. Orbiting the unnaturally sharp edges were what looked like small white balls on strings. These were pieces of bone that the tendons had torn off. Roger, standing next to my hospital gurney repeating over and over, 'Is not possible, is not possible.' That my wrist was also broken seemed inconsequential, but it would make using crutches for the next few months really awkward.

All I felt was calm. It was over, there was nothing I could do or think to change things. Even then, lying there, still in damp race kit, I knew this was not a healthy reaction.

Heavily pregnant, Sally had chosen to stay at home for the start of the Tour. She'd invited friends round to watch the prologue on television, laying on wine from the region and making a spread of French-themed food. The poor weather and limited number of live TV motorbikes meant it was Channel 4's Phil Liggett who first broke the news that I might have had a problem out on the course. Over the next 20 minutes, information was drip-fed from the race officials to the commentary box and from there to our front room in Meols. It was five minutes from the end of the live programme before they finally got some images of the crash. Eventually, Sally got a call from Roger to say that I was in hospital, banged up but fundamentally OK.

It was a long night in that small hospital room, staring at the clock and counting the pulse of my throbbing ankle. I eventually got some morphine and drifted off, dreaming about cameras in my face and giving an interview, trying to explain what had happened. At least I thought it was a dream until years later when Gary Imlach confessed that it was him and cameraman John Tinetti who had sneaked in the rear entrance of the hospital.

Although we've never spoken about it, I think Roger felt he was to blame for the crash, that his encouragement had pushed me that little bit too far on a rain-soaked descent. But it wasn't his fault. I was the man with his hands on the brakes – or not. They were my choices and I never held anyone else responsible. The team dearly wanted a result, but I chose to go along and try to win the unwinnable prologue.

Getting home from a small town in Brittany on a Sunday was not an easy thing to arrange, but it needed to be done fast, before the bones started to calcify. With no scheduled flights, Roger hired the Tour's private jet to take me directly to Manchester where an ambulance would be waiting to take me to my home hospital, Arrowe Park. Being carried onto a private jet in your underpants might, in other circumstances, be the start of an excellent day. Not this one, sadly. Anne O'Hare and Pete Woodworth travelled back with me and their in-flight entertainment was the sight of me repeatedly throwing up as we crossed the Channel.

I was operated on at six o'clock that evening. Two six centimetre screws were inserted into my ankle to hold all the pieces together and a cast was also put on my arm while I was under the anaesthetic. I was then dosed up with more morphine and largely left to sleep away the next week. By the time I was allowed home I was 64 kg, I'd lost nearly a stone from my already low racing weight.

I tried to read in a garden hammock, which made me feel sick, slept in the Wendy House with the kids and got to see Oscar Miles

Boardman born (ironic, as I haven't seen many of his birthdays since, due to them falling in the middle of the race I'd just crashed out of). I loved it. I'd stepped – fallen – off the performance train which carried on without me, taking all the madness, media and responsibilities with it.

CHAPTER 11
1996

In the movie version of this story, I would have come roaring back to the Tour de France in 1996 to win the prologue in a howling thunderstorm, conquering demons and rediscovering my passion for cycling along the way.

As it turned out, I came second in a light drizzle.

Despite the damp conditions in the Dutch city of 's-Hertogenbosch, it came as a shock to lose to ONCE's Alex Zülle, but in retrospect it shouldn't have. The year to that point had been full of unwelcome surprises. Burning to rectify the mistakes of 1995, I'd trained right through the winter and come into the new season at a lower weight and in better condition than ever before. Based on my form-to-results ratio from previous years, I'd expected to reap big rewards. But despite being both lighter and stronger – every cyclist's dream combination – I seemed to be using all of my increased power output just to cling on to other people's wheels. In time trials, my winning margins were being eroded – or erased.

I'd arrived at that year's Tour ready to prove that I was not only the best time trialist on the planet but a real contender for the general classification. Second place in the prologue was a blow, but I was still determined to finish high in the overall rankings in Paris. Fortunately, Fred Moncassin relieved the pressure on the team for a big result by winning the bunch finish on stage one. As a French-man on a French team, his victory probably meant more to GAN than mine would have.

The second plank of my Tour strategy snapped on the first real mountain day, stage seven from Chambéry to Les Arcs. I finished 47th, almost half an hour behind the leaders. The first long time trial of the race was the following day, and this was hilly too, a 30 km test from Bourg-St-Maurice up to the ski resort of Val d'Isère. After my struggles on stage seven, I didn't expect to do well but still chose to ride it flat out. I surprised myself by finishing eighth, ahead of some notable climbers. The performance might have been worth a mention in dispatches but it was still far from a win and did little to improve my mood.

On the morning of stage nine, scheduled to be the toughest day in the Alps, we woke to high winds, talk of snow and rumours of the leg to Sestriere being shortened, cutting out the climbs of the Iseran and the legendary Galibier. We sat around in the team cars waiting for instructions. Although it was spitting with rain and not exactly pleasant, the weather didn't look too bad to us, but we certainly weren't going to complain if the organisers wanted to remove the hardest mountains from the day's menu. An hour later, the decision was made: the stage would start just 46 km from the finish. I was ecstatic.

Since the alternative was a massive detour through valley roads clogged with traffic, we still had to tackle the Galibier by car. A long, snaking line of team and Tour support vehicles set off along the race route. On the lower slopes, we passed sodden fans who were none too pleased to see us cruising past in heated, motorised comfort. Some even spat at the convoy. At first I felt guilty, but as we approached the top the weather quickly deteriorated. By the time we crested the summit at 2,645 metres it was a full-on blizzard. The terrible conditions covered just a six-kilometre stretch of the race route, but with no feasible way to circumvent it the organisers had been left with no choice. What was supposed to be a stage of 189 km featuring the two biggest mountains in the race, had been turned into a mass-start hill climb. I finished 20th, conceding another two minutes. Still, it had been a very welcome gift.

By the time we started stage 17 to Pamplona I was over 40 minutes behind the race leader, Bjarne Riis, and almost totally drained. The 260 km route ahead of us would not only be the longest of the race, it would take us over five serious climbs. It was a daunting prospect, but for those who survived it Paris would effectively be in sight. The minute the race left Argelès-Gazost the road went up and so did the pace. After just five kilometres of riding, I was unable to stay with the peloton and found myself out the back, alone.

I couldn't believe it. I'd invested so much in this race, this season, and I'd been disappointed at every turn. After two weeks of suffering, and with the prospect of finishing the Tour for the first time the only prize left to me, I couldn't see how I was going to get to the end of the day inside the time limit. Certainly, feeling sorry for myself wasn't going to do it. At the summit of the Col du Soulor

I snapped out of my self-pity and on the short descent fought my way through the team cars and onto the back of the peloton. I rejoined just as the race started to climb the Col d'Aubisque and was immediately dropped again. It was a mental and physical process I repeated several times over the next 90 km until eventually, on the lower slopes of the Col de Soudet, the *gruppetto* formed.

The *gruppetto* or *autobus* is based on the old premise that misery loves company. It's a temporary alliance between riders from different teams who, without each other's help, might not be able to finish the stage inside the time limit. Together, they ride the climbs at a steady pace – one sustainable by the slowest member of the group – and once over the top, they descend at full tilt to claw back what time they can. On the flat they spread the workload until the next climb, where the cycle begins again. Because of this shared, often unpleasant experience, there is usually a strong sense of camaraderie amid the suffering. The bus has unwritten rules, which are usually enforced by an experienced member, a respected individual who takes it upon himself to coordinate matters for the greater good; controlling the pace on the climbs and cajoling people to work on the flat. The driver of our vehicle was the Italian giant, Eros Poli.

I'd lost time in races before but I'd never been in this situation: left behind by the majority of the peloton, beaten. Although I was relieved to have some company at last, my confidence was shot, and with more than 150 km left to ride I was still fretting about making the time-cut. That's when a grinning Eros dropped back down the line and with typical Italian brio said, 'Hey, relax! Is no problem – we ride easy on the climbs, *à bloc* on the descents and all is good.

No problem!' His reassurance, delivered in a warm and friendly tone with a lot of arm-waving, pulled me out of my miserable introspection. Eros put everything back into perspective: no one was going to live or die by this result, it was just a bike race. Everything about his demeanour suggested that this 260 km slog through the mountains was a cross between a day off and a day out.

At six foot four and nearly 90 kg, Eros Poli was a key member of the lead-out train for Saeco's star sprinter, Mario Cipollini. Cipo himself wasn't in the *autobus*, he'd had the good sense to abandon before the big mountains as he did every year. It was the first time I'd spoken to Eros, but I knew he was well thought of in the peloton; one of the last super-*domestiques*, a breed who respected the opposition, held themselves accountable to some invisible code of honour and spent their careers giving their all in the service of others, even when they had the ability to ride for themselves. The following year, Eros would join GAN to work for our sprinter, Fred Moncassin. We'd ride together until his retirement in 1999, and his positive outlook on life would be a godsend over the next few seasons.

Eight hours after we'd set off, our 32-strong group rolled over the line, more than 45 minutes behind the leaders but inside the time limit. We looked at each other and smiled. Pats on the back were exchanged and everyone headed off to find their respective hotels. It remains the hardest day on a bike I have ever had.

Fred Moncassin, who'd finished on the podium three times in the first week, got his second win in Bordeaux on stage 19. Having two victories took the pressure off team management, who were subsequently more inclined to look upon my just finishing the Tour for the first time as sufficient for this year. By the time we reached the penultimate stage, a 63.5 km time trial from Bordeaux to Saint-Émilion, I was actually feeling quite good. Very good, even. So I decided to give race-mode another go.

The flat smooth roads meant the stage was all about aerodynamics and pace judgement – my forte – but in the event I was able to finish only sixth, two minutes and thirty seconds off the pace. It was one of my worst ever results in a flat time trial. Incredibly, Festina's Laurent Dufaux, who never usually got within minutes of me on a stage like this, finished fifth.

To ride into Paris for the first time, see the Eiffel tower in the distance and feel the cobbles of the Champs-Élysées under my wheels, was an emotional experience. I'm not ashamed to say there was a tear in my eye. It had been a hellishly tough month, 3,765 kilometres of mostly despair and disappointment. I'd wanted to show myself as a possible podium contender. In the end, I was almost an hour and a half behind the winner. But for the next few hours all that was set aside.

The 100 km of the route from the start in Palaiseau to the centre of the French capital had been the slowest I'd ever ridden in an actual race. In a long-held tradition, riders took the time to reflect on what they had just been through, chat to friends and colleagues in other teams and celebrate their collective achievements. There was a sense of kinship I'd never experienced before. Everyone here – many, like me, for the first time – now belonged to a special club. The password for entry was your own name on the list of finishers in the world's greatest bike race. I might not have beaten the Tour but neither had the Tour beaten me.

On the circuit of the Champs-Élysées, the pace picked up for the final hour and Fred Moncassin came close to his third stage win, pipped at the line by Fabio Baldato of MG-Technogym. I rode the last few kilometres up at the front with the team, trying to control the race for Fred, and enjoyed being in on the action for the final stage. It was just days since the nightmare of stage 17, yet I felt fantastic, as if I could just carry on racing. It was too late now.

The post-Tour party was one of the few times in my life I've stayed up until dawn. In the basement club of the Concorde La Fayette hotel we danced and drank and I seem to recall being on a stage, shirtless. But that's another story: what happens in the nightclub, stays in the nightclub. Plus, it was pre-camera phone. Getting up for my flight was not fun, but I couldn't afford to miss it. I had just 48 hours to get home and repack before heading to Atlanta and the Olympics.

The 1996 Games were the first in history to allow professional cyclists to compete. I was the defending Olympic champion in the 4000 m pursuit – except that I wasn't going there to defend it. Graeme Obree had won the world title in Bogotá the previous year and he got the nod ahead of me. I'd have loved to ride both the time trial and the pursuit, but I could understand the selectors' reluctance to pick a rider whose preparation for a four-minute event had been a three-week stage race.

Unlike 1994, when it had taken me weeks to recover from riding just half the Tour, I came out of the 1996 edition feeling fantastic, ready to compete and desperate to get a result. But the season of unwelcome surprises continued. Once again our power-measuring devices told me I was in the form of my life, once again it wasn't enough. I finished third, behind Spain's Abraham Olano and Miguel Indurain. Even the time trial no longer seemed to belong to me. I was in a maudlin mood.

Graeme Obree had it worse in the pursuit, posting one of his slowest times ever, and didn't make it through the opening round. His result prompted the selectors to take a punt on me for the upcoming World Championships to be held on the newly built track in Manchester at the end of August. It was my last target of the year.

Conceived as part of Manchester's failed bid to host the 1996 Olympics, the velodrome had a difficult birth. It was a joint venture between Sport England, Manchester City Council and British Cycling, but they couldn't agree on what the facility should be: a multi-sport stadium or a cost-effective training venue for the British team. The squabbling continued until 1992 when my Olympic success finally gave the project the push it needed. A compromise was agreed and the funding secured. I now had a world-class facility just an hour from my doorstep. The velodrome would play a pivotal role in the next two decades of GB cycling success.

After six weeks away from home, I took a rare weekend off to go camping with Sally and the kids in Barmouth on the North Wales coast. 'Off' meant taking a bike but only training in the mornings. Along with friends, we spent our time on the long sandy beach, daring each other to go in the freezing water. On Saturday evening, we went to a local fair where Ed and I had a go on the waltzers, which made him sick. It was a token visit to the real world before diving back into sport. I rode home.

Early the next morning, Pete Keen and I arrived at Manchester Velodrome where we'd scheduled some track time before the championships to evaluate equipment. We used power cranks and the controlled indoor environment to compare different combinations of wheels, helmets, frames and positions. Since my gold-medal ride in Barcelona, the Lotus bike had achieved mythic status, but we'd never actually evaluated what the real difference was in performance between the famous S-shaped carbon monocoque and a conventional machine. Although the original Olympic bike wasn't available to us, we had the Lotus 110 frame that I'd been using for time trials. By swapping out the chunky aluminium rear ends, it could be converted to a track bike. We'd be testing the futuristic frame against a more conventional steel model, built by Terry Dolan from teardrop-shaped tubing and based on the bike I'd used in the Atlanta time trial. Both the Lotus and the steel prototype were married with a carbon fork/handlebar that I'd designed myself.

It was a compact component – the triathlon bars mounted directly onto the forks – and it allowed me to tuck myself low into my preferred time-trial position despite the Lotus's full-size wheels front and back. In fact, with this set-up I could adapt to whichever sponsor's bike GAN required me to ride. It was my first foray into the world of carbon design and I'd commissioned the small UK manufacturers Hotta to make the part for me.

Repeated trials indicated that the Lotus was superior to the steel frame. We surmised that this was partly down to aerodynamics and partly to the flexy nature of the steel with its flattened tubes. Having chosen our frame, we worked our way through wheels and helmets and eventually came to the most important thing of all, my position. You can tinker with tubes all you like, but it's the rider that represents about 80 per cent of the frontal area and therefore the great majority of the drag. Changes here would likely have the biggest impact on speed.

As well as the handlebars I'd designed, we had another set made by Peter Cooke, a friend and engineer at Liverpool University. These mimicked Graeme Obree's new arms-outstretched position – the 'Superman', as it had been christened by the media. Graeme had devised the new set-up after the UCI had banned his previous tucked configuration, and it had helped him win the 1995 world pursuit title. Having seen him profit from his pioneering thinking before, other riders were now following his lead; both male and female Olympic pursuit titles had been won using it.

I was reluctant even to try this new position because I thought a) it looked silly, and b) it somehow wasn't proper bike riding. Balanced against my curled lip was the knowledge that a) Pete and I were supposed to represent the rational, scientific approach to cycling, and b) we'd been caught out before. So for the final test of the day, I had my triathlon bars detached from the Lotus and the steel Obree bars mounted. They were as elegant as antlers on a shark.

Once I discovered what they felt like, though, I couldn't have cared less about the aesthetics. Within three laps of the track, and before checking any of the power data, I knew that this position was remarkable, significantly better than anything we'd tried so far. I could sense the change in speed and the increase in cadence. Without wind tunnels, power cranks, aerodynamicists or physiologists, Graeme Obree had done it again: discovered an advantage that would revolutionise the world of pursuiting. At least it would for another few months before it too was banned.

For the second day of trials, all tests were conducted using only Graeme's position. As we worked, both Pete and I could see the opportunity that had just opened up. These three-minute efforts were being run off at 55 kph, which was hour-record pace. My 1993 distance had since been beaten four times, by Graeme Obree, Miguel Indurain and twice by Switzerland's Tony Rominger. The 55.291 km he'd ridden in November 1994 had seemed untouchable to us, but here I was touching it in the Superman pose. To double-check, we quickly added an extra run to the schedule: a steady 20-minute effort at about the pace required to set a new record. It wasn't definitive but it was close enough.

At the end of that day we did something we'd never done before. We decided to put the cart before the horse and attempt a new hour record as soon as possible, using the form I'd generated during the Tour de France.

That evening, I phoned Pete Woodworth to tell him of our findings and intentions. Surprisingly, he was very much against the idea and wanted to schedule the attempt further in the future, so that it could be fully capitalised on as it had been in Bordeaux. Having had my confidence in predicting form badly shaken over the last few months, I didn't want to risk losing this opportunity. I dug my heels in. Pete, not understanding my emotional state and confident that we could reproduce this form at a time of our choosing, still disagreed. It was the first real argument we'd had and it strained our relationship severely. Two days later, after a four-and-a-half-hour meeting, Pete was on board and started to put measures in place for an attempt in three weeks' time, eight days after the Track World Championships.

That just left the familiar conflict between the bike I wanted to ride and the one I was contracted to ride. By now GAN's official frame supplier was Eddy Merckx, an even bigger legend than Greg LeMond to risk offending. We called Roger Legeay who flew over from France on 21 August for a meeting. As record attempts were extracurricular to my team duties, I put it to Roger that I would make this one only if allowed to set the best mark with the best equipment. Eddy was welcome to have his name and logo on the bike, even though it wasn't one of his. Roger called Eddy, who agreed. As for Lotus, they had no say. Roger had bought the frames and could put on any sponsor's name he liked.

My first big success of the 1996 season came in spectacular style on 29 August, in the pursuit final at the World Championships in Manchester. It was Superman vs Superman – Italy's Andrea Collinelli was using the position too. Collinelli started fast and died in the final kilometre, giving me the perfect lead-out to smash the world record for 4000 metres. The time of 4:11.1 stood for nearly 14 years (thanks to the UCI, who outlawed the position soon after the championships).

Celebrations were brief. The next day Pete Keen and I went back to the velodrome for a full-length trial at 53.5 kph. I circled the track to the sound of Pete's whistle echoing around the dimly lit and now deserted space. His signal indicated exactly when I should be hitting the pursuit line if I was on schedule. Sixty minutes later we were both happy. It had been hard but not hell – we could do this.

The trial also produced some valuable information about the Obree handlebars. Unnoticeable in a 4000 m pursuit, the arms-outstretched position had caused cramping in my triceps after 30 minutes. The configuration was tweaked to roll my arms inwards and under, so as to let my skeleton take a little more of the strain. Two 'arm breaks' – that is, getting out of the saddle for a stretch – were also scheduled into the attempt.

A special helmet had been constructed by Giro, GAN's official supplier, that was sculpted to fit the contours of my shoulders and back. In 1996 aero helmets weren't required to have any protective function, so it was little more than a wearable carbon fairing. On the tip of the helmet's teardrop tail we attached piece of velcro that stuck to my skinsuit as soon as I sat in position, making a perfect seal. Combined with the Obree position, the Lotus frame and my rounded shoulders – something I never thought I'd find a use for – it was probably the most aerodynamic package any cyclist had ever assembled.

Conditioned by the high temperatures of the Tour and the suffocating humidity of Atlanta, I was more heat-acclimatised than I'd ever been. We knew that air resistance dropped as the mercury rose – we'd had a lot of experience with that in Bordeaux three years earlier – and we experimented with the velodrome's thermostat to see just how much I could cope with: 28 degrees seemed to be the sweet spot.

On the day, even Manchester's air pressure joined the team effort, dropping to an unusual low and giving us a sort of altitude effect. Heat, low pressure, physical condition, aerodynamics, everything was optimal. At 6.32 p.m. on 6 September, I set off in front of a capacity crowd who made so much noise I was afraid for my hearing. Over the next 60 minutes, I produced the best performance of my sporting life. So good there's almost nothing to say about it. There was no drama or jeopardy. I wasn't fighting my body or the bike. The attempt didn't hurt and yet I felt there was no faster I could possibly ride: the sensation you get when you're genuinely peaking. By the end of it I'd beaten Rominger's untouchable record by over a kilometre to set a new mark of 56.375 km. My form had finally found an outlet.

The post-hour party was possibly more impressive than the ride. Friends, colleagues and family gathered in a private room back at our hotel for a marathon celebration. Unsurprisingly, I didn't last the distance, having been exhausted to start with. Eventually, long after I'd retired, Eddy Merckx announced he too was going to bed. His statement was met with a challenge from an incredulous and drunk Roger Legeay, 'The great Eddy Merckx, abandoning? Taking off his number and giving up? Surely not.' Suitably goaded – and also drunk – the Cannibal sat back down again heavily and took a bite out of his glass. He finished the evening wearing a Rolling Stones tie around his head singing 'I Can't Get No Satisfaction'.

CHAPTER 12

The Beginning of the End

It was 4.30 in the afternoon, 12 December 1997, and I was sitting in our office in Meols with the two Petes. We'd gathered for our annual post-season debrief and planning session, and we weren't far into it before I had a realisation.

For the first time since turning pro – since I'd begun racing – there were no suggestions on how to progress, be better, move forward. It was all about aiming to repeat successes of years past. None of us could identify any areas for significant improvement, any 'stretch goals' that would see me advance as an athlete. These gatherings were supposed to be our councils of war, identifying new fronts to attack. Now my team seemed to think the best I could manage was standing still. It was at that moment I lost interest in being a professional cyclist. Because I agreed with them.

We sat and plotted, but without the enthusiasm and passion of previous years. Pete Keen already had a new role as Director of Performance for British Cycling and his energy was now being channelled into setting up the World Class Performance Programme with the new Lottery funds that were flowing into the sport. I couldn't blame him (although I did at the time). He'd started to think of life after Team Boardman and so had I.

The 1997 season had been our all-out effort – in fact, an unacknowledged last-ditch attempt – at turning me into a real GC contender. The main goal had been a high overall finish in the Tour de France, with all my preparation aimed at being able to stay with the favourites in the mountains. In order to do that I needed a higher power-to-weight ratio, and since my power was pretty good to start with that meant losing weight. To provoke my body into a fat-burning response I'd spent the first half of the year on a relentless programme of low intensity, non-stop rides of eight hours or more.

For a week in May I set off around the country to make the all-day jaunts more palatable, with Sally driving ahead to meet me in obscure places for dinner. We wound our way through the Lancashire hills, across the Yorkshire Dales and the Lakeland lanes. Each morning I'd get up early and ride off towards the next destination, often 150 miles away.

Weight loss was supposed to be a means to an end: the missing element that might help place me on the podium in Paris rather than just in the prologue. Instead it became an obsession, something I could seize on and be in control of in my otherwise unpredictable and high-pressure world. I weighed myself three times a day and monitored the calorific content of every morsel I consumed. On one occasion, after six and a half hours in the saddle, I finally pitched up at the Eureka café near Chester, the local cyclists' watering hole, only to see the readout on my SRM computer screen showing 4940 calories burned. Instead of pulling in I rode past for a few hundred metres with my brakes on, just long enough to see it tick over to 5000.

By the time I got to July I weighed 67 kg, three kilos lighter than I had ever been as a rider. I took my second Tour prologue win, from Jan Ulrich, and with it my second yellow jersey. I wasn't too worried when I lost it the next day to Mario Cipollini: my energies were focused on the race overall, not a few days of glory in the first week. GAN regained the jersey in any case on stage five when Cédric Vasseur escaped to win alone. The management were delighted and as the race wound its way towards the Pyrenees the team was in good spirits.

Tactically, I'd not put a foot wrong through that first week, but almost as soon as the race hit the lower slopes of the first real mountain I was dropped. It was the Col du Soulor, the same climb I'd been distanced on in the Pamplona stage of the previous year's Tour. It wasn't by much, only a couple of minutes at the summit, but it was enough. I knew in my heart of hearts that was it. I was never going to be a GC contender: there was no way I could keep up. It all became moot on the descent when I crashed in thick mist and sustained a back injury that would force me to retire a few days later.

It had all started so well. In 1994 there'd been three stage wins in the Dauphiné, two world titles and a yellow jersey in the Tour. In 1995 I'd finished second in the Dauphiné to Indurain himself. But from that point on my GC trajectory flattened and results in general became more erratic. Prologues were still winnable, just, but in stage races I could no longer stay with even the second tier guys on the climbs, or recover from day to day.

Pro life had soured. Somewhere along the line it had turned from being a great adventure, full of elation and discovery, to a confusing, frustrating and depressing place where results didn't seem to abide by any predictable rules.

Earlier that year, while searching for a new sponsor, Roger had drawn back from the day-to-day running of the team and engaged Denis Roux, one of his old riders from the Z-Peugeot days, to take up some of the slack. Officially, he had come on board as a coach but Denis was soon fulfilling the duties of a team manager. After a short honeymoon period he'd become a champion of the blame culture. As far as Denis was concerned, the team's increasingly lacklustre results were all down to the riders, who were either too fat, too lazy, or too fat and lazy. The winter training camps that had seen us mix long, hard rides with drinking and fun on the rest day, were now only about training and critiquing what the riders ate. Roger didn't actively participate in this morale-sapping approach, but neither did he step in to stop it. It wasn't all the management's fault, I had already turned my head to look towards retirement, to dream about what was going to come after. The atmosphere in the team throughout the following year just quickened my pace towards the door.

In the last few months of 1997 Roger had finally managed to secure a backer. But there was a funding gap. The deal with GAN ran out at the end of the season and the new sponsors, Crédit Agricole, couldn't step in until they'd finished handling the ticket sales for the 1998 football World Cup in France. The potentially disastrous cash flow problem was finally fixed through the magnanimity of GAN, who agreed to stay on for an extra seven months, and the flexibility of the UCI, who sanctioned a mid-season change in sponsors.

The 1998 Tour would be our farewell race in the old white, yellow and blue, although I wasn't confident of being able to come up with the parting gift of a prologue win. Perhaps I was just trying to mentally prepare myself for another disappointment, but despite my performance ambitions now being refocused purely on winning time trials I headed to Dublin for the start convinced that I didn't have the form. A look at the circuit, though, gave me hope – and an idea. It had a nasty sting in the tail, a sharp left-hand bend less than a kilometre from home that forced riders to come to an almost dead stop before starting a shallow climb all the way to the line.

Thinking I had nothing to lose, I gambled everything on that bend. I held back, saving myself for the final minute of racing. When I reached the sharp left-hander I came to a virtual halt like everybody else, but once I was through it I was probably the only man in the race with the reserves to re-accelerate for the drag up to the line. That bend, along with race experience and better legs than I'd thought I had, got me the victory ahead of Abraham Olano of Spain. It was a welcome highlight in what had been a difficult year.

Two days later and still in yellow I was tucked in behind team-mate Eros Poli, who was dragging me to the front for the final 50 km of the stage to Cork, when I blinked and found myself staring at the ceiling of an ambulance. OK, I thought, lying there and trying to get a grasp on the situation, I've clearly been in some kind of an accident. I'm wearing a neck brace. Wiggle my toes; yep, they work, so not spinal. I wasn't in the Tour de France, was I? Arm and face burning, I know that feeling – skin-loss and sweat. I wasn't in the yellow jersey, was I?

I'd never been knocked out before and it took a fair bit of this self-interrogation before I mentally bridged the gap between my current reality and the last bit I remembered. Roger was there, but as soon as he saw I was coming round he disappeared back to the team car and sped off to rejoin the race. I was no longer the golden child, the overall contender that they'd hoped – and were paying – for.

It had been a freak accident. One of the riders in the line had flicked left around a cats-eye in the middle of the road just as I was passing his rear wheel. The front of my bike had been wiped out from under me and I'd gone straight down on my face.

I'd only had three serious crashes in my career and they'd all been in the full glare of the media spotlight in this race. Denis Roux took me to hospital in Cork where the medics insisted on cutting off the leader's jersey, which then disappeared. I'm told it is now up on the wall. The next day, having had the ragged skin around my left eye stitched up and my fractured wrist put in a cast, I headed home without fanfare. Then I sat in the lounge in front of the TV and watched the Tour de France explode.

A week before the race, French police had arrested the Festina team's masseur, Willy Voet, at the Belgian border and confiscated what were later confirmed to be performance-enhancing drugs, part of what had been a systematic doping programme in the team. Further arrests followed, confessions were made and the team containing some of France's biggest stars was thrown off the Tour.

I felt sorry for the race director, Jean-Marie Leblanc, a genuinely lovely man who was suddenly faced with a scandal that threatened to destroy the sporting monument he was in charge of. The Tour limped on, amid sit-down protests from the riders and more police raids. Cycling is still dealing with the fall-out today. What people thought was a single catastrophic event turned out to be the tip of an iceberg.

As grim as the situation was, I paid little attention to it. I had a much bigger crisis to deal with at home. I'd always been an obsessive, applying myself to whatever I was fascinated by to the exclusion of all else. At the beginning, Sally had put up with my compulsive character, had even enjoyed being involved. She'd coped with playing second fiddle to my needs and wants for years. Now, the disappointment and frustration of not being able to progress – of actually regressing – had made me moody and unpleasant to live with. Where previously I was dedicated, now I was simply self-obsessed, uncaring of the people around me and morose. And she'd had enough.

It wasn't an instant thing, Sally was – is – a strong and loyal person. She'd been telling me she wasn't happy for years but I just hadn't been listening. A turbulent few months followed and this time it was cycling that took a back seat as I tried to recover what I'd belatedly realised was the most important thing in my life.

By the time of the 1998 World Championships in the Netherlands Sally and I were still together but things were very raw and fragile. She came out to Valkenburg along with Pete Woodworth, who was due to meet with Roger. Whether I was ready for it or not, it was time to renegotiate my contract with the team.

I'd been thinking long and hard about whether to continue as a professional. Retiring was a definite option because even though I'd only done five years I knew the desire to explore my capabilities was all but gone. To simply stop, though, would have been a huge life-change, and with everything else that was going on I realised it was too much of a leap for me to make. I decided to sign another two-year contract, taking me through to the end of 2000, knowing it would be my last.

Fully aware of my waning performances, I was prepared to sign for half of my current salary, so I fought to keep a straight face when Roger suggested 'Same again?' at our meeting. 'Er, OK,' I replied, deadpan, and left hastily to let Pete finalise the details before Roger could change his mind.

From my narrow perspective I had viewed my worth only in terms of race results. It hadn't occurred to me that my public reputation could have a value, or that I might have been part of a package Roger had already promised his new sponsors to get them to sign on the dotted line. I was relieved to have concluded the deal in advance of the time trial where I finished 11th, almost two minutes off the pace. Roger put this down to my personal life but I knew that was only half of the problem.

Two days after posting my worst ever result I started my second task of the championships, this time not as a bike rider but as a broadcaster. Since I wasn't scheduled to ride the road race, the BBC had asked if I'd give my expert opinion during their coverage.

It wasn't something I was particularly interested in but I was there anyway and it didn't involve any preparation so I agreed.

It was wet and gloomy when I met up with lead commentator Hugh Porter on the morning of the race at our microphone position facing the finish line. I'd known Hugh to say hello to for many years. He was, quite simply, the voice of cycling in the UK. When I replayed my gold medal ride from Barcelona, in my head even, I heard his commentary.

Hugh was accompanied by his wife Anita, herself an Olympic gold medal-winning swimmer, who sat in the wings and handed him cards containing each rider's career highlights. She seemed to be the responsible adult of the pair. When Hugh got stressed or flustered, they'd bicker and squabble silently as only a totally devoted couple can. I liked them instantly. Throughout the event, Hugh kept picking out riders with extraordinarily difficult-to-pronounce names and, soundlessly laughing, tried to manoeuvre me into having to articulate them live on air. I quickly developed the knack of referring to 'the Czech rider' or 'the team mate of …' It's a technique I still use today.

The season over, I set off with Sally and the children for what was becoming a family tradition: an autumn break in an enormous, castle-like house just outside Hawick. Everyone was excited as we headed north on the M6 towards Scotland, the Verve playing on the radio and the kids piping up periodically with 'Are we there yet?' In the rearview mirror I noticed how unusually quiet the motorway was.

At the same moment the traffic news came on the radio, reporting that the northbound M6 had been blocked by an accident on the

Thelwall Viaduct which we'd crossed a little earlier. 'A vehicle has shed its load causing a number of shunts and it's likely to be several hours before the scene is cleared and the motorway is reopened.' We'd just missed it, I thought. That was lucky. I looked again in the mirror. Where was my bike? And where was the bike rack? A mile of silence followed before we pulled over and I phoned the police to report them as lost. The staff at Borders Cycles in Hawick were surprised to see me the next morning and even more surprised that I wanted to hire a bike for a week, but they were happy to oblige.

When we'd first holidayed in Scotland I thought that as visitors from England we'd be given a cool reception. The reality couldn't have been further from the truth, everyone we encountered was happy and welcoming. The hospitable atmosphere that allowed us as outsiders to slot straight into the community was one of the main things that made the area so appealing and kept us coming back year after year.

Each day, I'd head out on my mountain bike and ride for hours though the spectacular Borders countryside, often without seeing a soul. The kids and their cousins, who usually joined us for the week, explored the huge overgrown gardens and dammed the river that ran across the grounds. In the evenings we ate around the enormous table then sat in front of a knackered old telly next to a roaring fire. It was the start of my love affair with Scotland.

Two weeks later, I went to Knutsford police station to pick up the remains of my mountain bike and three penalty points for failing to secure it safely to my vehicle. The parts could have fitted into a shoebox.

CHAPTER 13

The Jens

It was a hot July day in the south-east German city of Karslruhe. Jens Voigt and I were sitting in the back of a VW Camper van, manhandling bottles of fizzy water. Shake. Pause. Quarter turn of the top – just enough to let out the gas without spraying the contents all over ourselves. Repeat. Another ten minutes of this and we'd have enough still water to see us through the 72 km of the 1999 Breitling GP two-man time trial.

The van belonged to our race support team, a crack outfit of enthusiastic local retirees assigned to us by the event organisers. Their main qualifications for the job seemed to be their availability and their access to a vehicle capable of ferrying us to and from the airport with our bikes.

Having stepped straight off the plane into the summer heat on the morning of the race, we'd asked if they had any supplies of water for us to fill our bidons from. No, but they were happy to run off and get some, returning with four large bottles. They hadn't asked us whether we wanted still or sparkling; it hadn't occurred to us we'd need to specify. Team Sky we weren't.

We looked at the start list, all giants of the sport. 'Oh my god,' said Jens – he started a lot of sentences that way – 'We are going be dead last.' He drew out the 'e' in the word dead to emphasis his point. He did that a lot too. Looking at the sheet, I couldn't help but agree with him, the majority of the invitees had been battering us all year. We were getting a healthy start fee for this event but it looked unlikely we'd be receiving a share of the prize fund.

I'd first met Jens at the end of 1997. He had arrived for his first training camp with the team ready to ride. His bike was the only one of 20 with mudguards, the tips of which, as he proudly pointed out, were the 'regulation ten centimetres from the ground'. I wasn't sure whose regulations he was referring to but we all scoffed ... until it started raining. A massive tussle followed as riders scrambled to be directly behind him on the group ride, the only place that it was safe from being sprayed with muck.

Jens's arrival on the team was a revelation. He was like a big puppy who saw everything as a game or adventure: whether it was a cup of coffee or an eight-hour bike ride in the rain, it was all to be savoured. His attitude to life was the perfect antidote to the sullen expressions of the management. I ended up rooming with him for his first season as a pro, which was pretty tiring; his batteries never ran down and he didn't seem to have an off switch. Even when I was showering he would insist on shouting a running commentary through the bathroom door on the cartoon he was watching on TV. His favourite was *Cow and Chicken*.

His enthusiasm for life was infectious. It was impossible to be glum when Jens was laughing at things like how he'd had a 'hunger flat' a hundred kilometres from home: 'Ha, ha! I was soooo bad I was asking people to just shoot me!' This was another favourite expression. On hearing that I had four children, he proclaimed that if he ever had that many he would gladly shoot himself.

In one early season race, we lined up at the start in temperatures hovering just above zero and as we set off it began to sleet. This is pretty much the maximum allowable misery in cycling: any colder and it turns to snow meaning the race is usually cancelled. Many in the peloton, including me, had already started to think about warm team cars and hot showers. Only one rider thought the conditions were the perfect excuse to attack or 'smash ourselves!' Jens did smash himself – a gloriously futile solo break followed by a predictable collapse. Some hours later, one of the last men on the road and nearly half an hour down, he finally crossed the line, where the team *soigneur* almost had to lasso him to get him to stop.

On the way back from a small race in Normandy – the Duo Normand two-man time trial – we found ourselves stuck overnight in an Ibis hotel at Charles de Gaulle airport. We'd been victorious that day so we dumped our bags in the room and headed down to the bar where Jens spotted they had draught Grimbergen, a particularly noxious Belgian beer. He'd never tried it before and decided to spend the evening putting that right. I cautioned him against this course of action, to which he just laughed, smacked his chest and said, 'I can handle it, I-am-a-man!'

Later that night I was thankful for his fastidious German nature, which compelled him to clean up every last trace of vomit before he left for his early flight. When we met up for our next race I asked him how it was that he'd managed to make it to the bathroom – which in an Ibis is about the size of a wheelie bin – but still failed to reach the toilet bowl.

'Oh my god, man,' he said, 'I was already happy to have made it to the bathroom!'

With such a chaotic lifestyle, constantly on the road and changing hotels every night, it's not surprising that pro riders like to room with the same person. You become like a married couple, but without the sex. When the UCI introduced its longitudinal medicals – regular blood tests to create profiles for every rider in the peloton – it was natural that Jens and I went for our first test together.

We'd been given the address of a clinic in Paris, where we were to stop on the way to our next race and have samples taken. Simple enough. Having navigated our way though the narrow streets, we arrived at the specified location, a majestic and ornate six-storey building. As we passed through the big oak doors the noise of the busy streets was cut off and we were left in a silent foyer without a person in sight. We set off down an echoing corridor in search of help and eventually found someone who looked as though they might work there. In my pidgin French I told them we were there for the blood test and asked where we should go. They shyly mumbled directions and pointed down another passageway.

When we finally found the waiting room there were a dozen men already there. 'Hi!' said Jens to no one in particular as we entered. No response. Some minutes of gloomy silence later we were ushered into an old-fashioned office where a stern doctor sat behind his desk. He directed us towards the two chairs in front of him and waited for us to speak. I reiterated that we were here for the blood tests. 'Which one of you?'

'Both of us.'

'You are both infected?' he asked.

At this point the sequence of events since we'd entered the building rotated slightly, clicked together and formed a picture I didn't want to see. I decided I'd better spell it out. 'We-are-here-for-the-cycling-blood-tests. Part-of-the-longitudinal-medical-scheme.'

'But this is a clinic for sexually transmitted diseases.'

We left the office swearing we would never speak of it again to anyone.

It was Jens's never-say-die attitude that turned the tables for us halfway though that edition of the Breitling Grand Prix. On a long straight stretch of road running back into the city he caught sight of the favourites, Laurent Jalabert and Abraham Olano, up ahead in the far distance. That glimpse was all he needed. Like a homing missile he went after them, with me in tow trying to match his ferocious desire to hunt them down. When Jens was in one of those moods it was visible in his body language. He rocked as he wrestled his machine, every muscle fibre pressed into service. Following behind, our support team pensioners also sensed the resurgence and gunned the engine of the camper van to bring them alongside, where they enthusiastically offered us the last of the now-only-slightly-fizzy water.

In the end we won the event by ten seconds and found ourselves laughing on the podium, both at the absurdity of the day and just how wrong we'd been in our pre-race pessimism. We each got a very nice Breitling watch for our efforts. I wear mine to this day and smile every time I look at it.

Jens rode professionally until he was 42, attacking for the sheer enjoyment of it right until the end, before being cheered into retirement as probably the most well-liked rider in the world. He lives happily just outside Berlin with his wife Stephanie, their six children and a menagerie of pets. To my knowledge, he has not yet shot himself.

I'd thought that signing my final contract would give me the stability and certainty I needed to concentrate on racing for my last two seasons, but my body had other ideas. In January 1999 a set of routine blood tests at the team's winter camp had produced some worrying results. I was low in testosterone and other metabolic hormones, and since recovery had been a consistent issue in my career I was advised to have this looked into.

Further tests back in the UK led to an appointment for a scan at the Royal Liverpool Hospital. That revealed I had low bone density, something quite unusual at my age except in people with depressed testosterone levels. It was suggested that the condition was almost certainly being exacerbated by my chosen career as an endurance athlete, constantly breaking down body tissues with high volumes of work. The standard treatment was hormone replacement therapy, which I was advised to start straight away.

If my job made the condition worse, it made treatment pretty much impossible. Testosterone is a controlled substance in sport.

To use it and still race I'd need a TUE, a Therapeutic Use Exemption. Unsure exactly what to do, I approached the UCI – there were no armies of team personnel then to do this stuff for you – and explained my diagnosis. I also forwarded copies of my bone scans.

The initial response was encouraging. I was advised to organise treatment while the TUE was arranged. Soon afterwards, though, I received a call from the UCI telling me, in embarrassed tones, that there would be no exemption. They weren't disputing my condition – it's hard to fake a bone scan – or that I needed the remedy prescribed, but it wasn't something that could be sanctioned. All this had happened at the wrong time: French police were still arresting people connected to the Festina affair, and despite the consequences for my career I couldn't bring myself to disagree with the UCI's stance.

I thought seriously about whether to pack it all in there and then. I met with my UK doctor to see if there was a legal interim intervention that might at least manage my condition if I did decide to keep on riding. There was: regular infusions of a calcium-binding agent that required me to be hooked up to a drip for four hours every other month. Logistically, the most efficient time to do it was in the run-up to competition when I'd be backing off training anyway, so I scheduled the first treatment for late March, just before flying out to France for a race. That was how I found out that the medication destroyed performance. From then on, sessions were carefully timed to coincide with my return home from racing.

With only six minor time trial wins, 1999 was a pretty thin season for results. Despite what I'd thought was an excellent build up to the Tour de France, I was only able to finish fifth in the prologue behind the eventual race winner, Lance Armstrong. I completed that year's Tour in 119th place, two and three quarter hours behind the American. There was no celebration: getting round wasn't what I was being paid for. The atmosphere in the team was almost hostile.

CHAPTER 14

The Final Hour

To usher in the new century we hired a local restaurant, The Green Room in West Kirby, and a one-man acoustic band. The poor bloke didn't realise he'd be providing a karaoke service, but when he failed to prise the microphone and his tambourine from Sally's grip he gave in with good grace and resigned himself to the role of backing singer. Sally worked her way through the bulk of Dolly Parton's back catalogue and the kids fell asleep under the table. It was a nice night.

The party marked not only the end of a century but the start of my final season and the countdown to retirement. I was looking forward to it. Sally, though, had a wider view and could see the shock I was in for when I stopped racing, so she had devised a strategy. She knew I wanted to continue exercising regularly and that I was, at least for now, utterly sick of cycling. The alternative was running: a pursuit with the added bonus of having no historical benchmarks for me to fail to live up to. She reasoned that this simple activity might give me the transitional structure I needed to adjust to civilian life. And what better way to encourage such a regime to take root than to have a regular running partner depending on me? It was a great plan. It was also doomed from the outset.

That August my birthday present was a lead and a collar. It was the first I knew of Project Beagle. Sally had visited Maccombs pet shop in Hoylake with a list of canine requirements: the dog needed to be a manageable size and cope well with car travel, it had to be good with children, obedient, a non-moulting breed and, of course, it had to like running. 'Easy,' said Jan Foster, the owner. 'What you need is a Beagle.'

Just how wrong on how many counts this advice was would only become clear once it was too late but Sally, knowing little about dogs, thanked Jan for the guidance and duly placed an order with a recommended breeder near Preston. A few months after my birthday we shoehorned ourselves into my tiny orange Lotus and headed off to pick up our new charge.

In the kennel was a large mass of brown and white fur that on hearing the door open dissolved into eight fluffy tennis-balls of energy. I say eight, in fact there were seven boisterous puppies and one snoring lump left in the corner. It had runt written all over it and naturally this was the one Sally had bought. She was undeniably a very cute dog. No larger than my hand, with huge sad eyes and floppy ears bigger than her body, her appearance gave no indication of the pathologically stubborn engine of destruction that lurked inside. In the car, as she nestled between Sally's feet, we tried to think of a name. The 90-minute drive home failed to produce anything suitable so we simply adopted her mother's kennel name: Cookie.

A few months later, after all the oohing and aahing over how cute she was had subsided, Cookie's true nature started to emerge. Despite its solid walls and high fences she made a series of escapes from the garden. None of these breakouts were witnessed, she was simply found on the wrong side of a boundary that logic said she couldn't breach. Unable to work out how it was happening, we called in a fencing expert to escape-proof the garden. When he arrived it seemed telling that he had his own Beagle in tow, presumably to quality-check his work.

Cookie was no less trouble indoors. Her ability to feign sleep, complete with loud snoring, became legendary. This ploy was used on many occasions to lull us into thinking she could be safely left unattended in a room, usually one in which food was stored. The moment she found herself alone, she set to work, often moving furniture to access worktops and tables.

Over the course of a year she ate a box of Weetabix, several pounds of cheese (blue preferred), three square metres of wallpaper, a chocolate cake, a kilo of butter, several books and a box of Thornton's toffee.

As Jan had promised, Cookie had no problems with car travel. In fact she loved to be with the family – her pack – at all times. It was the indignity of being left in the car, even for a few seconds, that Cookie objected to. In retaliation, she ate the seat belts, which cost £600 to replace, and projectile-moulted, an ability I still maintain she was consciously in control of. She wasn't left in the car again. It was our first obedience lesson.

*

Our inaugural run – supposedly the dog's *raison d'être* – was a leisurely jog in light rain along the Hoylake seafront. Sensing the consistent nature of the activity, she rebelled after 90 seconds and simply stopped. Every time I moved back towards her, making encouraging noises and enthusiastically slapping my thigh, she ran a few metres in the other direction, always staying just out of reach until we got home. Obedience lesson number two: she must have been pleased with my progress.

Determined not to be bested by a hound, I devised a new strategy. I'd start the run and get to my turnaround point before letting her off the lead. Then when she started her break for home it would be at a time of *my* choosing in the direction *I* wanted her to go. Cookie cottoned on to my plan immediately and simply sat down, refusing to move. No fuss, barking or biting, just passive-aggressive resolve. Gandhi would have been proud. As I yanked on the lead, she made choking noises, her claws rasping noisily across the pavement. Passers-by scowled at me for the cruelty I was displaying towards this poor beast with the big brown eyes and floppy ears. After two weeks I gave in. The dog stayed at home and ate the soft furnishings while I did the running around.

It wasn't that Cookie didn't like exercise, just that it had to be on her terms. She loved walks across the sandbanks of the Dee Estuary, following the many scents, straining to get off the lead, but I knew that letting her loose at the wrong moment could turn a short, peaceful stroll into an open-ended episode of 'seagull frenzy'. Once, I chased her around the sandy expanse shouting myself hoarse until the evening slid into dusk and the tide started coming in. As we ran back and forth – for considerably longer than any of the runs the dog had refused to take part in – a crowd gathered at the railings along the promenade. When Cookie finally decided she'd had enough and trotted over, ears drooping, eyes full of (false) remorse, I got a round of applause. At least I like to think it was for me.

Another advantage of living by a beach, for Cookie at least, was the number of people who liked to barbecue in good weather. One late summer evening, Sally and I were walking along the coastal track that ran from our house past the sand dunes separating the Royal Liverpool Golf Course from the estuary. Cookie, who had disappeared into the dunes some minutes earlier, exploded into view running at full pelt, ears flapping in time with the large steak protruding from either side of her mouth. We carried on walking in silence and pretended it wasn't our dog.

In the end, the only requirements on Sally's original list that the dog actually fulfilled were not getting car sick and not biting. Or licking for that matter. In fact, Cookie generally ignored people altogether unless they had food. She became the family eccentric – or at least the *most* eccentric – and the older and more crotchety she got the more we loved her.

If the 1999 season had been thin, then my final term as a professional was a disaster. In fact, it was so depressing I can barely bring myself to write about it. It was the only season of my career in which I didn't win a single race: second in the prologue of Paris–Nice was the best I could manage. The team management knew about my health problems but they didn't seem to make any allowances for

Elation and despair. I'm the surprise leader of the 1994 Tour,
but about to lose the jersey just hours from the start of the UK stages

Making a good show of hiding my terror ahead of my first Tour de France road stage

George about to have his first drink

My first Tour lion on the podium in Rouen, 1997

The 1995 Tour de France prologue. Two minutes away from the ambulance…

On the road with GAN boss, Roger Legeay

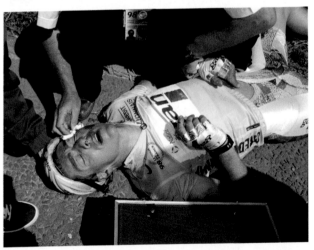

1998 Tour de France, Ireland. I have no recollection of this

The final hour, with Peter Keen track side, 40 seconds from the end of my career

This image speaks for itself

Track Centre with fellow Senior Management Team member and friend, Steve Peters

The ITV Tour team 2010 catching the last few kilometres of a stage (apart from cameraman John Tinetti who was catching 40 winks)

Discussing TT bike geometry with Ironman champion Pete Jacobs

The inimitable Boris Johnson. Love him or hate him, he's the first British politician to commit to a long term cycling vision

My dog, Cookie

The squad, 2016. From left: Harriet, Ed, Sally, me, Agatha, George, Sonny and Oscar

them, and the less valued I felt the less I wanted to be there. Even the combined high spirits of Jens and Eros couldn't get me to see cycling as anything other than a daily, weekly, monthly grind. So I did what everyone does when they aren't happy at work: I clocked off and looked outside for enjoyment. It arrived from an unexpected source.

Anne O'Hare seldom gave her friends and family actual, physical presents. She preferred experiences. Either something she would enjoy doing herself or, more often, something she wanted to see you do for her amusement. At Christmas 1999 she handed us a plain white envelope. I winced inwardly. Was it singing lessons? A bungee jump from a balloon? Maybe a session as a stand-up comedian? Grin fixed in place, I tore it open to find the best present I had ever received: scuba-diving lessons. Sadly for Sally, who was also included in the deal, it was possibly the worst present that she had ever received. This seemed to please Anne just as much as my elation.

On the night of Sunday 16 January, I went to Europa Pools in Birkenhead and breathed underwater for the first time since I was 13 years old. In a single breath my love for the life aquatic rushed back into me and I became fanatical about it all over again. It was a child's excitement and the immersion was almost total. Diving lessons became the focus of my life with my career fitted in around them.

Sally persevered with the course out of sheer stubbornness, hating every moment of it. She didn't mind the theory, sitting in a classroom was fine, it was just the bit that involved water she detested. After a few weeks our highly competent and patient instructor, Paul Chapman, took us to Astbury Water Park just outside Congleton. It was a rather grandiose title for some rotting wooden buildings the size of a couple of shipping containers sitting on the side of an old sand quarry.

The murky green water was a frigid five degrees. Despite the drysuit and several layers of clothing, the first time we submerged ourselves was a shocking experience, even for me. I can't believe Sally stuck with it. Part of the first lesson involved taking off our masks and replacing them while sitting on the bottom. When Paul indicated to Sally that she should perform this manoeuvre she fixed him with one of her stares and slowly shook her head. Over the course of three days we completed the required tasks and became qualified scuba divers. We were now allowed to experience the full wonders of Astbury. We saw a dead frog. I think it had committed suicide.

Having met the challenge and passed her tests, Sally has never dived since. I signed up straight away for more tuition. By May I was on to Advanced Diver training, the search and rescue part of which was performed in Liverpool's Salthouse Dock. From the course I got both a certification card and a virulent nasal infection that severely hampered my ability to train. Already in the team's bad books for my lack of results, I did not make the selection for the 2000 Tour. I had mixed feelings about this, partly wistful that my last shot at a stage victory had been taken away, partly relieved not to have the responsibility. I already felt like an outsider.

In late June I was out training in the Cheshire lanes when I stopped to take a call from Roger. He'd been thinking about my final season and wanted to make sure I went out on a high note.

While I stood at the side of the road with my bike in the warm afternoon sunshine, cars whizzing past, he reminded me of an account I'd given him of our Bordeaux hour record preparation. What had stuck in his mind was my description of a small side exercise that we'd done out of curiosity – mostly Pete Keen's.

Along with all our high-tech gear we had taken a normal track bike, a silk jersey and an old-fashioned 'hairnet' crash helmet to gauge how hard it would be to break Eddy Merckx's 1972 record using the same kind of equipment. I hadn't given any thought to it in seven years, but the tale of our experiment had inspired Roger. He proposed that the final act of my career should be an attempt to better the 49.431 km mark set in Mexico City by the world's greatest ever cyclist.

By this time it had become a record worth breaking again. Since my second hour ride in 1996, the UCI had not only clamped down heavily on bike design, they'd rewritten history. They ruled that every record holder after Merckx, from Francesco Moser though to me, had tinkered to some degree with what they saw as standard cycling equipment. So they split the hour into two categories. My 1996 record of 56.375 km had been designated Best Human Effort, while the traditional hour record or 'Athlete's Hour' had reverted to Merckx.

I told Roger I'd have a think about it and come back to him. Still standing at the side of the road, I called Pete Keen to get his reaction. Like me, he fancied the idea – it was just the kind of project we loved – but he was quick to point out that it wouldn't be easy. Having travelled more than six kilometres further than Merckx in 1996, I admit to silently scoffing at his warning.

*

I was seen by many as one of the riders responsible for a technological renaissance in cycling, using equipment to steal a march on the opposition. Many traditionalists viewed this application of aerodynamic knowledge as a sort of heresy, as though to rely on anything other than legs, lungs and a hearty breakfast was tantamount to cheating. So to finish my career with an exercise that eschewed almost all forms of science and focused solely on athletic ability seemed beautifully symmetrical, like tidying up before I left. The more I thought about it, the more it seemed this would be a poetic way to bow out. We booked the Manchester Velodrome for an afternoon in October, in the middle of the track world championships, and set to work.

Merckx had ridden under the regulations of the day, so his 1972 machine was state of the art – in 1972. The parameters that Pete and I devised to ensure comparability were very simple and we hoped that anybody who came after us – assuming we were successful – would adhere to them. Firstly, the bicycle had to have round tubes. Not almost round, or round to all intents and purposes with some hidden aerodynamic advantage cleverly designed in: just round. In addition, the main tubes could be no less than 25 mm in diameter. Wheels had to have traditional spokes and the rider position was to be in line with the UCI rules for mass-start road events. That was it, all the rules in one paragraph, simple boundaries that we hoped would allow a direct comparison between riders 30 years past and 30 years hence.

Within these constraints we could still experiment, which is how we found ourselves in Pete's garage with an SRM ergometer and a full-length mirror. In his role as Performance Director of British

Cycling, Pete was evaluating this piece of lab apparatus for the team. It was like an item of heavyweight gym equipment in which someone had hidden an exercise bike. The beauty of it was that it was endlessly adjustable: it could quickly mimic any rider position while precisely measuring the changes in power output produced by every tweak. With its programmable motor-controlled drive it could also dictate the rider's cadence, workload or any combination thereof. It was the perfect machine with which to explore.

The equipment limitations we were working under meant that I couldn't stretch out or otherwise radically change my shape on the bike. Still, drag was going to be a key factor so we set about minimising my frontal area. To start with, we put all the measuring devices to one side, placed the ergometer in front of the mirror and simply tried moving saddle, bars and stem around until we found what looked like the smallest shape that I felt I could adapt to. Once we had what was a promisingly minimalist silhouette, Pete set the rig to demand 400 watts of power and I did a ten-minute block to test it from an ergonomic perspective. Only after confirming that I could ride hard and still hold the position did we reach for the tape measure.

The numbers were insane. Although the position looked passably conventional on the ergometer, to achieve it would require a bike that married a 54 cm seat tube with a ludicrously long 63 cm top tube and a 16 cm handlebar stem! For anyone who knows cycling, this set of measurements is bizarre: no bike would ever be constructed with such dimensions.

It was a valuable lesson that would resurface years later when I was coaching coaches. The SRM rig, which had no tubes and no recognisable frame, allowed us to experiment, unconstrained by the historical template of what a bike should and shouldn't look like. By not measuring until the very end and using a device that gave us no visual clues as to where our experiments were taking us, we had been able to suspend judgement and focus solely on the demands of the event.

To have such an odd frame built there was only one person to go to: Terry Dolan. It would be the very last bike I ever rode as a pro, so it was fitting that the man who'd helped me from the very start would be intimately involved in creating the machine I'd use at the close. With his stream of jokes and his thick Liverpool accent, some people underestimate Terry, but he is one of the most perceptive people I've ever met. I'd learned the hard way not to ignore his advice in 1996 in the run-up to the Olympic Games.

Sick of people saying it was the Lotus bike that had got me my gold in Barcelona, I'd been stubbornly determined not to ride one in Atlanta. I designed a frame of my own, constructed from teardrop-shaped steel tubing, with all the cables routed internally. It looked fantastic. It also flexed like a diving board. Terry had warned me this would happen the moment I showed him my sketches. Arrogantly thinking I knew better than someone who'd designed frames for decades, I failed to listen. Feeling his job was done – Terry never once tried to force his opinion on me – he set about building the frame and letting me learn my own lessons. The bike bent out of line so much on the climbs of the Atlanta circuit that it had actually changed gear of its own accord.

I was curious to see what Terry would make of this radical track bike Pete and I were planning. A couple of weeks after sending him the measurements, I got a call to say that the first prototype was ready for inspection. It was an ugly beast and looked to have more in common with a barnyard gate than a world-beating bicycle. On closer inspection, I noticed the down tube was slightly oval rather than the specified circular cross-section. I delicately brought to his attention the fact that this rendered his creation obsolete before we'd even begun. He stared at the frame for some seconds, desperately trying to find a rationale that would render the frame usable.

'Well … it's roundish.'

I left poor Terry to redo the frame while Pete Keen and I turned our attention to the other component that we could influence within our self-imposed guidelines, the engine.

Pete had been looking into simulated altitude training. Through his contacts we obtained some equipment that filtered oxygen out of the atmosphere to create a hypoxic environment. We tried one of the company's prototype portable hypoxic chambers in my home office. It was a perspex cube so large that, once assembled, it filled the space completely making it impossible for anyone to open the door to enter or leave the room. We needed a more practical solution, one which was eventually provided by six-year-old George Boardman. Or more specifically, his bedroom.

Most of George's possessions were removed, along with George himself who had to share a room with Oscar for the duration of the exercise. I fitted seals around the door and drilled large holes in the window frame for three plastic tubes, which led down to the garage where the filtration systems were housed. Over the course of a day they slowly changed the atmosphere in George's bedroom until the tiny space mimicked the oxygen availability at nine thousand feet. I trained, slept and watched TV in this rarefied atmosphere for up to 12 hours a day over a period of more than eight weeks. Regular physiology testing in the run-up to the record attempt told us that this innovative training technique enhanced my eventual performance by absolutely sod all.

In May, after completing the final stage of the PruTour in Edinburgh, we loaded the car up with kids and Jens for the drive south. He was staying over for a week's training and change of scene from his base in Toulouse. Why he thought Merseyside would be more interesting than the south of France I don't know, but he was never one for choosing the easy option. While he was with us I introduced him to the beautifully quaint world of British time trialling.

During the spring and summer months, Thursday was the Chester road club's ten-mile time trial night, so for a quality workout we headed across the Wirral peninsula. It was a curious clash of worlds: Jens, famous German professional, lining up on the grass verge on Rake Lane with half a dozen local amateurs to put 50p in an old biscuit tin in return for a number. Being true Brits, none of the participants batted an eyelid at his presence. Never mind this namby-pamby Tour de France rubbish, if he wanted respect around here he had to get under 20 minutes for ten miles (he did).

That summer was packed with unusual episodes – unusual for me, at least. Sally relinquished domestic power and let me take over the refurbishment of the bathroom in our little flat in Chester. Oscar and I went on some rides with his tag-along bike attached to the back of mine and I tried my hand in the kitchen using my newly acquired copy of Delia Smith's *How To Cook*. Naturally, I didn't start with the boiling an egg page but the twice-baked soufflés. The whole summer felt like a series of day release sessions as I was gently groomed for reintroduction to society.

On Friday 27 October, I woke up knowing that by the end of the day I would no longer be a professional bike rider. I was excited. I spent the morning drinking coffee with friends before heading to the velodrome. The attempt had been slotted into a free afternoon session in the World Championship schedule, so I was guaranteed a packed house.

The hour before the record attempt was spent in a breeze-block physiotherapy room underneath the velodrome. I'd been in many such spaces during my career, convenient pre-race holding pens of a hundred different shapes and sizes: village halls, camping cars, hotel bedrooms and mechanics' areas. But this time was different, this time, when I walked out I would never need a space to warm up or mentally prepare for an impending battle again. I'd already sworn that there would never be another number on my back, that I would never carry a pulse monitor again or measure my power output. Whatever the result, when I left that velodrome, the bicycle would become something very different to me. I didn't know what and at that moment I didn't care. I was just glad it was about to be over.

Warm-up complete, Pete sprayed me with the same ethyl alcohol and water mix we'd used in 1993 to help cool me down for the first few minutes of the ride. We shook hands and headed for the track centre. I'd done this twice before and on the second occasion I'd been at my absolute physical best. After my nasal infection and a summer spent diving more than racing, I was far from my prime for attempt number three, but I was still hoping for a similar experience to 1996.

As I sat on the start line I gave my pacing strategy one last mental run-through, then at 3.45 p.m. I pushed off for the final time. I hadn't travelled more than ten laps before I realised this was not going to be the euphoric experience of four years earlier. My legs were heavy and my breathing laboured. It was going to be bad. I looked up at the stands, full of cheering people here to witness history being made. I already knew I couldn't sustain the pace required but neither could I abandon. This was the last thing I'd ever do.

Once environment and aerodynamics have been excluded, the governing factor in a cyclist's performance is aerobic efficiency – how well your engine runs. But unlike a motor vehicle, the moment you start the ignition on a cycling engine, it starts to lose capacity. With every turn of the pedal, muscle fibres are damaged and go out of commission, while the power requirement to maintain a constant speed remains the same.

In other words, I knew I was only going to slow as the hour wore on and I believed, rightly or wrongly, that if I just stuck to the even-paced schedule we'd set – 18.2 second laps – I would fail. I had to create a buffer. Over the first 20 minutes I stole a metre here, a metre there, until by half distance I had a 250 metre, or 18 second lead over Merckx. The crowd cheered, sensing success, but with 30 minutes still to ride, I already knew it was going to come down to a sprint. Timing was going to be critical and the outcome was far from certain.

From half distance I began to suffer terribly. As my legs burned and my arms cramped I started to lose ground. With 20 minutes to go the bad news reached the crowd. The PA announcer Mike Smith had a copy of my schedule and let them know I'd lost 12 seconds in just ten minutes of riding. I was now only six seconds ahead of Merckx. The noise from the stands changed to a low rumble. They'd finally got it: they weren't here to witness a choreographed swansong.

I battled with the pain, my entire world now focused on Pete Keen, who was walking alongside the track to indicate how far I was ahead or behind the target speed. Over the first half he had walked away from me until he'd been a full lap ahead, showing me I was 250 metres up on the old record. Now he shuffled towards me every time he came into view. With 15 minutes to go he had unwound most of the one lap gain and was back into the home straight, just a few strides away from the pursuit line, the place he'd started at a lifetime ago. I fought on, desperately trying to hold him in position or at least slow his pace.

With ten minutes to go Pete stepped onto the pursuit line. I was dead level with Merckx. Two minutes later he'd walked almost to the bend, indicating I was now nearly three and a half seconds behind our target. I fleetingly wondered how many calories he'd burned with all the exercise. The crowd noise dipped again: they had shifted from thinking it was going to be close to not believing I could do it.

But by now I was feeling the opposite. I'd had nearly two decades of time-trial training; I knew my body and what I could expect from it. For the last half an hour I had fought not to stay ahead but to stay in touch. Now, with the end in sight, I was convinced I was close enough for my last card to count. The goal was achievable as long as I timed the sprint right. I'd judged that the final push for home could start with 16 laps to go and not before. Despite appearances, I felt in control, at least I did until Sally stepped onto the side of the track.

Sally, always indifferent to my sporting exploits, had been watching from the infield with everyone else, seeing me slide behind. Suddenly she was within touching distance and screaming at me, urging me on, something she had never done before. It was an emotional moment and nearly overwhelmed me. I started to respond, pushing up the pace, but it was too soon. Once I ventured over my aerobic threshold it would be only a matter of moments before I ground to a halt. I got myself under control, at least physically, and held back for a few critical seconds.

With 16 laps to go, I began to accelerate again. Thirteen laps to go, I came into the home straight and saw Pete's face. He had guessed what I was doing and now, for the first time in 30 minutes, he could see the proof on his stopwatch. He strode away from me indicating the change in trend. Ten laps to go. The crowd, who had seen Pete reverse direction and step purposefully back towards the pursuit line, exploded.

The next few laps were a blur of noise and pain. At some point Pete had started holding up his fingers to indicate the number of laps remaining. Just five until the end of my career, but he was still 25 metres away from the line and success. Each agonising lap he edged closer but I was running out of time. I pushed harder. With three laps to go, he was less than 15 metres from the mark. Eyes full of sweat and almost unable to see, I poured everything I had left into the final effort, hardly a sprint, there was barely a change in speed, the tank was almost empty. At this point I no longer cared about the result, I just wanted it to stop. The bell rang, barely audible over the roar. I could see people jumping up and down; they looked happy. Pete Keen was beaming too, arms raised, standing ten metres the right side of the line, which was how much I'd broken the record by. I still didn't care. Then the gun fired. It was over. All of it.

CHAPTER 15

Retirement

The plan for retirement was a fairly simple one: do nothing. Taking a position as a team director or some other cycling-related role would have felt like a cop-out, letting myself be institutionalised for the sake of financial security. For at least the first two years I wanted to look outside the narrow world of sport: I could start doing woodwork again, see if I could get Cookie to run more than 50 metres, spend more time scuba-diving and generally see where the wind blew me.

To accommodate this utopian lifestyle, Sally and I had begun to economise: the flashy Lotus was sold, the kids were taken out of private school, health insurance and gym subscriptions were allowed to lapse. Without all the financial pressures, I'd have what I'd wanted for years: the freedom to explore and choose work simply because it interested me. It was all very exciting, and after I swung my leg off the bike for the very last time life was everything I had hoped it would be. For about six weeks.

The sudden removal of the central object around which my existence had orbited was disorientating, and the unfettered liberty quickly lost its lustre. I had no idea how much I'd needed pressure, challenges to overcome and problems to be solved.

I began to invent them. Things I'd never really noticed at home started to leap out at me. Sally's CDs were strewn around the house, left wherever she'd last listened to them. I spent a whole day hunting them down then carefully filing them alphabetically. I developed firm opinions on everything from the colour of Ed's shoes to which route the kids should take on their walk to school and generally began trespassing on territory that had always been Sally's.

It was no surprise that she wasn't too upset about my growing infatuation with diving, it got me out of the house for a few hours. With the local dive club I explored the delights of Liverpool Bay, scoured the bottom of Salthouse Dock and jumped into just about every flooded quarry in North Wales. When I returned from my muddy exploits I spent hours in the garage obsessing over my diving equipment (now installed in its own custom-built racking system) and even knocked up a self-contained underwater breathing pack for the children. Luckily for them it was never tested in earnest.

I wasn't short of invitations to rejoin society at large during this period. Even with the minimal methods of contact I maintained with the outside world, I was amazed by the almost daily weird, wonderful and worthy requests that reached me. The hardest to answer were generally in the last category: selfless individuals representing some wonderful cause or other who want nothing more than a bit of your time.

During what I've come to think of as my gap years, I received an email from a Squadron Leader Graham Staunton. It looked merely worthy to begin with but quickly turned both weird and wonderful. It was a heart-warming account of fun and fund-raising for a new gym at his RAF base. He didn't need me for that – after years of sponsored bike rides, three-legged-races and fêtes the gym had been built. All I had to do was come and open it. No problem, except that the RAF base was at Kinloss, way up on the east coast of Scotland. After a quick Internet search to confirm how long it would take me to get there and back from the Wirral, I sent Graham my apologies and wished him all the best with finding someone else. The next morning there was a reply. Not the 'thanks anyway' I was expecting but something almost as short: 'Oh go on, we'll send a Nimrod for you.' As offers-you-can't-refuse go, it was hard to beat.

So on an overcast early May morning I wheeled my bike into Liverpool's John Lennon Airport and made for the two figures in the green RAF regulation flight suits: Graham and his copilot Craig 'Mucky' Mackie, both Scousers born and bred. They might as well have landed from a different planet as far as airport security was concerned. There followed a stand-off between the worlds of military and civil aviation as the two pilots attempted to get their single passenger and his luggage onto the plane. My fully assembled bike was too big to go through the standard X-ray machine. Despite Graham's assurances that it was OK, the airport staff insisted it had to be scanned: 'For all we know, there could be bombs in the tubes.'

'That's OK,' said Graham. 'We can stack them next to mine.'

The dark blue uniforms weren't amused and we had to go and find an X-ray machine that could handle freight in the bowels of the airport.

Once the bike had been cleared of any terrorist threat, it was our turn. Graham set off the metal detector.

'It's all right,' he said, 'it's just my knife.' From his top pocket he pulled the razor-sharp folding utility blade that he kept for cutting himself out of his harness in an emergency.

'You can't take that on board!' said the flustered guard.

'What's he going to do?' I chipped in, mimicking holding a knife to my own throat. 'Hijack himself?'

On board, things felt no less bizarre as I was ushered into the cockpit and invited to try out the co-pilot's seat. Just like in the movies, every surface was covered in gauges, switches and dials. On the 'steering wheel' was a large red button with a bold letter N in its centre. I asked, tongue-in-cheek, if that was for releasing the nuclear bombs. 'Yes' came the answer. Apparently in its past, the Nimrod had carried nuclear depth charges. Having your hand right next to a button that launched weapons of mass destruction is a sobering experience.

After take-off we climbed to an altitude of just 300 metres which we maintained all the way along the Mersey towards the Irish Sea. It was an incredible, once-in-a-lifetime view of my home peninsula and the city of Liverpool. We were almost level with the Liver Birds perched on top of the building that bears their name. As we reached New Brighton and the mouth of the Mersey, Craig banked right, skimming the sand dunes at Formby, and headed north hugging the coast.

To justify using a multi-million pound reconnaissance aircraft as a taxi, the trip had been logged as a training exercise to track 'enemy ships', in this case a real Russian warship, the *Admiral Chabanenko*, that had been visiting Liverpool as part of the Battle of the Atlantic celebrations. It was known to be 'somewhere in the Irish Sea'. In the interests of post-cold war friendship the crew had agreed to take some aerial publicity photographs of the vessel. When we'd pinpointed it – which we seemed to do suspiciously quickly – I assumed that the millions of pounds' worth of spying equipment in the wing-mounted pods would be used to capture high definition images, taking in the tiniest details on the decks below. Instead Graham strolled back through the cabin to the domed window on the port side and removed it. He then reached for his own camera, leaned out and started snapping away.

After another spectacular low-level swoop, this time along the Great Glen to take us from west coast to east, we arrived at Kinloss, the home of 120 Squadron. The gym opening went well and I even had a go at piloting the base flight simulator, although it couldn't compare to being a passenger on the real thing.

The Nimrod flight was one of many bizarre money-couldn't-buy experiences I've been privileged to have as a result of simply being able to ride a bicycle round in circles faster than other people. In late 2001 came an invitation from the UK's leading scuba publication, *Diver*: would I like to go on an all expenses paid trip to the Abaco Islands in the northern Bahamas for one of their celebrity features? As a member of the Jesters Sub Aqua Club based in Chester, and used to dives that qualified as exciting if you could see your own fingers, I accepted.

My host for the trip and the man who would be writing about me was the slightly eccentric John Bantin, a bearded 30-year veteran of the industry, who had a talent for spinning yarns and seemed to be as interested in photographing women in bikinis as he was the various species of exotic fish. He was great company. We stayed at the luxurious Bluff House in Green Turtle Cay and dived with another veteran of the underwater fraternity, Brendal. A native of the island in his fifties, he had a 20-year-old's passion for life. His priorities were clear for all to see: rum, partying, women and rum all linked together by his love for the sea.

This was my first proper diving boat trip and it was to set a very high standard. After 20 minutes of bouncing lightly across the swell in Brendal's little boat, he killed the engine and with a big grin simply jumped over the stern leaving his deckhand in charge. After a couple of minutes had gone by I began to wonder if it was an elaborate suicide attempt. Then Brendal resurfaced, holding two large conchs. He leapt back onto the boat, quickly extracted the molluscs from their shells and turned them into fresh conch salad for lunch.

No sooner were we underway again than we took another detour. Brendal hauled the boat hard to starboard and cut the engine once more, this time so we could spend a few minutes watching a humpback whale feeding at the surface. I hadn't even been in the water yet and I was already struggling for appropriately gushing adjectives. Once I did go over the side there was no avoiding full immersion in Caribbean cliché: the warm clear water, the huge curious fish, the seabed below a profusion of colourful soft corals swaying majestically in the light current.

Near the end of the dive a Giant Barracuda appeared, about the same length as myself and almost the same girth. It was an intimidating sight and an increasingly detailed one as it headed towards me at speed. When it was within two metres I could see the finger-length teeth in its half-open mouth. It suddenly exploded into action, flashing past my ear to catch the fish it had been stalking behind me.

This was the world I'd read about in Ladybird diving books late at night under the bed covers with a torch, the place I'd fantasised about since I could barely walk. With my Lego I'd made replica models of the underwater habitat Jacques Cousteau built to study places just like this.

At the end of that incredible morning Brendal went over the side once more, armed with a metre-long steel rod, which he used to spear half a dozen lobsters. A few minutes later we were dropping anchor at Manjack Cay, a picture-postcard desert island fringed with palm trees. We fed the tame whip rays in the shallow water with left over pieces of conch while our host barbecued the lobster and served it up with the salad he'd made earlier.

Like many holidaymakers before me, I was determined to see if I could find a way to stay in this new world, or at least have regular access to it. I decided to invent a new job writing about diver training from a participant's perspective. I presented the idea to *Diver* magazine's editor, Steve Weinman, leaving out the fact that I'd never written anything for publication before and had left school without an English qualification. He liked it, and I began travelling all over the world with friend and photographer Craig Nelson, indulging my passion and writing articles on more than 20 different courses. I did everything from exploring the caves of Mexico to mastering re-breathers in Devon, learning to drive power boats on the Mersey to navigating wrecks in Southern Egypt. It was an amazing experience and a wonderful lifestyle. For a single man.

I was doing it again: I'd retired from one all-consuming activity only for my obsessive nature to latch straight on to another. While I'd been fixated on cycling my fanaticism had at least been feeding the family. Diving took up inordinate amounts of time and paid just enough to cover the parking at the airport. Sally had always been incredibly patient. It's a rare woman who will get up at 5.30 the morning after her wedding so that her husband can ride a hill climb in Lancashire. Now that I was retired there was supposed to be a fairer balance in our marriage, but I was still behaving in the same self-centred way.

Of all the adjustments to life as a former professional athlete, this was the one I hadn't seen coming. When people came round for dinner and I'd got up from the table and gone to bed when I'd had enough, it had always been accepted because 'Chris is training in the morning' or 'Chris has a big event at the weekend'. From my mid teens until I was 32, my career had encouraged me to put my well-being ahead of all else. This performance-first attitude was tolerated, even admired in an athlete, but I'd managed to stretch it to incorporate just about every aspect of my life.

I knew I'd never cure myself completely. I would always be the person who'd once popped into the garage to make a work surface and ended up spending three months fitting out an entire workshop complete with fully integrated dust extraction system. But it was clear I couldn't just keep doing what I wanted when I wanted. Sally had just given birth to our fifth child, Sonny, and my behaviour was driving her up the wall. I had to reintroduce some proper structure into my life – and earn some money.

Apart from a few guest appearances on TV and some ad-hoc commentary for the BBC, I'd had no meaningful contact with the cycling world since climbing off my bike at Manchester Velodrome. I was determined that my life would never again revolve solely around cycling but I couldn't deny that it was the sphere in which all my experience and expertise lay. And whatever my personal preferences, I couldn't continue to ignore the fact that this was the quarter most of the offers were coming from.

In mid-2002 I was contacted by Jeremy Whittle, the editor of *Procycling* magazine, who asked if I'd be interested in writing some bike reviews for them. I liked writing, or to be more precise, I liked anything that started with a blank piece of paper – figurative or literal – that required me to 'make' something, and so I agreed.

I was conscious of the impact reviews had on cycle sales and took the responsibility very seriously. I never wrote anything that I couldn't verify or expressed an opinion that wasn't backed up with a solid rationale that I'd be prepared to stand up for if challenged. Although cautious, I was also prepared to call a spade a spade. If something wasn't good I'd say so and if a claimed advantage was little more than marketing speak, I'd be happy to expose that too. In fact, it was a condition of my writing for the magazine that I be allowed to write responsibly but also truthfully.

One of the manufacturers I wrote about – I won't name them – churned out new bikes like a fashion house, with minimal development to justify devaluing the previous year's model. Their claim for the particular machine I was testing on the roads around Frejus in the south of France was that it was lighter than its predecessor. On investigation, I found the only difference between the two models was 60 grams and a £300 price hike. I advised readers to 'keep the previous frame, leave your 150 gram watch at home and go on a training camp with the money you've saved'. The manufacturer in question pulled their ads from the magazine.

Despite being under fire from the advertising department, who had got an ear bashing and lost revenue, Jeremy stuck to his guns. Sure enough, people enjoyed the candid articles, magazine sales were strong and the brand eventually came back.

While I was busy re-engaging with my former sport, at least in a peripheral way, I received a phone call from my former coach. In his role as Director of Performance at British Cycling, Pete Keen was now immersed in creating the World Class Performance Programme. We didn't know it then, but he was laying the foundations for what would become known as the medal factory.

Since taking up the post in late 1997 he'd been battling to transform what was an amateur organisation, staffed by people sometimes qualified by little more than passion and plenty of free time, into a professional, results-driven machine. It certainly wasn't that yet, but British Cycling had made great progress under Pete. At the 2000 Olympics in Sydney the GB track team had won two bronze medals, a silver and Jason Queally's gold.

The velodrome was where all of the success was coming from. The problem lay in the prevailing definition of success. Team GB were happy to win medals – any colour – which meant they weren't targeting golds. Apart from Jason Queally's, they weren't winning them either. They had become known as the plucky Brits who would give the opposition a good run for their money before padding out the podium while someone else's national anthem played. They just didn't seem to be able to find the formula to climb onto the top step in numbers.

Pete had called me because they had one particularly promising young athlete who had become disillusioned with his string of second places and was contemplating an abrupt change in direction. He'd already signed with a French professional team and now he was talking about breaking with British Cycling completely. Pete and his team were concerned that he seemed to have no coherent plan, and frustrated at having seen him get so close with the BC set-up only to contemplate ditching it all at the last.

What Bradley Wiggins seemed to want out of life was to do what I had done: carve a professional career for himself winning big time trials. Pete believed my track record might give me the credibility to make him reconsider. So in late 2002 I agreed to meet up with British Cycling Head Endurance Coach Simon Jones and his gangly young charge.

We sat in the canteen at Manchester Velodrome and I started by asking Brad three simple questions. What do you want to achieve? What do you think that requires? Tell me how what you are planning to do will get you those things? That was fundamentally it. His answers were woolly and every other word was 'y'know', which in my experience is a sure sign that the speaker doesn't know. To make sure it was clear and unambiguous, I asked him to write his plan down and email it over, which he agreed to do.

That was a big first step but it wasn't when Brad eventually responded a week later that I knew he was going to be OK: it was when he didn't shy away from the relentless and sometimes brutal follow up questions I asked. He'd clearly worked really hard to try and map out how it was he believed he was going to achieve his goals by abandoning everything he'd believed in until now. I wasn't directly critical, never said what was right or wrong, but I did drill down into his reasoning, asking him to explain what made him believe each particular step of his plan would work. What were his beliefs based on? How would he measure progress? Where he waffled and evaded I demanded evidence and clarity.

Brad courageously battled on but in just a couple of exchanges his plan collapsed under its own weight: he'd shown himself that he was unlikely to realise his ambitions by breaking with British Cycling. From that point the conversation turned towards what he and Simon Jones had to do as coach and athlete to make it work. I'm sure both Simon and Pete had been asking him the same kind of questions, but I had a dual advantage: not only had I been where Brad ultimately wanted to go, I had no vested interest in the outcome. The fact that British Cycling had so much riding on Brad's future was preventing the pair of them from taking what were necessary risks.

On one occasion we arranged to meet as a team and Brad was late. 'It's just Brad, it's normal behaviour for him,' said Simon. I left. Simon couldn't believe it and was clearly uncomfortable with my blunt approach. But for me it wasn't about ten minutes. I interpreted Brad's tardiness, possibly wrongly, as a clear indication of how important winning was to him, of how much he valued my time and Simon's. I would invest in 'Project Brad', as he later referred to it in his autobiography, as much or as little as he did himself.

It was seen as a risky, even reckless way to deal with a talented athlete British Cycling didn't want to lose. What Simon and Pete were too close to the situation to see was that there was no risk involved: the relationship was already broken and their star prospect was leaving. If it was going to work for them and for Brad then the philosophy, ground rules and relationships had to change. It was his career and he had to take responsibility for it. Which he duly did.

Contrary to popular belief, I spent very little time with Brad. He and Simon Jones did all the graft. I played the role of team mentor, proofreading their plans and asking them questions. I got involved in debriefs and attended races, mostly for moral support because they actually knew more about the topic of pursuiting than I did, they just didn't believe it yet. I travelled to several competitions with them in this capacity and eventually found myself in the Hanns-Martin-Schleyer-Halle in Stuttgart watching Bradley beat Luke Roberts of Australia to become the 2003 world pursuit champion. It was a deeply satisfying moment to see Brad and Simon celebrating, the culmination of what for them had been a long slog. I don't think any of us could have dreamt just how far he'd go from there.

As well as Brad's breakthrough, 2003 was also the year Peter Keen decided to move away from front-line sport and accept an offer to set up GlaxoSmithKline's Lucozade Sport Science Academy. I never actually worked out what that was and I'm not entirely sure he did either. Behind him, he left a terrified Dave Brailsford in charge.

Dave had been on board with Pete almost from the outset, first in an advisory role, then as Programmes Director. Although he'd worked very closely with Pete and had a business degree, to this point he'd always had a boss, someone to make the ultimate call. Suddenly he was holding the reins, a position he was not at all comfortable with, at least at first.

Right from the start, Dave began organising things – or disorganising things – in a way that would eventually become his signature modus operandi: lots of good people with vague titles, no job descriptions, no formal training and no appraisals. His style and character were hugely different from mine in nearly every regard. I enjoyed structure, a framework inside which my imagination could work and explore. Dave saw structure as constraining. One of his favourite phrases was 'We are comfortable being uncomfortable'. What he actually meant was 'I'm comfortable with *you* being uncomfortable'. It was emotionally tough for people around him; there was no yardstick for them to measure themselves against, no way for them to be recognised as having done their part well. However, it also meant that there were no false goals for people to be distracted by, no 'I've done my bit, it's not my fault'. There was just one goal for everyone no matter what their position in the organisation: winning gold medals.

Perhaps Dave's greatest strength was to know his own weaknesses. From the beginning, he surrounded himself with people who didn't see the world the same way he did, even if that made his life

difficult. I think this courageous tactic was the single most overlooked aspect of his success as a leader.

It was over a coffee outside our team hotel towards the end of
those Stuttgart World Championships that Dave asked if I'd stay on
and continue working with the team up to the Athens Olympics.
True to form, there was no clear job description, just a flattering
approach backed up by a winning smile. And that was how I got
sucked fully back into the world of cycling.

I started out with the title of Technical Advisor, a moniker
that fitted with my desire to remain independent. I was able to
have high-level input at BC but also continue my outside interests.
Now I had another fascinating challenge, another blank piece of
paper. Meetings with Dave and a small steering group followed to
plot how the organisation could move forward. The set-up, like
all Dave's set-ups, was fluid. It wasn't uncommon to agree a plan,
be away for a week and return to find that it had been changed
beyond recognition. The business of the World Class Performance
Programme waited for no one: you were either all-in, all the time,
or you were left behind.

In December 2003, a staff conference was organised at the Ruthin
Castle Hotel in Wales. I remember walking in through the crowd
gathered in reception and over to Dave who was chatting to someone I'd never seen before.

At this point in my life, I was not very good with people and
wary of conversations with anyone I didn't know unless I was sure
of the context: either it was social or it was work and I was meeting someone to do X or Y. I certainly didn't know this almost

furtive-looking middle-aged man so I said hello, politely shook hands and then got on with what I wanted to talk to Dave about.

A few minutes later we filed into the conference room, which unusually had chairs placed around the edge of the space rather than in rows facing the front. To start the day, we took it in turns to say who we were and what our role was. When we got to Dave's guest, he introduced himself as 'Doctor Steve Peters, I work with mass murderers and psychopaths'. He now had the room's rapt attention, which of course is why he'd said it.

Steve is a great showman and he knew the importance of first impressions. Now he needed to do something with the opportunity he'd created. Standing confidently in the centre of the floor he described the start of the day from his perspective. He recounted what he'd seen people doing back in the lobby and what their body language had told him about what they were thinking. People laughed as they realised he'd correctly identified motivations, feelings and actions that they hadn't even consciously perceived themselves. Steve's point was that the unconscious mind has more of an impact on our actions than we'd like to believe. He was there to show us that it was possible to control some of its more unhelpful elements to aid performance.

The Steve Peters show was just getting started. His account of people-watching on the way in was an entertaining party piece, but to convince his audience he really knew what he was talking about he needed a subject with whom he could go into more detail, preferably someone known to everybody present and who had a bit of status within the assembled group. Steve asked me to join him in the middle to re-enact our brief exchange that morning.

As I walked over, he described the minimal eye contact I'd made with him and the closed body language that had left him no opportunity to engage with me. When I took his hand to mimic the greeting we'd exchanged, he froze me midway through and pointed to what I was doing. I'd subtly turned our hands so mine was on top, showing dominance. Then he showed how I'd gently but firmly pushed it back towards him and away from myself, sending an unconscious message of, 'Hello, I'm being polite but don't really want to talk to you.' I'd reinforced this by not asking him a single question, instead directing all my attention to Dave.

I wasn't sure whether I was being told off for my lack of basic manners but if so I deserved it. I certainly learned a lot about myself in the space of that short demonstration. I was able to see and understand just how visible my feelings really were to others, and I accepted the lesson because it was being delivered by a confident individual with irrefutable credentials. More fun followed and Steve achieved just what Dave had hoped he would: he'd got almost everyone in the room to embrace the prospect of delving into the subconscious as a way to access untapped potential.

In fact, as I found out later, Steve had already been working individually with a number of the riders, one in particular, with remarkable results. In a matter of a few hours he had helped turn a non-coping, virtually non-functioning human being into an athlete who was able to go out and win a medal. Dave was convinced this was a service that had a crucial role to play in the BC set-up and he'd persuaded Steve to join his new regime on a similar basis to my own, part-time. What Dave hadn't envisaged was how valuable Steve would be in managing the coaches. We had just as many unresolved issues as the athletes.

I really admired Steve, not just for his evident brilliance but also his honest, refreshing directness, and I was pleased when Dave drafted him onto the four-strong Senior Management Team, the successor to the informal steering group. The fourth member of the SMT was the men's sprint coach Shane Sutton, a man Chris Hoy once described in an interview with the *Observer* newspaper as follows:

'My first impression was that he was a complete nutter. He has incredible enthusiasm. His willpower is astonishing. And he's a stubborn bastard ... a force of nature, a bundle of contradictions ... the ultimate people person, he's in your face, intense and scarily perceptive.'

That's as good a summation of Shane Sutton as any I've seen. Regardless of the various job titles he held during our time together at British Cycling, he was never more than a few centimetres away from the riders, involved in their lives to an incredible degree, from helping wallpaper one team member's flat to breaking the news of another's family bereavement.

The four of us couldn't have been more different: Dave, the risk taker and embracer of creative chaos, across the table from me with my love of process and structure; Steve with an understanding of human psychology second to none, alongside Shane who was guided through life by gut feeling. He was the resident agitator, never afraid to upset the status quo. With Steve's arrival things got slightly more organised, but only slightly.

*

Meetings were held once a fortnight, either in Dave's office or Steve's, a windowless room which had been annexed off from the physiotherapy suite. Although there was usually an agenda it was largely ignored. Steve would generally go first, working his way through a list of problems that staff and athletes had brought to him. Shane would latch on to one of these topics, then veer off to talk about whichever individuals and issues were currently pre-occupying him. As the discussion lengthened and the focus drifted, I would become increasingly agitated, interrupting to try to drag the debate back towards its original point. Dave played the role of liberal referee – reluctant to step in until the squabbling got really out of hand. So we would quarrel our way though the two-hour slot, overrun and leave having covered less than half of the original agenda. The process was messy and difficult but somehow, despite itself, productive; our different vantage points ensured that we clashed but they also gave us a panoramic view of the operation that none of us could have achieved alone.

I was still managing to write a few bike reviews during this period, although by 2005 the diving articles had fallen by the wayside. They'd been crowded out by my latest obsession: developing the capabilities of British Cycling's coaching team, something Dave had asked me to do. As usual, I couldn't go and take advice, I had to start from a blank piece of paper. I wanted to understand coaching and coaches in every detail – and, of course, I had to own the outcome.

The first thing I did when I took on the role was go back and look at everything Pete Keen and I had done over more than a decade working together. We'd developed a coaching process directly analogous with business planning and this was the basis of the grand vision I wanted to present to the team. I arranged for all the coaches to meet in a hospitality suite at the velodrome on a Monday morning.

Desperately wanting them to understand and buy into my coaching philosophy – and disregarding the fact I'd never coached myself, nor asked them for their thoughts on the topic – I worked furiously over the weekend to get everything I knew about performance planning into a Powerpoint presentation. Being a black hat thinker – the type of person who looks for threats rather than opportunities – I tried to imagine all the possible objections they could make and cover them in advance. I was going to batter them into understanding.

Monday morning arrived and all 20 coaches were crammed into the tiny space of Hospitality Two. Over the course of 30 minutes I took them through my recipe for success, from selecting goals for the year and setting intermediate targets, to monitoring processes and gathering athlete feedback. At the end of my half-hour monologue I stopped, expecting rapturous applause or at least looks of awe and perhaps a few tears. Nothing. Silence. Didn't they understand? This was it, THE formula for winning medals. Eventually there were a few positive grunts and a couple of nods.

In my arrogance and ignorance, I'd overlooked the fact that these people had given their lives to this topic: they'd shed blood, sweat and tears striving to be the best coaches they could. Now here was a man standing in front of them with precisely zero coaching experience telling them to forget all of that, THIS is how you do it. I didn't realise any of this at the time, I was just mystified that a group of professionals could be presented with such a foolproof plan and not be jumping for joy.

A few days later I was having a coffee with Dave and recounting my experience to him. By now it was late summer 2005 and London had just won the bidding process to host the 2012 Olympics, flooding UK Sport with both enthusiasm and even more money. Determined to make the most of this once-in-a-generation opportunity, they'd set about identifying what was needed for Team GB to get the best possible results in their home Games. One of the ingredients was world-class coaches.

When Lottery money had first come on stream, various British sports had tried to buy in coaching excellence, selecting candidates from nations around the globe who'd had long-term success. With a few exceptions, they'd been used as a dumping ground for said countries to offload their excess coaching baggage. After a few years the penny dropped and UK Sport resolved to manufacture its own talent.

To create this coaching excellence, the most ambitious and expensive development scheme British sport had ever seen was put in place. The Elite Coach Programme would have a maximum annual intake of just ten candidates. Those selected would each have a lavish three-year customised course built around them as well as attending four intensive, week-long 'residentials' a year with their fellow cohort.

'We could put one of our coaches forward for this,' Dave said, 'but why don't you go? If there's anything that you feel is really good, we can replicate it here.'

I knew a bit about the initiative, specifically just how much time it would take up. I was already plate-spinning, and knew that if I did this it would be 'as well as' not 'instead of' my other responsibilities. Reluctantly, I agreed.

Task number one was to be accepted onto the programme in the first place and the assessment was like nothing I had experienced before. For a full working day, I was to play the role of a government department head from the fictitious country of Simlandia, with all the associated duties such an official would perform, from writing reports to managing a hostile press interview and making a presentation to the country's Prime Minister. I even had to mediate in an argument between two other department heads. All of this took place in Manchester United's executive suites at Old Trafford, each of which had been turned into an office complete with Simlandia notepaper and computers. Moving between the offices was a gaggle of actors playing the various parts. Sledgehammers and nuts sprang to mind. When the news arrived that I'd passed the assessment I wasn't exactly thrilled.

On 9 October 2005 I walked into a beautiful oak-panelled room in Slaley Hall, Hexham for the first group session of the Elite Coach Programme and briefly met my classmates-to-be before ignoring them and burying my nose in a laptop. All I could think about was how much of my valuable time this course was going to take up, and I couldn't see how speakers such as Bill Endicott, a former White House aide to Bill Clinton, were going to make being here worth my while. The language of self-improvement didn't help me warm to the enterprise. The sessions had titles like 'Being Elite'. I sneered inwardly and kept to myself as much as possible. Thank God Steve Peters wasn't around to observe me.

But slowly, over the span of a few of these weeks away, my cynicism began to fade as I noticed a trend emerge. All of the sessions I thought were going to be useful turned out to be merely interesting, while a high proportion of those that looked pointless – voice coaching, talking to polar explorers – produced revelations. Performing stand-up comedy in front of a live audience, walking around swearing at the top of my voice, these were activities from which I gained a huge amount of personal insight. Left to my own devices, I'd never have tried either of them in a million years – and certainly not in the cause of self-development.

But perhaps the best thing about the programme was meeting my classmates. The people I'd ignored at our first get together at Slaley Hall turned out to be fascinating characters who taught me as much as the course did.

Jim Mallinder and Nigel Redman both came from rugby union and coached in the England Academy. They couldn't have been more different. Jim, who'd started out as a maths teacher before becoming a highly accomplished player, fitted the stereotype of a leader perfectly: smart, charismatic, loud and likeable. If he were cast as an historical figure, it would be as a gladiator. His talents were spotted by others too and his time on the programme was cut short when he resigned after a year to take up the head coaching position with England Saxons.

Jim was a giant but Nigel was a marginally bigger one: six foot four of battle scars. His elbows wouldn't lock out and little was left of his ears. Despite looking like a seasoned bouncer, a warmer, gentler character you couldn't imagine. He had a quiet strength, choosing to listen long and hard before forming an opinion. In our second year we did an exercise to help us understand our own characters. This involved defining both ourselves and each other by one of four animal types: Dolphins (caring and supportive), Lions (commanding and single-minded), Monkeys (playful and extrovert) and Elephants (careful and analytical). Nigel, convinced he was a monkey, was deeply shocked when the group labelled him an elephant. It took him two days to formulate and express his feelings on the matter. I fancied myself as a monkey too, but according to my classmates I was a lion.

Definitely in the 'monkey' group was GB Olympic Triathlon Head Coach Dan Salcedo whose violently stripy socks and Sideshow Bob hair complemented his fun personality. Diving coach Steve Gladding was much more reserved. He was an emotional thinker and naturally assumed the role of listener. He couldn't have been more different from me, which is probably why it was with Steve that I learned the most about myself and how to adapt my style to get the best out of others.

Undoubtedly the toughest person in the room was double Olympic judo medallist Katie Howey – though you certainly wouldn't have guessed what she did for a living because she was probably the quietest of the group. Public speaking was her nemesis and became her personal focus over the three-year course.

Ian Barker had won Olympic silver as a sailor in 2000 and multiple golds since then as a coach. He was an interesting guy who seemed to spend the entire course wrestling with his own character. Both Ian's website and his Wikipedia page reflect his personality perfectly:

factual and without embellishment to the point of being terse. He started off dismissive of 'soft skills', as he called the ability to engage with people on an emotional level. By the end of the course he seemed to have glimpsed that this area, alien and uncomfortable to him, was where his personal breakthroughs were likely to be.

Scottish Swimming coach Ciaran O'Brien was a monkey/ elephant hybrid. Although a lover of fun and easily sidetracked, when a topic did engage him he'd often ruminate on it for weeks before resurfacing with some profound observations. He was perhaps the most changed by the three-year journey.

The final member of our group, the one I admired the most and who was perhaps the most capable of us all, was hockey coach Karen Brown. Karen had the rare ability to both listen and lead, to work through intensely personal issues with individuals and also think strategically. She was disciplined and always put the mission, whatever that was, ahead of herself. The only other place I have seen such a breadth of capability in one person is in business, amongst some of the most highly respected – and highly paid – CEOs. I have no doubt she would have made an excellent leader in any sphere she chose, had she not been missing one vital ingredient – an ego. I do have an ego and enjoy leading, so it came as something of a surprise to me when I realised that Karen was someone I'd love to have as a boss.

Despite the diversity of their characters, my classmates had two traits in common: their total commitment to each other and their willingness to explore, to try new and often uncomfortable ways of doing things. That just left me, slowly getting to know these intriguing individuals. And through the tasks we took on together, getting to know myself a bit better.

The swearing exercise – all of us walking around a room while a voice coach egged us on to shout the worst obscenities we could think of – made me realise that my discomfort was rooted in the need to control how people saw me. If I wasn't prepared to risk looking foolish, I'd never be more than I was now.

Stand-up comedy made me even more uncomfortable. For someone paranoid about losing face, it was about as stressful an exercise as you could possibly devise. Before tackling this excruciating task I'd been convinced I'd only ever want a straight-talking coach, someone who would tell me the uncomfortable truth no matter what. Instead, I learned that when I was under extreme stress I just needed unconditional support. Different approaches were needed not just for different people, but sometimes for the same person depending on the situation. Top teachers varied their style.

Towards the end of our time together we found ourselves in yet another hotel, off the A55 just outside Queensferry in North Wales. It was the last day of a gruelling residential when we trooped into our work room for the final session and met our host for the afternoon: marine biologist and expedition leader Monty Halls. A passionate and animated individual, Monty didn't look wholly comfortable in a suit. We knew each other a little as we'd both written for *Diver* magazine, but on this occasion he'd come to talk to us about his early days in the Royal Marines, where he'd quickly discovered his passion was less for killing people and more for organising expeditions.

As a young soldier, Monty had been charged with leading a group of scientists into the Brazilian rainforest, keeping watch over them while they did their research, then getting everyone safely out again. He recalled how he'd treated the scientists as baggage, just something to be transported from A to B. From the outset he had hardly bothered to give them the time of day. As soon as the expedition was underway things started to go wrong. The monsoons arrived early, the camp was washed away, a team member was bitten by a poisonous snake and couldn't be evacuated because of the weather. It was an unmitigated disaster. After two miserable weeks they all managed to get out of the rainforest, if not entirely intact then at least alive.

Throughout the whole calamitous experience, though, there had been one quiet scientist who with cool alacrity had simply dealt with everything that was thrown at him. It had been this unprepossessing figure, not Monty, who had galvanised the party. He'd led by example, and in doing so inspired the group to see their ordeal as an adventure to be talked of for a lifetime rather than endured and forgotten. Monty recalled how he'd thought of this man and his colleagues at the start of the trip and how he'd treated them. He was humbled and felt compelled to confess and apologise for his behaviour. Before they all went their separate ways, Monty sought the scientist out for their first proper conversation and asked him how he'd managed to cope so well under stress.

'Well,' said the scientist, 'I recognised that all of those things were beyond my capacity to effect. I couldn't change them. But one thing that is always within my control, no matter what is happening around me, is the attitude with which I choose to face those challenges.'

That was the grand moral of Monty's story: attitude is a choice.

I sat there, a bit like my team of cycling coaches had that Monday morning in the hospitality suite at the velodrome, slightly underwhelmed. I could appreciate what was being said to me on an intellectual level but I wasn't inspired to leap out of my seat and punch the air. It seemed so simplistic. 'Choose your own attitude.' There was only one thing for it: I resolved to put it to the test.

Monty's session had been the last one of the week. I was only a 40-minute drive from home – and an evening of ceilidh dancing that Sally had committed us to attending with friends. I hated those things. When I couldn't avoid them altogether my usual strategy was to bitch, moan, make sarcastic jokes and then get out of the door as quickly as possible. Not tonight. This time I was going to have fun.

When I arrived home Sally was getting ready. I informed her of my decision to have a good time that night. 'That's nice,' she replied looking at me in the dressing table mirror with a raised eyebrow. I think she might have misunderstood what I was referring to. En route to the evening's venue, Caldy Rugby Club, I controlled my nerves and reminded myself of my mission. What did I hate the most? Easy – the dancing. I decided that I'd be the very first person on the dance floor. And I was. Sandwiched between two women I'd never met before, I proceeded to Strip The Willow, which would have been impressive had the dance not been a Britannia Two-Step. For the next half an hour I proceeded to mangle every instruction given by the dance master. And I was enjoying it: it was liberating and daft.

Inspired by the progress of the experiment, I considered what else I usually avoided. Talking to people I didn't know. Challenge number two was to find a stranger, have a conversation, find them interesting and discover something new. I accosted people at the bar and discussed philosophy with individuals I'd never met before in my life. It was fantastic, another revelation. And other people noticed too, because a couple of them asked Sally if I was high.

Attitude is a choice. For years I'd shared a hotel room with the walking, non-stop-talking embodiment of the idea in the form of Jens Voigt, who'd chosen to be positive about everything and everyone he encountered. But it hadn't really registered then as a choice that might be available to me. A five-minute story had finally encouraged me to try it out for myself.

During my time on the Elite Coach Programme, Monty Halls was just one of 46 deliverers of valuable lessons: leaders of armies, musicians, comedians, polar explorers, psychologists, psychiatrists, body language specialists, even hostage negotiators. Dave Brailsford's suggestion over coffee led to three years that taught me twice as much about myself as I had learned in the previous 39.

From then on, my mission with the BC coaches and every other team I worked with changed: from having to come up with all the answers to coming up with the right questions; from striving to be the best to getting the best out of others.

The original idea had been for me to filter the contents of the Elite Coach Programme and bring back the most useful elements so that we could replicate them with our own coaches. Sadly, this plan was never implemented. I desperately wanted our coaching team – and even more so the senior managers – to have the same experiences I'd had. But in a system that had no job descriptions, let alone appraisals, a formal education process was just too big a cultural leap. My proposals for personal development were met by the management team with what I'll describe as benign indifference, an outward enthusiasm for the concept but a reluctance to actually do anything. The lack of appetite for significant exploration outside what we already knew was further dampened by the biggest of all enemies of change: success.

British Cycling had made significant strides, going from a single gold in Sydney to two in Athens and five at the 2005 track world championships in LA. Everyone had moved from a state of open-minded desperation to improve, to one of growing confidence in their own methods. From Dave's perspective things were going well, so he was understandably reluctant to support wholesale change, especially since he was ambivalent about the kind of change I was suggesting. Without his continuous, full and visible backing, the other key opinion leaders at British Cycling remained passively resistant to doing anything differently and the coach development programme withered on the vine.

To escape my frustration at having failed in this area that I believed to be so important, I scaled the scheme down to a few mentoring sessions and ploughed my energies into my other role, as head of research and development. This was my natural habitat and I was free to explore it however I saw fit. As it turned out, the work of the R&D team would make more measurable contributions to Olympic success than any other department.

CHAPTER 16

Secret Squirrels

I'm not sure how many business decisions around the world are made in coffee shops, but the proportion was pretty high at British Cycling. In late summer 2004, Dave Brailsford and I had sat down with a couple of cappuccinos to discuss the squad's performance at the recently finished Athens Olympics.

'We're good at timed events, good at the physiological stuff, but it gets patchy when tactics are involved,' Dave said. It was true, people referred to us as the kings of qualifying. 'We've got a couple of people working on that aspect but what about everything else?'

'What do you mean?' I asked.

'Well,' he mused, pausing to sip his coffee. 'This is a technical sport, there is a lot of other ... stuff. Bikes, wheels, helmets, clothing, all that stuff. Is there anything we can do to improve that?'

And so, at a corner table in the Manchester Piccadilly station branch of Starbucks, I became Head of Stuff and the 'aggregation of marginal gains' philosophy was conceived.

I'd already started to take a lead on equipment, overseeing the race clothing design for Athens and a new carbon handlebar to match the frame Peter Keen had commissioned back in 2002 before his departure. Perhaps because Pete had now joined UK Sport as Director of Performance, they too had decided to invest in R&D. Whatever their motivations, the announcement of their Research and Innovation programme was music to my ears.

In early autumn 2004, I officially took on the role of British Cycling's Director of R&D for the GB Olympic programme. It was a long title with one key word, Olympic. The criteria for spending Lottery funds were very strict; they couldn't be used to simply improve performance, increase participation or even to win world titles, they could only be used to improve the chances of winning Olympic gold medals.

It was a few weeks later at Loughborough University that I first met Scott Drawer, the new head of UK Sport's Research and Innovation department. Resplendent in his pristine business suit, he bounded over to greet me and Simon Jones. Bursting with enthusiasm, a big grin plastered across his face, he talked on fast-forward, leaping from topic to topic. I was out of breath just listening to him. Despite his apparent youth – late twenties I guessed – he would be the person deciding who would get access to hundreds of thousands in funding. And who wouldn't. But his biggest contribution to our cause wasn't financial; it was his insatiable curiosity.

We'd come to the university to attend an event Scott referred to as 'Boffins Day', to meet people he thought could be helpful in our search for speed. Scott ushered us into a large room set with several round tables, each festooned with paper, flip-charts and pens. Around them sat experts in the fields of aerodynamics, mathematics, composites, computer modelling, data analysis, textiles and more. All had been sought out and persuaded to come along by Scott. He was like Face, the fixer in *The A-Team*: 'You want experts? How many?' And here they were. These were some of the UK's best and brightest minds, most of whom knew nothing at all about the sport of cycling.

The format decided on for the day was deliberately simple. We would show them videos of the various cycling events and ask a single question: how would you make the riders go faster? The room's occupants attacked the challenge with gusto and over the course of the next three hours I was able to observe how they worked with each other, who wanted to lead, who wanted to listen and, ultimately, what their imaginations could come up with.

Their requests for basic information inadvertently revealed our own Achilles' Heel: we knew how bike races worked. 'How wide are handlebars?' was a typically naive question. Everyone in the cycling world knows the universal standard for bar width is 42 cm, a convention so old it's probably what Douglas Adams based his famous number on. But the follow-up question stopped us in our tracks: 'Why?' 'Because ... well, because it is.' Even to our own ears this sounded ridiculous. Under external scrutiny, many of our long-held beliefs were exposed as little more than opinions, repeated so often down the years they'd become accepted as fact.

Some of the ideas generated that day were fantastic in the true sense of the word: fans inside frames to suck air through micro-scopic holes to reduce the 'boundary layer'; kinetic devices that stored the rider's energy at low speeds and returned it at critical moments in a burst; pedal axles that locked on a particular part of the stroke to provide extra leverage. Over the course of those three hours I learned two important things. The first was that ignorance is an essential ingredient in innovation; these people didn't know what you couldn't do. They looked at cycling not as a sport but as a collection of technical challenges to be identified, examined individually and prioritised. It was the approach I'd first encountered in the figure of Richard Hill at Lotus more than a decade earlier. Now I really began to grasp the power and potential of it.

The other big lesson of Boffins Day for someone who'd supposedly spent years studying aerodynamics, was that my understanding was embarrassingly rudimentary. We needed to go to a wind tunnel.

On a cold morning in late January 2005, our embryonic team drove on to the Highfield Campus of Southampton University. Following directions, we turned into University Crescent, a narrow cul-de-sac lined with careworn terraced houses, and came to what looked like a dead end. A quick phone call confirmed that we hadn't made a mistake: the facility was accessed via a tiny alleyway at the end of the close. A minute later we arrived at a grey, windowless metal box with the words Wolfson Unit stencilled on the outside. I rang the bell next to a small access door and waited.

I hadn't set foot in a wind tunnel since my visits to the MIRA test centre in 1991, an exciting few hours that had changed the way I thought about bike racing. Although that experience had provided some answers, it had also raised many questions that were still unresolved. More than a decade later, I was finally going to get to the bottom of things. Or so I thought.

We were met by research engineer Sandy Wright and his colleague Martyn Prince. Martyn was mild-mannered and happy to chat, while Sandy seemed to enjoy scowling and swearing at inanimate objects. Both would become valued members of the team. On entering, I discovered that what had looked like a big shed on the outside looked like a big shed on the inside. The corners were crammed with scale model boats and racing cars. Bits of scientific equipment and random tools lay about, all covered with a light coating of dust. The air had a faint smell of oil and epoxy resin. In the centre of the space, looking like a truck-sized belt sander lying on its back, was a rolling road. The top of it disappeared three metres above us into a huge doughnut-shaped structure fashioned from wood and steel: the tunnel.

Like most people, I associated wind tunnels with the latest technology, so I was astonished to learn that this one had been constructed in 1920. It emphasised just how far behind we were in getting here; 85-year-old technology seemed cutting edge to us. We climbed the steps to the control room, a tiny green Formica-lined box that looked more modern – the 1950s, at least. In it was 'Big Mike', the tunnel's operator.

Mike didn't seem keen on talking to outsiders and his conversational repertoire appeared to be restricted to 'Does anyone want tea?' Over time, we realised he wasn't really grumpy, he just took a little while to warm to people – in our case, about six years. In all the time we worked there I only ever saw Mike outside the confines of the tunnel building twice. I wondered whether he'd claimed right of sanctuary. He was a character and I liked him.

One of the boffins we'd brought with us was composites expert Dimitris Katsanis, although defining him with a single label would be misleading. A former cyclist on the Greek national team, Dimitris was a cross between an artist and an inventor. His endless reserves of energy and curiosity meant that he wasn't the most relaxing person to be around. But the fruits of his labour – usually delivered just in time rather than on time, and seldom for the budget discussed – were uniformly exquisite, making it more than worth the stress. Over the eight years we would work together, he helped conduct nearly 15,000 tests and experiments, produced more than 200 unique designs and oversaw the creation of bikes used to win 51 gold medals. Dimitris was more than a founder member of the group, he was its lynchpin.

Jason Queally, gold medallist in the kilometre time trial in Sydney, was our first tunnel test pilot. His primary role was to be the shape of a cyclist. This involved him sitting on a bike in a cold tube for hours on end while we blew air over him. It was not glamorous. Despite not having any evidence, Jason was adamant from the start that the skinsuit he'd used back in 2000 to win gold was special in some way. He eventually brought it along to show the experts who passed the now faded Lycra garment around and confirmed it was indeed ordinary, with nothing to set it apart from lots of other clothing we'd already tried and discarded.

I was reluctant to use up valuable test time just to prove its averageness, but Jason was determined to back his own gut against the scientists' knowledge and doggedly championed his cause. Finally, to shut him up more than anything else, I agreed to work it into the schedule. Wearing his old suit, Jason's drag dropped a full 10 per cent compared with the current best race clothing we had. I had the equipment checked, re-calibrated and ran several repeat trials. The results remained consistent with the first test. The experts were baffled. Over the following sessions the garment was tried on other athletes, and even on those it didn't fit we still saw big gains.

Thanks to Jason's tenacity, that piece of clothing – christened the pixie suit as we could find no earthly reason for its performance – served as a reminder to us not to be too clever for our own good, not to rule anything out just because we 'knew' it wouldn't work. Months of research by Sally Cowan, our materials specialist, revealed that the factory that had made the suit was no longer in business and no one knew the whereabouts of the machines that had produced the cloth. There would be no short cuts, we would have to try and understand it from first principles.

The pixie suit never did give up all of its secrets, but its magic properties seemed to have something to do with the roughness of the fabric. The final race clothing it led to looked nothing like it, but without the proof of potential it provided, we – I – would never have believed enough to invest. The research programme it kicked off is still going on at the time of writing.

Early in our exploration, while we were trying to get to grips with making the human form more slippery, Rob Lewis, our lead aerodynamicist, showed us an old photograph on the Internet. It was a tennis ball in a wind tunnel being hit with smoke as a way to make the turbulent air visible. A second image showed the same ball with a ring of fine fuse wire wrapped around it roughly halfway between its leading edge and its apex. The smoky air hitting the ball 'tripped' over the carefully placed wire and stuck to the surface a little longer before breaking away. The barely visible intervention had halved the ball's drag.

Rob reasoned that if we could do the equivalent to the riders' approximately cylinder-shaped legs, then we could get a huge drag reduction. I pointed out that we couldn't stick wire to riders: that would be illegal. Not willing to give up the idea immediately, Rob assured us that the height differential needn't be big; a long, well-placed scratch with a nail or a string of nettle stings would do the job. He was a practical if immoral man. I stopped the line of theorising when Rob and Dimitris got into an enthusiastic discussion about just how many nettles they might need and whether a rusty nail might yield a more advantageous ridge.

Most of these brainstorming sessions took place in the bar at Chilworth Manor, our home-from-home while we worked at the wind tunnel in Southampton, and they often led to important advances. In this case, nettle stings and scratches were replaced by raised seams on riders' clothing, a way of joining fabric panels together that dramatically improved performance. All perfectly legal.

On one occasion we were joined by Ed Clancy, our team pursuit anchorman. Installed in a pair of Chilworth's leather chairs next to the fire, Dimitris and Rob looked at Ed's broad frame and speculated that if they broke his collarbones and re-set his shoulders in a more rounded form it would improve his aerodynamics no end. It was another conversation that went on for an uncomfortably long time – with Ed himself even joining in – before it was consigned to the unethical bin. But it was the starting point for a research programme on garments to help the riders train to maintain a more streamlined shape.

On another evening it was former world champion Rob Hayles, one of our regular test pilots, who sat with the team. Rob, always full of ideas, suggested that we should test a rider (him) naked, in order to get a true baseline measurement against which we could check all aerodynamic improvements. Looking back, most of Rob's suggestions seemed to involve him with no clothes on. Partly out of interest and partly to call his bluff, we agreed. Our computer image-capturing system was accurate enough to map every inch of his undressed form. Rob asked if all the flopping about would adversely affect his aero performance. Sandy, who was running the test, told him that he doubted the wind tunnel instruments were sensitive enough to pick it up. To be fair to Rob, it was cold.

The session showed, to our great relief, that bare skin wasn't the fastest option and made us consider with more urgency just why covering the body with material made it faster. We continued to experiment with controlled roughness and other interventions that I am not able to discuss without the fear of British Cycling operatives breaking into my house under cover of darkness and neutralising me and my family.

Within a few months of using the wind tunnel and testing some of the less inhumane ideas, we'd begun to gather practical, performance-enhancing knowledge that had never before been used in competition. The thing about that kind of knowledge, though, is that it only has a high value so long as you are the only one holding it.

The office set-up at the British Cycling HQ in Manchester was open-plan and made for sharing information. The 30 or so people who worked in the space assigned to the Performance Programme team all knew each other well and readily chatted about anything and everything that they were doing. Coaches would come back from trips abroad and everyone enjoyed hearing their news, being involved. It was a brilliant environment for enhancing communication. Now, for the first time, there was a small group of people who wouldn't share, because the knowledge they held was so precious it was too risky to discuss in the open, even with friends. It was an abrupt change in practice and not one that went down well.

In late 2005, I was walking around the curved corridor under the track at Manchester Velodrome, discussing performance improvements with Dan Hunt, the Women's Endurance Coach. I can't recall the exact details of the conversation but I do remember the way it came to a dead end.

'Well, I don't know,' he said in frustration, 'I'm not in the "secret squirrel club", am I?'

We parted company in reception and I considered what he'd said. This small group of people, whose names the public would probably never know, were doing remarkable work that they couldn't talk about, even to their British Cycling colleagues. They deserved an identity. From that point onwards, we became The Secret Squirrel Club. I spent a few hours messing around on the computer and created a logo – a silhouetted squirrel whose outline was filled with the union flag. When I showed it to the team, one of them pointed out that the squirrel I'd used was Canadian.

For wind tunnel sessions the small control room was always crammed. There were plenty of other places for people to work in adjacent buildings, but the process of discovery kept everyone tied to the result screens in that cramped space.

Athletes, technicians, sports scientists, aerodynamicists, engineers and the occasional coach would all wait for the drag numbers to be shouted out by Martyn the instant he finished collating the latest data. Our collective mood went up and down with the readings on the dials. The outcome of the trials matched the pre-test predictions of our experts only about 50 per cent of the time, a poor correlation rate, that I was surprised to find was quite normal in the research game.

Each unexpected outcome spawned another experiment to find out why, and our 50/50 hit rate meant the testing bill was going up fast. We had to find a faster, cheaper way to make progress. It just so happened that a member of our team had the answer: Computational Fluid Dynamics, or CFD for short. Instead of blowing air over a live subject in a real space that had to be staffed and heated, we could create the same environment virtually and let powerful algorithms run the tests for us. We'd done a little bit of CFD work with Sheffield University in 2003 to guide the shape of the pursuit handlebars for the 2004 Olympics, but what we were about to embark on would be a whole new level of sophistication.

Like Dimitris, Rob Lewis had quickly become a key member of the R&D team. He knew almost nothing about cycling and almost everything about aerodynamics, which made him a perfect addition to the club. He probably came up with more new ideas than anybody, something he was able to do partly because he had no fear of getting it wrong. When experiments didn't work out, he just shrugged and moved on to his next theory. Vast as it was, though, Rob brought much more than just his scientific knowledge to the team. His character, committed, supportive and above all fun, made him an invaluable asset when the going was tough.

Led by Rob's company, Advantage CFD, later TotalSim, we embarked on a programme of virtual modelling to try to unpick the reason we were getting so many surprises in the real world. To make sure the simulations were as accurate as possible we intended to put everything, including the riders themselves, into the aerodynamic models.

Sports scientist Matt Parker, another long-term Squirrel, spent several days in a windowless room in Manchester overseeing the laser scanning of key athletes for use by Rob. Vicky Pendleton, Brad Wiggins and Chris Hoy were all painstakingly recreated in cyberspace. Using their avatars, we could work on optimising riders' positions while they trained, raced or slept. With CFD we were able to explore and try new concepts quickly and cheaply. More than that, it gave us access to an intelligence greater than our own. Rather than designing a virtual component and then testing it on the computer for aerodynamic efficiency, we now had the option to ask the software to tell *us* what the best shape was. Its main limitation seemed to be the quality of the questions we were able to come up with.

Being able to see the airflow on a computer screen had a huge impact on every project, not least helmet development, which early tests identified as an area where significant gains could be made. The teardrop-shaped aero lid used by the team and individual pursuit riders was a fairly straightforward design because their head positions were exactly that – straight and forward-facing. For the sprints and bunch racing events, though, things were less clear cut.

'Do you want to optimise the shape for the final dash in the last 100 metres or for the majority of the race, where the riders are turning their heads from side to side to watch the opposition?' This was a question posed by Matt Cross, one of Rob's CFD engineers, as we reviewed a video of a sprint race. Matt's inquiry led to a carefully compromised design: the bulbous sprinter's helmet used in Beijing. It was a form later used by Team Sky for time trials and is now widely copied by helmet manufacturers.

To make sure the CFD was telling the truth, we still went back to the wind tunnel to validate early results. Jason Queally was dressed in a wetsuit and sprayed with a mix of solvent and bright pink chalk, a process that caused much hilarity. With the wind blowing, the mixture streamed, covering everything before quickly drying and leaving a visible pressure map all over Jason. When pictures of his painted form were compared to CFD stills, there was a satisfying correlation. Despite the best efforts of Martyn and Sandy, pink chalk can still be seen in the cracks of the tunnel to this day. I suspect it's still in Jason's ears, too.

Involving the various squad members in our testing certainly helped with validating results, but including them was expensive, time-consuming and often frustrating, so the bulk of our experimentation was conducted with our regular guinea pigs: Jason Queally and Rob Hayles. My intention was for us to find performance gains with a small, secure team and then take the findings back to the squad as a whole and convince them with the irrefutable evidence. It was a reasonable plan. It was also naive.

Late in the first Olympic cycle, as the GB riders headed into the final World Cup series to qualify for the World Championships and ultimately the Olympics, I turned up in Manchester with the first few aero helmet prototypes. To minimise their frontal area and still maintain sufficient strength to meet safety standards, a lot of carbon was used in their construction, making them quite heavy compared to the off-the-shelf foam models that had traditionally been used. I knew the aero gains far outweighed the negligible effect of a few extra grams, but when the athletes and coaches saw the helmets for the first time, they ignored our explanations of the advantages and obsessed over the weight.

In February 2008, I travelled out to the final round of the World Cup in Copenhagen and watched in disbelief as 80 per cent of the riders carried on wearing the helmets they'd used before. I was angry that we'd worked so hard to give them proven performance-enhancing equipment and they'd dismissed it. All that costly research, and only one in five of the squad had adopted all of the new equipment and positional advice.

But there was a pattern: the adopters were those who had helped us in the wind tunnel. I remembered my own reaction a decade earlier to Graeme Obree's riding position, a highly advantageous approach that I'd dismissed out of hand because it was different – until I tried it myself.

So we quickly arranged for all of the Olympic riders to have the opportunity to go to the tunnel. Sessions were organised so that each individual had a 'freeform' session, where they were allowed to experiment. While they tinkered, we projected their live drag data onto the floor in front of them, not in Newtons of force, our usual unit of measurement, but in seconds saved or lost. Bars, forks, clothing and helmets were all given to them to compare against their current set-up.

It was no longer our information, our findings: it was the evidence of their own eyes. To a man and woman they adopted the new kit and most of the positional advice that was offered. The tunnel had become as much a psychological tool as a scientific one.

In the end we conducted just shy of 10,000 tests and boiled down a long list of projects to the most advantageous – a still daunting 24 – to be made into real products fit for Olympic athletes to use in battle.

Production started in early spring, the hardware largely overseen by Dimitris and textile projects the responsibility of Sally Cowan. If they'd known just how hard these last few months of the process were going to be, I wonder whether either of them would have signed up for the journey. With manufacturers now involved, bringing with them their own issues and priorities, things got very complex. We had parts being produced all over the country and sections of helmets being fabricated as far away as Italy. I spent my time trying to unblock bottlenecks, cajoling suppliers who weren't delivering on time, ensuring everything met safety standards and managing the dwindling budget.

In late June, Sally Cowan turned up in the track centre in Manchester with the last of the products: the finished skinsuits for the riders to try on. In the large cardboard box she carried were the fruits of three years' labour – smooth, form-fitting plastic garments very different from the faded Lycra of Jason's suit that had started all this off. She plonked the box down in the athletes' pen and everyone crowded around to see the new kit.

Having now produced dozens of the plasticised prototypes with their high-tech bonded seams, Sally was confident they'd be up to the job. These final versions, carrying the full Olympic livery, had been produced in bulk by a British manufacturer to her specifications. Or so we thought.

The honour of putting on the first one went to sprinter Chris Hoy, who'd barely got his arm into the sleeve before it ripped all the way from cuff to shoulder. There was a pregnant pause before Sally reached for another suit and checked it. The seams of this one came apart easily too. Almost the entire batch – the only batch – was the same. With just weeks to go until competition started, we didn't have time to make replacements.

Other members of the R&D team gathered around a clearly upset Sally and without missing a beat began to exchange ideas about what could be done. There was no looking backwards, no deciding who was to blame, they had instinctively assumed it was their problem, not Sally's, and moved immediately to looking for a solution. I couldn't have been prouder of them than I was then.

Over the next few hours, a solution was found to repair the clothing and Sally set about implementing the fix. It turned out that the manufacturers had changed her design in an attempt to simplify the assembly process for themselves. The sleeves were made from two pieces of plasticised fabric. One featured a narrow painted stripe on the reverse side, which overlapped the seam by

5 mm so that when the two halves of the sleeve were heat-bonded, only this 5 mm would remain on the outside. The result would be a perfect red stripe: slightly raised, nicely aerodynamic. It was fiddly, but doable. Instead, the manufacturers had extended the paint to the full width of the fabric on its reverse side. There was still only 5 mm visible on the outside, so they reasoned that it wouldn't make a difference. It did. It meant that instead of heat-bonding two pieces of fabric, they were sticking one piece of fabric to a layer of paint, which, of course, peeled off with little resistance.

In the last week of July, having added a second layer of glue to the other side of the painted stripe on the sleeves of all 75 suits, Sally delivered the now perfect garments to the Olympic holding camp in Newport. It was just days before the squad set off for Beijing and we had no time to do anything else. If these didn't work, then we'd wasted years of work and a serious amount of money.

We stood in the centre of the track and watched the riders don the clothing. All good, no rips. One by one, they took to the track where Matt Parker conducted the final trials. To our relief, using both new clothing and equipment, their times dropped significantly.

There were no high-fives or whoops of joy, it was more like the fountain scene at the end of *Ocean's 11*, but without the fountain. We just shared smiles and let the warm sense of relief wash over us. We'd started with nothing – a blank piece of paper – and less than four years later we'd delivered. Perhaps not everything we'd intended, and in time rather than on time, but we'd delivered. Now it was up to the riders and coaches to do the hard bit.

CHAPTER 17
Boardman Bikes

Long and rambling, with little punctuation, the message that landed in my inbox in late 2004 had the hallmarks of a nutter email. Still, I hesitated over the delete key. The sender was Alan Ingarfield, a former triathlete who'd held the British Ironman record, and the gist of his proposal was to start a company together to make bikes.

I've always loved making things. As a teenager there was barely a component on my bike that wasn't drilled out for lightness or filed down for – well, I don't know what for, I just liked filing things. As a professional I'd designed the custom carbon bar/fork assembly that I used to break the hour record in 1996 and win the 1997 Tour prologue. Even in retirement I'd stayed in touch with the latest technology. The bike reviews I'd written for *Procycling* had allowed me to try the best – and worst – that the world's manufacturers had to offer. So by the time I received Alan's email, I had loads of thoughts on what makes a good bike.

I also had loads to do at British Cycling and almost no spare time. The prospect of being backed to engineer and design on a grand scale was tantalising, but Alan's proposal contained no real detail on how he planned to make it all happen. Eventually, curiosity got the better of me and I hit reply. Like the call I'd made when I was 13, choosing the evening club race over going diving, it was another mental coin toss.

We met up for the first time a few weeks later in a Liverpool café. Dressed in a white shirt and black jeans, Alan was tall, fit-looking and wore a big smile. The initial finance was no problem: Alan's partner, Sarah Mooney, was a successful businesswoman and keen to invest. Alan was just keen. Every comment I made, no matter how off-the-cuff, was met with unbridled enthusiasm and he instantly tried to incorporate whatever it was I'd said into his offer, which in turn changed shape every time I opened my mouth. I quickly realised that he didn't have a well-defined plan or even a clear direction: he just wanted to 'do something great'. That something – and this was as much as I could make out – involved me designing bikes that I would then put my name to, while he would find a way to both manufacture and get them to market.

Alan certainly didn't seem cut out to be the head of a venture on the scale he was talking about, but by now I'd met a lot of high achievers and few of them fitted the stereotype of the successful businessman either. He was just a bloke who wore his heart on his sleeve, looking for an adventure. I didn't really think anything would come of it, but as always there was the tiny voice in the back of my head interrupting the naysayer: 'Yep, I know it's not going to work – but you're going to do it anyway.'

Despite the vagueness of it all, I tentatively agreed to form a partnership. A pessimistic former pro cyclist and an enthusiastic former triathlete, with no relevant experience between them, setting out to mass-produce some sort of as yet unspecified bikes.

Leaving Alan to get to grips with the world of bicycle manufacture, I got back to juggling my work at British Cycling with a home life that was very much in flux. Sally was pregnant with our sixth child, meaning the Meols home that we'd once considered enormous would soon be bursting at the seams. We considered converting the attic to create more living space and looked at some larger houses in the area without much enthusiasm. Then we discovered that my childhood dream house had just come onto the market.

When I was growing up, my mum had worked as a cook at Red Rocks nursing home: a grand whitewashed building in Stanley Road on the western corner of the Wirral Peninsula. The home took its name from the sandstone outcrop on which it was built and had unique 180-degree views out over the sand flats of the Dee Estuary towards Hilbre and across to the hills of North Wales. I say unique: it shared the headland with one other house, Wirral Point. I'd walked past them both countless times on my way to play in the sand dunes or swim in the tidal pools on the far side of Periwinkle Island.

Not even when I was a pro earning hundreds of thousands of pounds did I dream of owning a 'big house' on that exclusive road. That was where the posh people lived. But with my position at British Cycling now secure and a small retainer coming in from the Boardman Bikes project, we thought it might just be possible. The sale was via sealed bids, so Sally worked out the most we could afford and put in an offer for a bit more. She sent it off in a pink envelope to make sure it stood out. It was accepted.

The reason we'd been able to afford the place was the amount of renovation it required, so much that we'd need to move into rented accommodation for nearly six months while floors were replaced, wiring was renewed and plumbing upgraded. The fact that Sally was pregnant didn't faze her in the slightest. She set about finding our temporary abode and co-ordinating the tradesmen.

On 31 January 2005, Sally went into labour and we made the familiar journey to the maternity suite at Arrowe Park Hospital. I was surprised she hadn't been issued with a loyalty card. At 7.20 in the evening, Agatha Wallis Boardman arrived and by 9.30 both mother and daughter were back at home on the couch. First thing the next morning, with Aggie in her arms, Sally was at the new house getting quotes for putting up walls from Barry the builder.

At the end of February we received the keys. While Sally scurried around measuring things, I went to stand on my own in the large garden and listened to a silence punctuated only by the crying of distant seals on West Hoyle sandbank. I wasn't quite sure how to feel. Wirral Point wasn't just a house but a physical representation, a waypoint in our life, and I think that moment, standing on the grass, was the first time I'd stopped 'doing' and put my head up to see where we were. I was almost shocked to realise how far we had travelled since heating one room in our first house behind Birkenhead Technical College.

Despite not yet having moved in, we had our housewarming party to coincide with the birthdays of Sonny and my grandmother. Proudly installed in the window seat of our new residence, my Nan said, 'It's got an awfully big garden.' It took a while to explain that we didn't own the whole estuary.

While we were busy with babies and builders, Alan had been making progress with prospective manufacturers for Boardman Bikes. Which meant I had to get down to designing some.

From the start I'd told Alan that, in my view, Dimitris Katsanis was the best frame designer in the world and the only person I wanted to work with. But any collaboration between us had to be handled carefully, since we were both part of British Cycling's Olympic R&D team. Neither of us was a full-time employee, so we were free to take on other work, but the potential for a conflict of interest was clear and I was keen that we were upfront with our BC colleagues.

In fact, as soon as I'd decided to take Alan up on his offer, I'd told Dave Brailsford and offered to resign if it was going to be a problem. But Dave was happy with my dual activities as long as I ensured that they stayed strictly separate. Since most of the BC products we were developing were highly specialised components for elite track athletes, it wasn't difficult to ensure there was clear ground between the two projects.

Having cleared Dimitris's involvement, we set about designing our first Boardman Bikes product: a carbon time trial/triathlon frame. The guiding principle was one we both held dear: the demands of the event would drive our design, and function would always take precedence over form. I'd seen so many gimmicks over the years and I was determined there would be none on a bike that carried my name. We would celebrate the simple beauty of functionality. When we'd finished, I wanted to be able to point to any part of a Boardman bike and know that I could explain why it was how it was.

With all our other duties, it was a protracted process, crammed into evenings and weekends. Computer designs were emailed back and forth as we went over and over every detail. It took a year before we were satisfied. Armed with our blueprints, Alan toured the Far East and eventually found a suitable manufacturing partner: a factory both big enough to have all the required skills and small enough to be passionate about our start-up venture, an operation with a conscientious staff we knew we could rely on. It was a long haul, but by mid 2006 we'd established what we wanted to make and the method by which it would be created. Now we just had to nail down a way to sell it.

In parallel with his Far East factory tours, Alan had been exploring all possible routes to market and attending dozens of meetings with retailers and distributors across the UK. The most promising response came from the biggest seller of bikes in the country, Halfords. Halfords CEO Ian McLeod was a brusque, no-nonsense Scot with a clear vision of how to improve his company's fortunes. He wanted to expand their presence in the bike market further, adding quality to quantity along the way. But as a place known better for car parts, Halfords was largely scorned by the Lycra-wearing, leg-shaving community of 'real' cyclists. Consequently, the big bike manufacturers refused to deal with them for fear of damaging their image. And since Halford's own-brand bikes didn't have the credibility to draw in more discerning customers, they were stuck.

So when Alan had approached them for an exploratory meeting, the timing couldn't have been better. If they weren't able to get the elite manufacturers to deal with them, maybe they could strike a deal to grow their own. Over the following months, a strategic alliance was forged between the embryonic Boardman Bikes and Halfords. The contract would give the chain sole rights to sell our bikes in the UK and me the right to sign-off on every product that bore my name.

It was a huge opportunity, but it meant the mission had to change to accommodate the needs of our new partner. Halfords wanted to move upmarket, but steadily – and not quite as far as the carbon-fibre works of art that Dimitris and I had designed. Their preference was for gentle evolution rather than wholesale reinvention. Our first offerings would be high-quality machines based on the principles we held dear, but with the initial emphasis on affordability rather than the last word in cutting-edge technology.

Through the second half of 2006 and on into 2007 I worked with their team to create a whole new set of designs, including mountain bikes. I loved mountain biking but I was far from an expert, so the head GB MTB mechanic was drafted in to advise on both geometry and equipment choice. For the road models, I led on the frame-design and sizing. All the bikes were aluminium, and for extra strength, every weld was 'double passed' and then filed smooth: a process that reduced the chance of stress fractures and had the secondary benefit of looking beautiful. For their part, Halfords were prepared to cut their profit margins to ensure that the bikes were class-leading, and so each was fitted out with equipment usually seen on machines twice the price. The finished article was stunning: simple, elegant and incredible value. Product we could be proud of.

Frustratingly, the beautiful carbon frames that Dimitris and I had worked so hard on found themselves in a retail cul-de-sac, no longer appropriate for the new mission. In the end, without having an appropriate route to market for them, we manufactured fewer than 200. Terry Dolan helped us distribute them under the Boardman Elite banner, before we mothballed the range and concentrated on the needs of our mass-market partner. It was a great product but it had arrived three years too early.

Over this period our tiny team grew from three – myself, Alan and Sarah – to a slightly less tiny six. Mark Harper, from the design house Bonbon, came on board to create the branding, and his partner Sasha Castling to oversee promotion. The final member of the team was Halfords' product manager Andy Smallwood.

Just as Dimitris Katsanis was the lynchpin of the Secret Squirrel Club, Andy Smallwood was and still is the hub of the Boardman brand. Warm, passionate and deeply knowledgeable about cycling, he was instantly recognisable as one of those rare individuals who I can only describe as gold medal material; people with that special something to set them apart from their peers. A keen cyclist with an engineering background, Andy was the perfect liaison between us and Halfords, and from the outset it was clear that the Boardman range belonged as much to him as it did to me.

In July 2007, just before the Tour de France got underway in London, Ian McLeod and I travelled down to the capital to announce both the new brand and the partnership. It had taken a year of designing, prototyping and testing before we were finally ready to launch our range of nine bikes, along with branded clothing and accessories. Being surrounded by walls covered with pictures of myself and products plastered with my name was uncomfortable and flattering in equal measure. I couldn't get used to thinking of and referring to myself as a brand. But it was certainly exciting and I hoped people were going to like the work we'd done.

I needn't have worried. Over the following few months, the bikes were rated best-in-class in every magazine review. Like a fanatical bird watcher on the hunt for a new species, I scanned the traffic everywhere I went, waiting to get a glimpse of the first model in the wild. When I did, it was in London, as I walked down Woburn Place, not far from the British Museum. A genuine Boardman customer. 'Nice bike,' I remarked as nonchalantly as I could to the guy as he waited for the traffic lights to change. I think he thought I was trying to chat him up.

Customer recognition aside, I knew that my name and racing history were a big part of what had helped get the brand off the ground and into Halfords. I also knew that they wouldn't sustain it in the long term. The company needed a pedigree of its own, which meant a presence in the peloton. Luckily, timing was on our side again, and this time the perfect partners were people I was already working with.

The GB track team was performing strongly. At the 2007 World Championships in Majorca they took a record seven golds, five of them in Olympic disciplines. Everything was on course for Beijing. On the road, though, it was a much more hit and miss affair.

Due to the healthy professional scene, it wasn't possible, or even really necessary, to run a men's national road squad. Talented male riders were quickly snapped up by continental teams and so were kept fit and technically sharp by their employers, only coming together under the GB banner perhaps once or twice a year.

Women's racing was not as self-sustaining. Quality national competitions were scarce and pay was poor, even for the very best who could find backing to travel abroad. Nicole Cooke, ever the vociferous champion of a national women's team, campaigned for British Cycling to finance one, so that riders might get sufficient racing and learn to work together. It was a reasonable request but not one we could act on.

Lottery money, the bulk of the GB stipend, was specifically allotted for maximising Olympic medal chances. Of the 14 gold medals available to our men and women in Beijing, ten were on the track and only four on the road, two of those being time trials. Funding a women's road team would suck up a huge chunk of the available budget in pursuit of a single road race medal. In coldly logical terms, it would not be a good investment.

No one understood this dilemma better than Dave Brailsford. In late 2007, we approached Halfords to see if they would back an entirely British professional team that Dave would control. They agreed and in January 2008 Dave announced his first pro outfit, Team Halfords Bike Hut. Oddly, the launch event was held by the sloth enclosure at London Zoo.

Nicole Cooke was the team's leader but there were many other stars of the future on the roster too, including Joanna Rowsell and a very young Emma Trott. Although it was primarily a women's team, we also wanted a male contingent to represent us on the domestic scene. Rob Hayles and Tom Southam agreed to come on board and fulfil that role. With our own racing team, we now had a reason – and a responsibility – to develop machines fit for them to ride. During the first half of 2008, Andy and I designed our first carbon fibre frame together, the Pro Carbon. Even fully built up, it was well under the legal weight limit and had to have lead stuck to the underside of the saddle to reach the UCI specified minimum of 6.8 kg. Halfords had never stocked anything remotely like it. During that inaugural season, Rob Hayles produced one of the best rides of his career to win the national road race title. Nicole Cooke made it a Boardman Bikes double with her eighth win in a row.

It signalled the start of an extraordinary summer. I was already exhausted before it got going: the hectic first year of Boardman Bikes had run parallel to the final delivery of kit and equipment for the GB team. July was a busman's holiday, working for ITV on the Tour de France, and from there I headed to Beijing to do the same for the BBC. The 2008 Games would be the first I'd ever travelled to as a spectator, albeit one getting paid to talk about what he saw. It felt strange to be outside the competition bubble, but I was excited to see what both riders and bikes could do. There was also the luxury of being able to have a beer in the evenings.

Soon after stepping out of the airport into the humidity and the smog, I headed off for dinner with my new Radio 5 colleagues, former sprinter Darren Campbell and ex-swimmers Steve Parry and Karen Pickering. Steve and Karen had a particular talent for sniffing out social freebies and soon had us inside London House, the British Olympic Association's hospitality centre, where we drank complimentary Pimms and loaded up on nibbles.

Over the following days, I settled into a new and very pleasant routine. A crew of off-duty media types would gather in the hotel bar and head off to the many eateries lining the shore of Qianhai Lake. The menus were brutally translated into English – presumably using Google – and contained descriptions ranging from the incomprehensible ('the lemon deep sea snow fish digs up') to the downright disturbing ('delicious roasted husband' and 'steamed red crap with ginger'). On one occasion I found myself invited to an intimate Chinese banquet with TV presenter Adrian Chiles, athletics star Steve Cram and senior staff from the British Embassy. I don't think I've ever sat at a dinner table before where the conversation spanned sport, sociology and spying.

The other side of the fence at the Olympics was proving to be everything I had hoped it would be: social, fun and free from pressure. With a few days to go until the start of the track competition, the holiday atmosphere was marred by news from the outside world. Lounging in my plush hotel room, I received a phone call from the GB head mechanic Ernie Feargrieve. There was a loud cracking noise coming from Chris Hoy's bike.

With a feeling of trepidation, I got in a taxi and headed for the velodrome. There was no visible reason for the noise but it had everyone severely rattled, including me. Phone calls were exchanged with Dimitris Katsanis and he prescribed a cure for the likely cause;

bearings shifting in the bottom bracket. Somehow, Doug Dailey, head of logistics, sourced Loctite 7471 and its activator in Beijing on Sunday afternoon. A makeshift autoclave was rigged up using a hairdryer in the mechanics' cabin at the track and the fix was implemented. The noise ceased and disaster was averted. From that point on, it was all upside.

The fun started on day two of the cycling schedule, as I settled in next to Simon Brotherton at our commentary position for the women's road race. By the midway point it was pouring with rain, resulting in numerous crashes on the slippery descents. Heading into the final few misty kilometres, five riders held a fragile lead over the remnants of the bunch. One of them was Nicole Cooke. I winced as they negotiated the last treacherous corner into the home straight and Nicole lost some ground. From there it was uphill all the way to the line, making it more of a long soggy slog than a sprint. Inside the last few hundred metres, our cameras switched to a long shot down the finishing straight and even though the figures were largely obscured by the spray, it was clear that one of them desperately wanted – needed – the win more than the others.

We stood and screamed as the drenched figure of Nicole clawed her way past the others to cross the line first, the shock on her face giving way to elation as she realised she'd done it. It was a joy to see, an outpouring of emotion that encapsulates why we watch Olympic sport. For me, the slow-motion footage of Nicole wining was the image of the Games. She conveyed without words how years of work and sacrifice can be justified by the intensity of an experience that lasts seconds. Nicole's was Britain's first gold medal of the games, the country's first ever in an Olympic road race, and she'd achieved her record-breaking feat astride a Boardman bike. I couldn't have been prouder.

Five days later, Simon and I relocated to the Laoshan Velodrome and watched in awe as the GB squad won eight golds. We seemed to be constantly out of our seats cheering – in a very BBC, non-partisan way – as British athletes challenged for victory in almost every event. Having been party to the tough journey they'd all endured to get here, I was delighted for them: Brad Wiggins's early disappointments before finally making his breakthrough in 2003; the team pursuit riders, forever second to the Australians, at last getting their noses in front; Dave Brailsford, terrified at taking it all on in 2004 when Peter Keen left, and sweating over every detail for four years. Now they were all finally seeing their tenacity pay off.

From my place in the commentary box, I could see everyone jumping up and down with delight as GB athletes delivered. It was magical. And we'd done our bit too. The Squirrels' work contributed a performance advantage of … well, I'm not allowed to divulge that. Let's just say that it justified UK Sport's investment many times over.

When it all ended on 24 August and the final totals were added up, Great Britain's cyclists had won a staggering 14 medals, eight of them gold – enough to put them in the top ten as a country in their own right. In the timed events, they'd broken every Olympic record and two world records. It was the most successful GB Olympic squad of all time.

*

The reaction at home to the Beijing results was extraordinary and widespread. The press hailed the team – and its staff – as sporting messiahs. It had a notable, and in some cases unwelcome, effect on their self-confidence. Some of the coaching team began to believe they were the kingmakers. Their healthy self-doubt was erased and their ability to listen to criticism diminished – all standard effects of winning big. I recognised the symptoms because I'd suffered from them myself. In 1992, I had gone from being an unemployed carpenter to the most successful British cyclist of his era, someone who could do no wrong. I began to believe everything that was written about me and it felt good. Those around me, the people I'd always relied on for counsel, were also affected by the press and spoke more quietly at exactly the moment I was less inclined to listen. Only failure brought me down far enough to start heeding their advice again.

As the only staff member who had been through anything like this before, I knew the process couldn't be avoided or short circuited: everyone had to experience it for themselves. Although I knew it was both natural and inevitable, I was still saddened to witness the unsavoury change in the team's dynamics as more and more people felt they had been undervalued, that their slice of credit just wasn't big enough.

Away from the fanfare and public adoration, the Squirrels had their own small gathering in a hotel in Chester to celebrate. Only a few people had publicly acknowledged the huge part they had played in the Olympic success story, Dave and Steve Peters amongst them. Just two athletes took the time to thank the R&D team personally.

It hadn't been a bad year for Boardman Bikes either. Barely 18 months in, and we had seen national, world and Olympic titles all won on our bikes. Frames out of the same mould as Nicole's Olympic machine were sold in Halfords stores for a shade under £1000, a price almost unheard of for carbon fibre. Sales soared and we became the fastest growing bike brand in British history.

With so much going on in my life outside, I was intending to resign my role with British Cycling. But Dave, charming and loyal as ever, convinced me over another direction-defining coffee to stay. We struck a deal: I would do another four-year term on the Senior Management Team and he would make some of the changes we'd discussed to the BC staff structure. In the end, neither of us would keep our word.

CHAPTER 18

Secret Squirrels Part Two

The rep in the Thomson Holidays advert scampers around, waving clouds away, smoothing the waves and tweaking the thermostat to make the temperature for their clients just right. Lying beneath the palm trees, with the cool breeze blowing and a turquoise sea in front of me, I could believe that was exactly what had happened here. It was September 2009 and Sally and I had come to the Maldives to celebrate our 21st wedding anniversary. Sally wandered over to show me the picture she'd just taken on her phone. It was of me, frowning and staring at a computer screen. Laptop on my knee, I was spending my time in this beautiful place ploughing through British Cycling emails, trying to stay on top of things while I was away.

The last 12 months had been like a fantastic party, but every party has its morning after, when the spilled food needs to be scraped off the carpet and the beer bottles collected from under the sofa. The scale of the aftermath is usually in proportion to the success of the night before and the 2008 Olympics had been a doozy.

I don't think I had really sobered up from the experience when I'd sat in the coffee shop with Dave Brailsford and signed on for another four-year stint on the Senior Management Team. Now, the realities of that commitment, and the more problematic effects of success, were making themselves felt. Fellow SMT member Steve Peters was in high demand away from cycling, giving lectures and advising businesses on the psychology of winning. Dave was also taking a well-earned break away from the front line, doing some corporate speaking and accepting invitations from high-profile entrepreneurs to critique their organisations. One of them, James Murdoch, son of media mogul Rupert, was a big cycling fan and they were hatching a plan to create a new professional team.

I was happy for them. They deserved their rewards and, in any case, I'd been doing plenty of outside work myself. Boardman Bikes Limited was booming. I'd undertaken several lucrative speaking engagements and TV work was now taking up more than two months a year. As well as these expanding external interests, my in-house responsibilities had increased too. As well as running the Secret Squirrels Club I'd revived the coaching development programme by organising a series of workshops and I seemed to be taking on ever more administrative work. It might all have been manageable had the other SMT members not frequently been AWOL.

No one wanted to stay home and mind the shop, never mind dedicate every waking moment to the task of trying to outdo ourselves at the next Olympics. It was also clear that the management restructure Dave and I had discussed over coffee a year earlier was not going to come about. As a consequence, much of the unglamorous everyday work of counselling disgruntled coaches and mediating staff disputes had fallen to me. I'd got on with it, stuck my finger in the proverbial dam, because I had seen there was a hole that had to be plugged and there was no one else around. But I didn't want to be the permanent solution.

The week before our holiday, Sally and I had even started discussing my taking on a personal assistant to cope with the saturation workload. But her photograph on the sunlit beach had made me take stock. Did I want to adapt my personal circumstances so I could cope with even more work? On 28 September 2009, sitting in Dubai airport waiting for our flight home, I made the decision to resign as a member of British Cycling's Senior Management Team and sent the email from the departure lounge. It was a bit of a cowardly way to do it, but I wanted to be able to set out my reasons clearly without getting flustered – and to give Dave a bit of time to absorb it. There was an instant sense of relief, mixed with a feeling of guilt. Dave had always been good to me, supportive and flexible, and I'd gone back on my word. But I could see no other way to deal with the overload.

The one thing I had been enjoying was leading the small R&D team, so I offered to continue managing this department, fully expecting to be told that a clean break was preferable. But Dave agreed and so I kept my title as Head Squirrel for the next three years.

In that first phase, 2004 to 2008, we had been pioneers, breaking new ground and finding rich seams of success almost everywhere we looked. After Beijing, the landscape was very different. Instead of hunting for nuggets, we were reduced to panning for dust, a tedious activity that required a different, more refined approach.

For the first 12 months back at the Southampton University wind tunnel, the team again experimented with the weird and wonderful: strategically placed sequins and patches of fake fur to create local roughness; devices to channel high-pressure air from one place and deposit it somewhere else. Athletes tried riding side-saddle to alter the shape of their wake and pedalled backwards to see if it offered any advantages. We even spent three months exploring naturally inflating clothing that would subtly change its shape as air speed increased.

As in the previous Olympic cycle, most of these bizarre experiments had been spawned by tantalising CFD imagery that showed how the air might be flowing over the riders and their bikes. But the computer models had shown that most of these avenues offered only tiny gains. The benefits, assuming they were even there, often proved too small for the wind tunnel's sensory equipment to pick up. In the build-up to Beijing, potential improvements had been easy to identify and we'd been able to test ideas quickly, proving or disproving their benefits and moving on. Now, the results were often ambiguous, with choices about what was worth pursuing necessarily driven as much by personal belief as by science. Naturally, opinions often differed and arguments became frequent.

Things came to a head at a meeting early in 2010. We pooled our problems and boiled them down to one big question: should we sacrifice a large chunk of our budget and remaining research time making more sensitive measuring devices, or keep using the existing set-up but dramatically increase the number of repeat tests to at least produce a believable average? Option two was the one I went for: the accuracy problem would need to be solved on another day and by another boss.

I'd thought that restricting my workload to the R&D programme would be the answer to all of my work-related woes, but it hadn't brought the contentment I'd been expecting. I'd been kidding myself. The sad fact was that I'd fallen out of love with bike racing, first as a rider, now as a staff member. It was loyalty to great people, not passion for the sport, that had made me agree to stay on, and in a game that demands total commitment that could never be enough.

If I stayed, I was obliged to give my all, which I'd resent – already did resent – otherwise those who still fully believed would start to resent me. Making space to do more away from the gold medal business had allowed me to see clearly that the activities I was enjoying were no longer in the sporting arena. Designing bikes with my company, helping shape strategy to grow the brand and making TV programmes were the things that excited me.

The only solution was to pull out completely, something I should have done after the Beijing Games. Still, I felt bad – it was only a few months since I'd stood down from the SMT. Caught between the need to get out and the realisation that I couldn't leave people I cared about in the lurch, I made a deal with myself: I'd give it everything up until the next Olympics, then make a clean break. London 2012 would be a fitting and symmetrical place to bring my career in competitive cycling to a close.

I broke the news to Dave, although it wasn't exactly news to him – he'd watched me getting ever more emotionally detached. He probably understood my feelings better than anyone, since he was following an almost identical discovery path. His plan to form a brand new professional team had come to fruition and his time at the velodrome was a fraction of what it had been before.

Running parallel with all this soul-searching, was perhaps my biggest challenge of the second Olympic cycle – and it wasn't one that was susceptible to extra testing or more sensitive equipment.

After Beijing, several fanciful articles had appeared in print, including one which claimed that all of Team GB's Olympic outfits had been burned to guard their secrets. In fact, the clothing in question was unusable simply because the livery had been specific to that one event, as is always the case with an Olympics, and the garments were still in a cardboard box in the BC storeroom. The facts notwithstanding, and stirred up by the media speculation, comments began to appear from the UCI President Pat McQuaid. He proclaimed his wish to see 'a level playing field' at the next Olympics, adding that 'some teams were using £50,000 prototypes'. He went further: 'It's against the Olympic charter, it's against the UCI rules and against the spirit of fair play.'

Pat McQuaid's statements, clearly directed at the GB team, were tantamount to accusing us of cheating. His conclusions had been drawn without having had a single conversation with the accused. I decided the best way to deal with the growing raft of inaccuracies was a visit to UCI headquarters in Aigle, Switzerland. I flew out in August 2009, accompanied by Dimitris Katsanis, who was not only the engineer responsible for making the '£50,000 bikes' but also a qualified UCI *commissaire*. On arriving at the futuristic egg-shaped headquarters we were met by a small party headed by Jean Wauthier, the UCI's technical chief. As soon as we entered the building he guided me over to a case displaying one of Eddy Merckx's 1970s machines, pointed at it and proclaimed '*This* is what a bike should look like.'

After the initial skirmish, we said a quick hello to Pat, who was very pleasant but simply refused to believe that the GB bikes cost us less than commercially available products. This was despite my offering to show him invoices to that effect and having their designer standing next to me. He didn't attend the meeting proper.

In a large conference room with views of the surrounding mountains, I laid the various parts of the GB bike and clothing on the table for Jean Wauthier and his colleagues to examine. I asked that they tell me which ones they felt were infringing the rules in any way. Mumbling followed. There were no actual objections but it was clear that they still weren't happy. It was as good as I was going to get.

Apart from politely challenging them to justify their public stance, one of the main questions I had come to ask was whether they were intending to change the equipment rules before the next Olympic Games, making any of the components set before them illegal. 'No' was the answer.

With so many emotion-based public statements flying about, I wasn't convinced. But we left having at least established a good line of communication and a solid, if slightly worrying, understanding of the political climate we were operating in. Sure enough, on 15 March 2010, British Cycling received a letter from Pat McQuaid informing us that, despite no rules having been changed, our bikes would now be deemed illegal for competition because they weren't available to the public. This seemed to be a wilful misinterpretation by the UCI of their own long-standing regulations. The rule in question, Article 1.3.007, stated that:

> 'Bicycles and their accessories shall be of a type that is or could be sold for use by anyone practising cycling as a sport. The use of equipment designed especially for the attainment of a particular performance (symmetrical or other) shall be not authorised.' (Article 1.3.007)

The wording was very clear: 'of a type that is **or could be** sold'. It showed that the UCI knew the difference between 'for sale' and 'saleable'. Despite our pointing this out, and the fact that the regulation had been in place for nearly a decade (the same GB bikes had been classed as legal since 2002), the UCI said that the wording now meant strictly for sale.

To comply with this new interpretation, all the BC bikes and equipment were listed on an obscure page of the UK Sport website and are still available today. The words 'or could be' were quietly removed from Article 1.3.007 in October that same year.

The bike episode was just one of the curve balls thrown at us by the world governing body. The UCI has a long-standing memorandum of understanding with the IOC on regulations for an Olympics. With 12 months to go, the rules and regulations are handed over and no amendments are made until after the Olympiad. Yet with ten months to go until the teams gathered in London, the UCI announced that the plasticised materials we'd used in the skinsuits in Beijing would now also be deemed illegal. They had broken their own agreement with the International Olympic Committee. It was evidence to me that the sport's leaders wanted to direct cycle racing like a theatre production, rather than define the sporting arena and judge the outcome impartially.

Fortunately, after the charged meeting in Aigle we had chosen to keep a second strand of research open into more standard materials, so we were able to produce an equally high-performing garment for the team in time for London.

Knowing that I was approaching my second retirement date, I had started to invest more and more energy in my activities outside of British Cycling. One of those commitments was working for ITV on the Tour de France, which would take up the entire month running up to the Olympics. Hardly ideal.

If someone had wanted to call my intention to continue with both roles in this critical period negligent, I don't think I could have disagreed with them. I was only able to get away with it because of the broad shoulders of Matt Parker. Upbeat, supportive and fun to be around, Matt had come on board with BC in 2006 as a sports scientist, but it was soon clear that his talents went beyond physiological know-how. Because of his methodical approach and easy manner around often tetchy sports people, he rapidly became an integral member of the trackside coach support team.

Less than two years later Matt was made coach of the men's endurance squad. In that role he stood in the Laoshan Velodrome in Beijing as his charges won gold in both team and individual events. After 2008, he changed roles again and became head of Marginal Gains, using nutrition, biomechanics, and performance analysis to do with the GB riders what the Secret Squirrels were doing with their equipment. Matt too would move on from British Cycling after 2012, taking his skills to the England rugby team as Head of Athletic Performance.

Matt had been involved in much of the Squirrels' activity as the liaison between athletes, coaches and the science team, so in my absence he was the natural choice to oversee the final delivery of hundreds of pieces of equipment and clothing. With a month to go until the London games got underway, I handed over the reins and hightailed it over to Liège for the start of the 2012 Tour.

CHAPTER 19

The Tour on TV

The alarm went. I opened my eyes and took in my surroundings. Dirty grey carpeted walls, equally grubby lino, and the crowning glory, a cracked toilet half hidden by a stained plastic shower curtain. As hotel rooms go, it had all the charm of a semi-derelict safe house for some criminal hiding out in the Pyrenees and waiting for the police to pass.

It's always the same when the Tour hits the mountains: tens of thousands of people swarming into sleepy villages looking for shelter. The race organisation secures all the prime real estate for the riders, teams and their own staff before the route is even announced. Wealthy fans take the next tier of desirable accommodation and we, the media, scrabble for what's left. However, it doesn't always follow that being the last in line condemns you to the worst quarters.

The Tour hotel list is a bit like those games of chocolate Russian roulette that people buy at Christmas: sometimes you're rewarded with a hazelnut praline and sometimes you find yourself chomping down on a chilli surprise. Twenty-four hours prior to waking up in the Bonnie & Clyde Hilton, we'd stayed in an exquisitely converted farmhouse, nestled in an equally beautiful valley, with rabbits and chickens roaming free beneath the terrace where we ate a home-cooked meal. The only sounds were those of distant cowbells.

It's not just the hotels: the whole annual road trip is a bit Forrest Gump. In terms of getting something to eat in the evening, the result is usually a ham and cheese sandwich at a motorway service station. But when there's no *autoroute* between us and the next day's stage finish things can get interesting, not to say desperate. Late one night in the middle of the 2010 Tour, starving hungry after a long, twisting journey through the Pyrenees, we saw a flashing neon sign in the distance.

As we drew closer, an American diner appeared mirage-like on the otherwise deserted stretch of valley road. It was past 10 p.m. and we were only heading deeper into the wilds, so we weren't going to look this strange gift horse in the mouth. As we entered, the strangeness doubled. Random car parts and bits of motorbike sat on the Formica-topped tables and red leatherette benches. It was as though an airborne piece of the American heartland had collided with a mechanics' workshop over Europe and crashed to earth on the French/Spanish border. It might all have been a bit off-putting if it hadn't been for the food: I had the best burger I'd ever tasted. And if our car had needed servicing, all the chef would have had to do was shuffle across from the grill to the repair shop counter.

The chef, it turned out, was the owner and when he spotted our Tour accreditation he insisted we follow him out to a storeroom at the side of his establishment, where things got even odder. His real passion, it turned out, was his collection of homemade trick bicycles. Contraptions that required you to pedal backwards to go forwards, that steered the wrong way or had wheels with the hubs off centre. All pointless, all constructed with a mad craftsman's care.

'Look,' he shouted in his heavily accented English as he turned tiny circles on a machine that hinged in the middle, 'Zey iz all crazy shit!'

When we drove the same stretch of road a couple of years later only the sign was left, the windows dark and dirty. Evidently provincial France had not been ready for his vision of a garage/restaurant hybrid.

We could, of course, log the good, the bad and the ugly as we trek around France each year and build up a reliable list of hostelries and eateries. That way we'd never have to suffer the same grubby lino twice. But if we did, we might never have found ourselves as accidental guests of honour at a wake somewhere in Provence, toasting 'Old Tom', or eating the most sublime pizza in the world served from a rusty transit van, or have met the mad bike mechanic-cum-chef. As John Syer told me back in Barcelona, elation and despair are two sides of the same coin. If you want to experience one then you must risk the other.

The ITV production team who make the 3,500 km road trip each year are no less strange and varied than the places we end up. If there was any kind of formal recruitment process for staffing the Tour, Matt Rendell wouldn't have a job; he'd have received a polite letter informing him that his application had been unsuccessful due to his being ludicrously over-qualified. But there isn't, so he does. He is a supercomputer often pressed into service as a calculator.

It's hard to define his role in the production because he can fit in just about anywhere. He conducts daily post-race interviews in various languages, he's the team historian, the statistician and the man we turn to if there's a rider we know nothing about. He acts as an adviser on ad-break timings for the director during hectic stages and he's the lead voice on the Tour podcast. After Jens Voigt, he's also probably the world's greatest source of enthusiasm on the subject of cycling, roaming the technical zone every day looking for people to share it with.

He once ended up on the now-defunct *Velo Club*, a live post-race TV chat show of the kind the French seem to love: an endless talking shop with a huge cast of journalists, pundits, team directors and riders, still in their kit from the stage just finished and desperate to get away for a massage. It was pretty tedious viewing usually, but we all gathered round the monitor for Matt's appearance and we weren't disappointed. He was there to talk about his recently published biography of Marco Pantani, but the discussion drifted onto the subject of whether or not riders should have sex during competition. Undeterred by his lack of expertise on the topic, Matt pitched in with a lengthy contribution in perfect French, to the great amusement of the woman sitting next to him and all of us in the truck. Years later the director still insists on calling him Dr Sex.

Matt is a walking encyclopaedia on many more subjects than just cycling (or sex): he's even written a book on Latin American dancing, *Salsa for People Who Probably Shouldn't*. In many ways, he's the glue that holds the production together. Each morning of the race he comes into the Outside Broadcast truck with three copies of *L'Equipe*, one for Gary Imlach, one for himself and one that he always puts on my desk. I don't think I've ever read one – my French isn't good enough – but I imagine he performs this daily ritual with a tiny internal sigh as he says a silent prayer for my intellectual redemption. Gary takes his copy outside to spare us all proximity to his breakfast: a bowl of mackerel and quinoa. This is after he has lovingly crafted the first of his two daily espressos.

I'm a firm believer that the composition of someone's desk provides an insight into their personality. In the tiny area of the truck that I have claimed as my own, I spend hours each year crafting shelves from cardboard and gaffer tape, ducting the mess of cables behind to produce a clean workspace. To my right sits Matt, whose endless notes, newspapers, various recording devices and reference books threaten landslides in all directions. Territorial disputes are common and I have been known to repel trespassers with cardboard barricades. This isn't required on my left flank because that's where Gary sits. He doesn't need bits of old boxes to mark his dominion, he uses a force field.

Approximately 40 per cent of 'Imlachville' is dedicated to making the perfect cup of coffee. He not only brings his own nitrous oxide-powered hand-held espresso machine, there's also a carefully calibrated grinder to pulverise his beans of choice. In addition, he has a special tool (only available via import from America) to realign the grinder's burrs if they get knocked out of true on the journey round France. Perhaps the most telling item of paraphernalia, though, is the set of digital scales used to weigh the beans and make sure he has exactly the right dose for each cup. The term 'that'll do' is not in his lexicon.

Gary's eccentricities pepper more than just one corner of the truck. Once, as we walked across a piece of scrubland doubling up as a TV compound for the day, we came across the site of a burnt-out car. The vehicle's husk had long since been removed; blackened debris and the smelted remains of an aluminium engine block were all that was left. Gary stopped, stared at the mercury-like blob and proceeded to prise it free. He then transported it all the way around France and took it home as an *objet d'art*.

Gary has a sharp sense of humour too, which sometimes gets him into trouble. He concluded one on-air discussion of the latest insinuations of doping against Chris Froome with the words, 'So, we still don't know when Chris Froome stopped beating his wife.' There was stunned silence on the set as he linked to the next piece of video.

'What?' he said, looking at the horrified faces around him. To Gary, the context had made his remark perfectly clear. 'When did you stop beating your wife?' is a classic example of the loaded question, one that assumes guilt and makes it almost impossible for an innocent party to answer. Some elements of the French media seemed to be doing the same to Froome, putting him in the position of trying to prove a negative. It might have been clear to Gary, but it wasn't to quite a few other people, including Froome's wife Michelle, whose text to Ned Boulting – 'WTF?!' – arrived about 30 seconds later. The director suggested that he might want to clarify his comment once the recorded item was over.

The joke was typical Imlach. He works harder than anyone I know to make every word count. The two words that led to our least professional on-air moment, though, weren't so much crafted as mangled. We were on the set, watching the closing stages of a key mountain climb and waiting to take over from commentators Phil Liggett and Paul Sherwen once it was over. The pair of them were going full tilt and somewhere in the excitement, the Dutch rider Bauke Mollema became Bob Malka: 'Bob Malka's been dropped.'

As mistakes go, it wasn't really that funny, or unusual for commentators at the end of a four-hour stint, but as any schoolboy will tell you, there's something about a situation where mirth is absolutely forbidden that renders even the tiniest spark of it especially dangerous. And once the fire is lit, the flames spread. I spluttered with laughter and that set Gary off, which was unfortunate as we'd just been put on stand-by to go live.

'Boardman, pack it in,' he said, forcing a straight face, as if just telling each other to stop laughing would work.

'I'll be alright,' I said, although it was obvious I wouldn't. The deadpan voice in my ear said 'Fifteen seconds'. Gary, sensing impending disaster, began to really lose it. Evidence that the occupants of the Outside Broadcast truck had been infected was clear in the director's voice as he wobbled through the count: 'Three, two, one … cue Gary.'

The unsuspecting ITV audience was suddenly presented with two twitching figures, oddly reluctant to make eye contact with each other. I fixed my gaze on my notebook. Unfortunately, for reasons I can't explain, I'd written the words Bob Malka in bold capitals in the centre of the page. Tears and snot began running down my face. Gary tried to simultaneously welcome the viewers while frantically gesturing at me to get down under the desk. How my helplessly giggling three feet lower down was going to help him regain his composure I don't know. He fought on valiantly for a few seconds, before squeaking out, 'We'll be back when we can treat the race with the solemnity it deserves,' before giving in to the inevitable and collapsing into an impromptu ad break.

The Outside Broadcast truck is the centre of our summer. Driven through the night from one stage finish to the next, it takes the strongman tag-team pairing of Richard Gaines and Pete Howarth to get it round the route, over Alps and Pyrenees, while staying within EU rules for maximum allowable hours at the wheel.

At dawn each day, it arrives with a hundred or so of its fellows on a predetermined patch of France – a car park, a town square, a diagonal quagmire at the top of a mountain – and disgorges its cargo of cables, cameras, bikes, gazebos and God-knows-what other equipment. As every other OB truck does the same, the ground is quickly hidden beneath thousands of coloured cables running in all directions. Somewhere in the cramped chaos a spot is found to pitch the two gazebos that serve as our TV studio.

People say the camera doesn't lie but I can tell you it bloody well does. I've looked at the monitor and seen myself and Gary, standing on a pristine set in front of a brightly coloured backdrop of cyclists and sunflowers. If the camera zoomed out you'd see the pair of us standing in mud, an umbrella gaffer-taped in place to stop the rain coming through the roof, and a gutter, cunningly improvised by cameraman Rich Hayward from plastic Vittel bottles, to drain the flood water away.

The exterior of the truck is unremarkable and so, I suppose, is the interior if you work in television. But for an outsider, to walk up the steps and through one of its heavy doors is to be transported to an alternative near-future: a cold, dark space, all sound dampened by the carpeted walls, a bank of TV screens providing most of the light. I imagine wars are orchestrated and rockets launched into space from places like this. I could easily envisage the man perched centrally on his swivel chair, producer/director/dictator Steve Docherty, doing either of those things. He sits each day in his mobile mission control, issuing assignments to the troops, each of them sent out into the fray with orders not to return if they fail.

'Good' or 'No, do it again' are common pieces of feedback from the Doc, usually preceded by a long pause and a flat stare. He is not a man to waste syllables or sugarcoat his criticism. He keeps his praise in a jealously guarded jar hidden away in his desk. On rare occasions, he'll crack it open, fish out an M&M sized morsel of warmth and hand it to a starved member of the team.

The Doc's leadership style is seen by many as harsh. It is, but it's born of a passionate pursuit of perfection and the resulting shows are all the better for it. For those that come every year and give it their all, he is a deeply loyal and appreciative colleague.

And it's not as if he's without a sense of humour. His impromptu, high-pitched impressions of Carol Kirkwood, the BBC weather presenter – who I suspect he secretly has a crush on – have to be heard to be believed.

To the Doc's right, at the rear of the truck, tucked behind a little curtain, is engineer Dave Thwaites, or Iron Dave as he's known. He arrives each year at the start of the race on a Brompton folding bike, all his possessions for the month stowed neatly in the basket. Dave regularly gets up at dawn or even earlier to ride it over some of Europe's highest mountains. Alpe d'Huez, Mont Ventoux, the Tourmalet: Dave has conquered them all on two small wheels.

When I started full time for ITV in 2003, the entirety of my job was to stand on the set and answer questions when asked. That task, filling the gaps between interesting stuff happening, took up a full ten minutes of each day. My responsibilities expanded slightly the following year when the Doc, finding himself staring at the prospect of televising a long and particularly boring flat stage, asked me to go and describe the last kilometre, where all the action was likely to be. I felt like a kid who'd been allowed to cross the road on his own for the first time.

The entire morning was spent crafting a minute-long script. Just before midday, I headed out to the finish line to record my monologue with our Aussie cameraman, John Tinetti. Experienced, mild-mannered and patient, John was the perfect partner for a newbie like me. The process of speaking a single sentence without stumbling was surprisingly difficult and my focus wasn't helped by cycling legend Sean Kelly squirting water at me from the second-storey window of the commentary box. I pretended it was all very amusing, all in a day's work for 'us pros'. Mentally, I was throttling him. The feature, though, earned me one of the Doc's rare praise-nuggets. After that they became my regular little contribution.

Sitting between Gary and Steve often feels like being on Dragons' Den: having to explain an idea to straight-talking, poker-faced industry experts, then wait while they mull it over, wondering what form the feedback might take. It's not a process for the sensitive, but it is a unique, even privileged, learning environment. Over the years, the Doc has shifted from specifying tasks to prodding me to generate ideas. Along with Gary, he'll take what I come up with, help me scope out how it might be illustrated, and proofread my scripts. The process feeds into my love of making things and their professional generosity is a big part of what keeps me going back. Well, that and the Doc's impressions.

In May 2011, sitting in a West Kirby café with Sally, I had an idea (OK, she had the idea) for something more involved than anything I'd done to date: a series of features to explain the technical aspects of bike riding to the non-expert audience: three-minute packages to enlighten the uninitiated without patronising the more experienced viewers. To do them properly, though, would mean planning and shooting them in advance of the Tour and that would take some of the show's precious budget. I emailed an outline to Carolyn Viccari, the executive producer, and to the Doc. The next day, I got a reply from the latter:

OK.

Steve.

I was immediately daunted by the responsibility those two confirmatory letters had put on my shoulders. As previous attempts to explain the inner workings of the peloton had been done using plastic figures and sugar cubes arranged in formation on a café table, I suppose the bar hadn't exactly been set high.

Although I knew how I wanted to illustrate my points – on a bike while riding – I realised I couldn't do it on my own; a single rider in a crosswind looks very much like a single rider in no wind. I needed an accomplice. Ned Boulting was the perfect candidate for the role by virtue of being the only candidate.

Ned and I started working on the race for ITV at about the same time. We are often mistaken for each other, something we've never really understood as we are very different people: I'm a planner, Ned thrives on busking it; I'm a worrier, he's happy to go live on air with no idea of how he's going to fill the space until he starts talking; he's been known to wear cowboy hats and sing badly in public, I'm normal.

The day before the 2011 Tour started, we assembled on a nondescript country lane in north west France – an out of condition ex-pro, a novice cyclist and a bemused TV crew following along in a Renault Espace. We had six features to film, the first of which was to show the effect of a crosswind on the peloton: how the riders fan out across the road to take shelter and what happens if one of them is forced to ride into it alone. The direction notes I'd written for the piece read: *Ned rides behind, moves out into wind and is slowly dropped. In front, CB explains to camera what's happening and why.*

As I rode at a steady pace down the lane, delivering my lines on the finer points of echelon riding, Ned brought the full force of the amateur dramatics training he's never had to bear on his supporting role. He swerved out into the road and began rocking with exaggerated effort from side to side, straining, gurning, head bobbing like a piston. He wobbled to a stop, dismounted and threw his bike into the hedge in mock frustration. I ploughed on, playing it straight, mostly because I didn't know what else to do. I was so nervous that I made myself scarce when the rushes went back to the truck for viewing. Oddly, though, the combination of the deadpan and the daft seemed to work. The pieces went down well and have now become a staple of the show. Over the past few years I've put Ned in a wind tunnel, hosed him down in a car park and subjected him to analysis on a psychiatrist's couch. I've no idea what to do next with a man who simply refuses to be humiliated.

Rob Llewellyn the responsible adult, Scottish Liam, Thumbless Tinetti, Blincoe the guitar playing soundman, Suave Mike the technical producer, Phillippe, Odette and Romain our wonderful caterers ... there are whole books to be written about the Tour de France cast – and that's without mentioning Carolyn, Brian and James back in London. Suffice it to say that they are my summer family, for better or worse. And like a family, we squabble, fight, walk out and walk back in, touching all points on the emotional compass every year regardless of the route.

For all the drama, though, we keep coming back year after year, I'm not sure we can help ourselves. There's a definite touch of Groundhog Day to the Tour; the same jokes and conversations and characters on what, a couple of days into it, begins to feel like an endless loop.

The 2012 race was different, though. A British rider was going to win it.

Three years earlier, I'd stood in one of the nondescript meeting rooms underneath the track at Manchester Velodrome, listening to Dave Brailsford predict exactly that to Christian Prudhomme, the Director of the Tour de France.

After Beijing, the new Sky professional team had become Dave's all-consuming passion and I'd enjoyed playing a small part in getting it off the ground. Although it was brilliant seeing him turn another dream into reality, and it was always tempting to get involved, this was clearly another 110 per cent all-in DB project, so I had reluctantly declined any full-time position with the outfit.

Under his leadership, the GB squad had achieved so many unthinkable results that people had began to doubt their own judgement before questioning his, but when he assured the Tour boss he'd win the race with a British rider inside five years, even I had raised an eyebrow. I'd have raised both if he'd said the rider was going to be Bradley Wiggins. But here we were on top of the Col de Peyragudes, the final summit finish of the 2012 Tour, and Brad had just comfortably defended his yellow jersey on what was realistically the last chance for anyone to take it off him. With just a flat stage, a time trial and the procession into Paris to come, Dave's dream was all but realised and he'd done it in just over half the time he'd allotted himself.

I'd watched as Brad, supported by a team clearly much stronger than the opposition, rode a tactically perfect race. Day after day, we waited for someone to cock-up, or someone to crop-up and take the jersey from him because, well, Brits didn't win the Tour. It felt akin to my own experience in 1992, where I'd sat on the start line for an Olympic final, knowing I had been the fastest all the way through but still not believing for a moment that people like me could win events like this. It turned out they could.

Post-stage, the work continued at a frantic pace for the TV crews, as evening highlight shows were crafted and beamed out to a waiting world. Around us, the crowd noise slowly ebbed away to nothing as people drifted off to bars, hotels and their cars to head home. On the slopes below us only a Sky Jaguar and camper van were left in the team parking area, probably waiting for a police convoy to escort them down into the valley. Leaning against the side of the sleek black Jag was Dave B, chatting away to the last few reporters. My work for the day was finished, so the normal thing to do would be to go and say hello to my friend and colleague. But I hesitated.

From the moment I retired, I have always felt uncomfortable around sporting stars or anyone having their moment in the spotlight. I've never been able to pin down exactly why, but I do know a large part of it is not wanting to be thought of as a hanger-on, someone trying to capitalise on another's success. Here, though, I was torn. I didn't want to intrude but I would have felt even worse if I hadn't at least gone down to say well done. Eventually, I pushed my feelings of awkwardness aside and scrambled down the embankment towards Dave and the handful of people milling around him.

The quietness of the mountainside felt wrong after what had just taken place: a jarring contrast I'd experienced many times around sporting high spots but never got used to. One moment, you are in a soup of noise and emotion, the deafening sound of low flying helicopters and blaring motorbike horns egging on tens of thousands of frenzied fans. Then, an impossibly short time later, it's all gone, and you're picking up your bag and heading home just like everyone else.

Down in the dusty car park, I shook hands with my British Cycling boss and offered congratulations. The words seemed wholly inadequate for what had been achieved. As I leaned against the car next to him, I watched the few Sky staffers left on the hillside shuffle about looking slightly dazed, trying to come to terms with the job being almost done. I hadn't realised that Brad was actually still on site, holed-up in the camper van behind me, probably enjoying the peace after defending his lead for ten days straight. Urged on by Dave, I reluctantly interrupted the race leader's quiet time and popped my head around the camper van door. There was Brad, skeletally thin and still dressed in yellow, sprawled on the bench seat, not looking at all like a man about to achieve something no other Brit had done before. More inadequate congratulations followed, then we had a brief chat about the next objective on his list, the looming Olympic time trial.

Although the Games weren't due to start for another nine days, they had already made their presence felt in the ITV truck in the guise of what I first thought was a hoax email. Apparently sent by an assistant to the director of the London 2012 opening ceremony, its subject was '*A fabulous cycling sequence that Danny Boyle would love you to be a featured part of*'. It was very short notice for what was a global event, and oddly vague. I strongly suspected a prank was being orchestrated by one of the people around me, so I proceeded with caution.

After obtaining permission from the BBC to take part if I wished (as they would be my employers for the period of the Olympics) I was sent a very legitimate-looking non-disclosure agreement to sign before I could be given any more details. That done, the following arrived from the cast co-ordinator for the ceremony:

'In brief, the segment is known as the Bike ballet and show-cases a variety of different skills, from BMX and Flatland to a forty-strong peloton and giant pyrotechnic bicycle. As you may know, one of the compulsory elements in any Olympic Opening Ceremony is the release of doves. Danny has chosen to do this using bikes with a cyclist whose costume is an enormous set of wings. The role we would like you to take is that of the Hero Dove Bike. This is an aerial role and would be the dove being "released" into the air.'

Now I was stuck. The source had been authenticated, so it wasn't a joke, yet what they wanted me to do seemed to be exactly that: fly across the Olympic arena dressed as a giant pigeon, complete with flapping wings.

I shared the information with Gary and the Doc. Big mistake. Steve turned to me, wearing his most serious expression: 'Chris, you've got to do it, the nation has called, it needs you to be … its Hero Dove.' The pair of them fell about laughing, describing possible scenarios: 'Now! Now! Flap harder, Boardman!' It kept them amused for the last couple of days in France. I politely declined the invitation but was still called Hero Dove until we reached Paris.

The rest of the race went as expected and Bradley marked his overall victory by delivering a devastating lead-out for his teammate Mark Cavendish to win the final stage in Paris. I winced a little as the Manxman crossed the line, fearing the damage he'd done to his chances in the Olympic road race. It would have taken superhuman restraint and strategic foresight from the reigning world champion to lose in Paris in order to give himself a better chance in London. But there was no getting away from the fact that his victory on the Champs-Élysées had just sent a message to his rivals: 'If you want to win the Olympics, you absolutely do not want me to be there when you arrive on The Mall.' It was arguably the moment he lost the chance of a gold medal.

After the teams had paraded up and down the Champs and the VIPs had quaffed the last of the champagne, we started the long and final pack of the truck. There's no good way to end a month like that. Everybody who works on the Tour dreams about the fantastic final party waiting in Paris, but every year, by the time we get there, we are all knackered.

Some immediately head off for planes and trains. Others dash back to our regular Paris base, the Hotel Alison, a lovingly maintained 1970s time-capsule, to dump bags before stubbornly heading out, bleary-eyed, in search of a restaurant still serving at 10 p.m. Having been in the latter group, I woke up next morning thick-headed and threw the last of my stuff into my old GAN team-issue suitcase. The red Samsonite relic saw service precisely once a year, for this event, as it kept a month's worth of TV shirts pressed and ready for duty. One taxi ride later, I arrived at a heaving Charles de Gaulle and joined the 300 metre-long easyJet queue. As I shuffled forward, I wondered if Brad and the other guys would be on the same budget flight back to Manchester. Probably not.

CHAPTER 20

London 2012

The Holiday Inn Express in Newbury Park was my home for the duration of the 2012 Olympics. It wasn't exactly The Ritz, but it did have one redeeming feature – it was just 150 metres from the extraordinary Curry Special, a fact that made floor manager Matt Wayne very happy.

There are people in life who can make pretty much any situation fun and Matt is one of them. We could have been in a plane crash and he'd have admired the view and cracked a few jokes on the way down. In 2010, Matt and I had worked for the BBC at the Commonwealth Games in Delhi. On our first evening in the Indian capital a group of us hailed Tuk Tuks – petrol tanks with three wheels crudely welded on as far as I could make out – and headed on to the chaotic streets in search of a curry. After the many media scare stories about security in Delhi, we were pleasantly surprised by the lovely people and vibrant nightlife. It was certainly heart-wrenching to see abject poverty living cheek by jowl with wealth, but at no time did we feel anything other than completely safe.

The next night, Matt suggested jokingly, 'Why don't we go for another curry?' Which we did. The question was repeated the following evening, with the same result, and what had started out as a joke turned into a challenge and eventually a nightly chorus: 'Of course we're going for a curry!' In the end we managed 12 in a row and in the process formed what became known in BBC circles as The Curry Club. Myself, Matt and presenter Jill Douglas were its founder members.

In London, the tradition was continued. After our third visit to Curry Special in as many days, the management realised they were on to a good thing and assigned us our own corner. It was from there, Peshwari naan in hand, that I watched the opening ceremony. No one could identify the Hero Dove but at least I had an alibi. Over the period of the Games, we hosted several well-known guests at our table – the photographs, I believe, are still on the wall – and even appointed Sue Barker as the club's honorary president, a proud moment in her career.

On 28 July, the day after the opening ceremony, I dashed down the crowded Mall after completing an interview with Tanni Grey-Thompson for radio. At the second security check in just 200 metres, I did the 'I'm late' shuffle and sighed as loudly as I could while the journalists in front of me took ages removing laptops from their bags for inspection. I ran up the gantry steps to the commentary box to join my colleague Hugh Porter, slipped my headphones on, deadening the crowd noise, and hit the red talk button on the console in front of me. Seconds later the first Olympic cycling event, the men's road race, got underway.

The GB squad's tactics for the day were already widely known and had even been fully rehearsed a year earlier in Copenhagen to help Mark Cavendish take the world title. On that occasion, the British team had sat on the front for the majority of the 266-kilometre race, stifling all attempts to form a winning break-away. I'd commentated on Mark's win and remembered my mixed feelings at the time. I was happy to see the British flag flying over the podium, but I also knew that the team had just publicised every aspect of their Olympic plan in order to put it there, something the riders had confirmed enthusiastically to reporters in post-race inter-views. Cavendish's victory in Paris the previous weekend had been a reminder of both the plan and his form.

The GB squad had been kitted out with every advantage the Squirrels could provide: smoothed helmets, tailored clothing, over-socks, even the bikes they relied on as professionals had been swapped for custom machines. But no amount of technology or athletic ability could compensate for the one big difference between this event and their victorious outing of the year before: Great Brit-ain's team at the World Championships had been made up of eight riders, the Olympics allowed a maximum of only five. That meant four men – with Cavendish held in reserve – charged with control-ling a field of the best cyclists in the world. Given this reduction in troop numbers, sticking with the same tactics seemed outlandish, even arrogant. But in the light of recent events, with the British regularly achieving the impossible, no one wanted to say it out loud – including me. And as *domestiques* go, the group of Brad Wiggins, Chris Froome, Ian Stannard and David Millar might well have been the strongest ever assembled.

Early in the race, a group of lesser-known riders slipped away to form a break. It was standard stuff and nothing to be too concerned about. As expected, the GB riders lined up at the front of the main field and began to ride tempo. As the laps ticked by, though, some of their more dangerous rivals began to test the water. In the peloton, everyone watched and waited for the big acceleration: the moment when the British would put the hammer down and reel in the escapees, but there was no miraculous injection of pace. They kept things steady and the other favourites kept following. No other nations came forward to share the work because no one wanted to help Cavendish win a bunch sprint. The situation was crying out for a Plan B: a British rider attacking, perhaps – anything to disrupt the grim pattern the race was settling into. Never mind the high-tech kit we'd designed for them, this was more like The Emperor's New Clothes. Everyone – riders, press and commentators – could see the truth of it but no one was voicing their doubts.

As the Brits continued to toil away, more and more of their rivals attacked off the front. By the time they entered the final lap of the finishing circuit, more than 20 riders had coalesced to form a strong, well-coordinated group nearly a minute ahead of the British-led bunch.

Slowly, it began to dawn on those who had kept the faith to this point that there wasn't going to be a miracle. Team GB had let their chance of victory escape. The breakaway riders might not have been of the same quality as Cavendish's helpers, but they were working well together and their numbers were now overwhelming. The British team, who had prepared for this day for years, never figured in the race. Alexander Vinokourov of Kazakhstan won the gold medal. Mark Cavendish came in over five minutes down.

It was an inauspicious start and the British media were a little shaken to see that the all-conquering Brits were fallible after all. Maybe the home Games weren't going to be the fairytale they'd expected.

The national mood brightened 24 hours later when Lizzie Armitstead opened Britain's account with a thrilling, rain-soaked performance in the women's road race to take silver behind Marianne Vos of the Netherlands. And on day five the gold rush finally got underway with Brad Wiggins's victory in the individual time trial. The Tour and Olympic double was an astonishing achievement and should have heralded the start of a long reign at the top of professional road racing for Brad. Incredibly, it marked the beginning of the end.

For the exhausted R&D team, Brad's win was a morale-booster. He'd done it on a Squirrel-supplied bike, wearing the first of the new aero helmets we'd worked so hard to perfect. The bulk of the products we'd developed, though, had yet to be used in competition. All through the Tour de France and since I'd arrived in London, I'd been in daily contact with Matt Parker who had been frantically managing the final delivery of clothing and equipment on my behalf. The schedule was incredibly tight and a handful of the items were still being manufactured as the Games got underway.

The road races completed, Hugh Porter and I decamped to the new Olympic Velodrome in Stratford and took our seats in the commentary box for the first of the track events, the men's team sprint. This would be the first test of a piece of equipment that Matt had been sweating over: the new super-stiff cranks that had been designed primarily for the sprinters. These were the men who would strain the new carbon parts to the maximum, driving more power through them as they burst from the start gate than two endurance riders combined. As they'd arrived only days earlier there had been almost no time to use them in training, so although they'd been fully tested in the lab they'd never been used in anger.

The stadium was packed to capacity and the heat was stifling. The noise dropped away as the GB trio of Philip Hindes, Jason Kenny and Chris Hoy took to the track for their qualifying ride. No one knew what to expect. Great Britain were the reigning Olympic champions, but they'd lost one of the best starters in the world when Jamie Staff had retired after Beijing, and they hadn't won a major title since.

In an event often settled by hundredths of a second, the lack of a strong lead-off man had seen Great Britain slip behind the other major nations. Ironic, then, that it should be one of their big rivals, Germany, who had provided the solution. Carrying dual nationality, 19-year-old Philip Hindes had started out on the German national squad and represented them at the 2010 Junior Worlds. Shortly after, his father's military career brought him to the UK where he was asked by GB sprint coach Jan van Eijden – also German – to try out for the British squad. Despite his youth, he had been a revelation and progressed rapidly. Even so, he'd made the team relatively late and was short on experience under pressure. He'd certainly never performed on a stage like this.

The familiar countdown beeps sounded. Half a second after the penultimate tone, the three riders threw their weight backwards in perfect unison. An instant later, as if they had been leaning on invisible giant springs, they catapulted themselves forward in anticipation of the start gate's release. For a moment it looked like a textbook start, perfectly timed. But there was a problem. Hindes seemed first to wobble, then stall after the first few pedal strokes. Kenny and Hoy passed him and as they entered the first bend he fell sideways in slow motion to the boards.

Up in the stands, I was shocked into silence – which is not great for a commentator – convinced that it was the new cranks that had failed, perhaps robbing three great athletes of their chance at Olympic gold, years of work destroyed. I looked on, stunned, leaving Hugh to do the talking as replay after replay passed before us on the screens. Looking at the images, it eventually became clear that it wasn't the equipment that had failed after all. I breathed a sigh of relief.

We still didn't know what the cause of the crash was as the team rolled back to the line for their second and final chance – another botched start and they'd be out. This time the GB three got away cleanly. 43.065 seconds later their qualification ride was over and what had looked like a disaster had been turned into an Olympic record. In the next round they also broke the world record, then broke it again in the final as they beat France to take gold.

It was only once he had the medal round his neck that Philip Hindes explained his fall. Interviewed alongside Hoy and Kenny after they stepped off the podium, he told Jill Douglas he'd gone down deliberately because he thought his start wasn't good enough and he knew that a 'crash' would ensure a restart! I thought the press – and the French – would have a field day with this admission.

It was hurriedly corrected by the GB team and put down to Hindes' poor grasp of English. The major fallout never came and the standard had been set for six sensational days in the velodrome.

That evening, my hopes of celebrating by closing in on the consecutive-curry record set in Delhi were dashed. I was drafted in by British Cycling's Policy and Legal Affairs Director, Martin Gibbs, to make an appearance on BBC Two's *Newsnight* to discuss cycling, both as a sport and a viable alternative to driving.

My first foray into the world of transport policy had been in 2003 when I'd sat on the National Cycling Strategy Board, a body set up by government supposedly to advise on ways to increase cycling. It took me just under two years to realise there was zero appetite to do anything meaningful to achieve the stated goal and that setting up the committee represented the entirety of government action on cycling. I resigned soon after.

Now, though, the climate was different. The unprecedented success of the GB team ever since the Beijing Olympics had given both the general public and the press an awareness of cycling that had been missing a decade earlier and their interest seemed to be intensifying. Something which had been viewed by many decision makers as a frivolous leisure pursuit that got in the way of the serious adult business of driving was now being discussed as a genuine transport solution.

It was an easy cause to champion: it lowered pollution, reduced congestion, improved health and was cheap to implement. There was just no logical downside to cycling as a means of transport. In a civilised society it should have been the obvious way to get about, particularly since nearly 70 per cent of UK car journeys were under five miles. Yet despite the mountains of evidence in favour of promoting cycling – much of it generated by government departments – many in Westminster were just as uninterested in two-wheeled transport as they had always been. They simply didn't like it and had no intention of letting facts guide their decisions. Unfortunately for them, public opinion and a good press were something that couldn't be ignored. But the smiles and positive words would never lead to actual change unless some traction could be gained while the sun was shining on the sport. That's why my appearance on a programme that usually dealt with matters of state was so important.

The interviewer, Emily Maitlis, was used to grilling thick-skinned politicians so I wasn't sure what to expect. In this instance, it seemed neither was she; I was given a very easy ride and was able to segue from Olympic sport to extolling the wider virtues of cycling without challenge. Perhaps because it was novel to see a former athlete on a grown-up programme, my *Newsnight* appearance caused quite a stir. For me, this period marked a new relationship with cycling; I became an advocate, a political activist for the two-wheeled cause.

For the rest of the week, I commentated on the track racing alongside Hugh, hardly believing what I was seeing. I'd thought we had made a rod for our own back in Beijing by showing just how much technology could enhance performance. It had seemed like an invitation to the opposition to spend the next four years emulating the GB approach, so I'd come to London expecting to see a much closer contest. Instead, what I was witnessing, with increasing delight, was the other nations using the same equipment, clothing and techniques as they had at the previous Games. To my mind, this was tantamount to negligence on the part of their national associations, but an unexpected gift for a GB team on home soil.

It's one thing to have a technical advantage, but no amount of clever carbon can help individuals deal with pressure, cope with career-defining challenges measured out in millimetres, or make good decisions in less than a heartbeat. Throughout the week, British riders showed themselves able to deliver lifetime bests on demand: Laura Trott displayed the most sophisticated bike-handling skills I have ever seen to win the inaugural Olympic omnium event; her boyfriend Jason Kenny surprised everyone by taking the men's sprint title; and Victoria Pendleton, in her last event before retirement, bounced back from disqualification in the team sprint to take gold in the keirin.

The performance of the Games, though, came from Chris Hoy. On the final night of track competition, the Scotsman added to his gold in the team sprint with victory in the keirin. That brought his lifetime total of Olympic golds to six, beating rowing legend Sir Steve Redgrave who was in the velodrome to congratulate him. Ten track events and the British squad had won seven of them.

Due to the security arrangements unique to an Olympics, it was almost impossible to interact with the team, but I was happy to watch from a distance. I was delighted to see riders and coaches who had been such a big part of my life for the last decade fulfil their potential, some for the first time, others for the last. I wasn't the least bit sad that it also signified the end for me: who could have asked for a better note on which to bow out? Back in Newbury

Park, we celebrated the team's victory in the traditional BBC way: biryani and beer.

My focus at the Games wasn't solely on cycling; triathlon was also on my radar, even though I wasn't commentating on it. Four years earlier I'd watched a tenacious 20-year-old, Alistair Brownlee, compete at his first Olympics, and enjoyed his take-no-prisoners approach to the sport. He had made quite an impact on the Beijing race until he cracked spectacularly near the finish and fell out of the running. Alan Ingarfield had spotted both Alistair and his younger brother Jonny in 2006 and was so taken with their style that he'd backed them even before we had a company. Boardman Bikes had sponsored them ever since, so it was with delight that I watched Alistair win his Olympic title and Jonny take bronze. Our young business had supported a handful of athletes at two Olympics now and on both occasions we'd seen them win gold.

The end of my time in Olympic sport was fast approaching. As I had been in 2000 when my riding days ended, I was ready for it, excited for what was coming next and relieved that I hadn't cocked it up at the last by trying to juggle too many balls at once. The only thing I was going to miss was the company of the people I'd grown close to along the way. It was cycling that had brought us together, and given how intense the world of sport is I knew it would be hard to maintain relationships once we were no longer working side by side. It was time for us all to move on.

As the competition drew to a close, I had one last TV duty to perform, a short interview with Gary Lineker in the Olympic Stadium at the start of the closing ceremony. After that, my time was my own.

Seeing and hearing a stadium packed with 80,000 people, all gathered together to watch the end of the greatest sporting show on earth, is a spectacular, even daunting thing to witness. Yet, despite having a prized spot from which to watch the pageantry, I felt no compunction to stay. I no longer felt as if I belonged, or wanted to. I was happy to catch a lift with one of the BBC cars ferrying celebrities and sports stars to and fro. One of them happened to be heading to the Holiday Inn where my little car was already packed and ready for the trip north, back to Sally, the kids and my stupid dog.

I settled into the seat and set the satnav: 238 miles to home. I put my earphones in, started my audio book, Iain Banks's *The Wasp Factory*, and set off for the M25, using the dying moments of the Olympics as my cover to escape.

It had been bloody brilliant.

Epilogue: The Kids

Telling people how many children I have invariably gets the same response: 'Six?!' followed up with one of four questions:

>'Are any of them cyclists?'
>'Are you Catholic?'
>'Are they all yours?'
>'How do you cope?'

My replies have become equally standardised:

>'No, they're all normal.'
>'I'm an honorary member.'
>'You're asking the wrong person.'
>'Oh, you go numb after three.'

Having such a large family, it might seem strange that I've barely mentioned them in these pages but it has been an intentional omission. Having a fairly public life, I value being able to walk away from the spotlight and have a private existence. That said, the kids are the most important part of my life, which makes it impossible to write an autobiography without at least telling the world a tiny bit about them. My children have been a constant source of surprise, not least because of how different they all are from each other in both appearance and character.

Ed is our oldest and so was our learner-child; everything we did with him was for the first time. We were so young when he arrived – 20 – that in a sense we all grew up together. From the start he was a sensitive soul, scared of loud noises and reluctant to try anything new. Despite being dyslexic, as a child he loved to write, a passion that stayed with him and eventually led him to Southampton University where he studied creative writing. He was the guinea pig for one of my first parental decisions; we would not financially cosset our offspring. I thought this would encourage (force) him to get out there and make his way in the world. It never occurred to me that I might simply be teaching him to find ways to live on next to nothing. Which is what Ed did.

For the three years he was in Southampton, rather than give him a budget that he could blow on beer, Sally paid online for a weekly delivery of Tesco's basics. If he wanted to party, he'd have to find a job. Although he couldn't see why we wouldn't trust him, he did condescend to help us out and sent a list of his essential requirements: ciabatta, Parma ham, hummus, extra virgin olive oil and Lavazza coffee. We laughed, before signing him up for some bumper packs of super noodles and value bread. We did send him some decent coffee, though. We weren't monsters.

Since university, he has continued to eschew a material life and frequently spends months away, backpacking around Europe, picking grapes in Bordeaux and strawberries in Denmark. It's a lifestyle I dare say I'd have enjoyed. But had I ever mustered the imagination to even consider it, I'd have focused on all the things that could go wrong and talked myself out of it before breakfast.

Next to come along was Harriet, who is also imaginative and courageous but in a very different way. Although not the oldest, she was the first to get her own place and move out of the family home. When she told us she had got a job looking after mentally disabled adults, I was surprised that she would take on such an all-consuming task. Only in her late teens, I was sure she wouldn't last for more than a few weeks, but I thought it would be a good experience for her. She proved me wrong.

When someone in her care died, I was touched both by how much it meant to her and the steel she showed in dealing with a situation that would have had me in bits. 'If you can't change things you have to crack on with making the best of them. Someone's got to care, why not me?' was her response when I asked her how she coped. Five years later, she's still in the job while simultaneously taking a degree in psychology at Liverpool's John Moores University.

Harriet is the person I turn to whenever I can't work out what Christmas/birthday/anniversary present to buy her mother. She never fails to bail me out.

George, sadly for him, is the closest in character to me: an obsessive and a worrier. At 14 he got interested in tennis. Rather than play a bit with friends, he became fanatical and volunteered as an assistant coach at the local David Lloyd tennis centre until he was old enough to take his LTA qualifications. Three years later, he was coaching full-time at a world-renowned academy in Boca Raton, Florida. Now back home, he has followed Harriet in studying psychology. I'm not sure how to feel about that. I suppose in a couple of years one of them will be able to tell me.

If George is a fanatic and a worrier, his brother Oscar, 18 months his junior, is his alter ego. Although 20, he still spends full days holed up in our TV room with his mates playing *Magic: The Gathering*. If you don't know what that is, you'll have to look it up online, as I had to. His favourite drink is a cosmopolitan, which must look odd when he's in the pub with his cider-drinking student mates – he is also at university, studying chemistry. Oscar has already stated his intention not to engage with the real world. There is no history in our family of anyone going into the teaching profession – I barely made it through school – but Oscar was made for academia. With his quiet demeanour and floppy hair cascading down his bespectacled face, he is so geeky he's the height of cool.

My youngest boy, Sonny, could not be more different from our firstborn. While Ed was quiet and sensitive, Sonny is outgoing, loud and already displaying strong theatrical tendencies. In the winter of 2010 we took him and his sister to a pantomime in Chester. Halfway through, Old Mother Hubbard asked for three volunteers. Unbeknown to Sonny, who was streaking down the aisle towards the stage, these had been chosen in advance by the producers, but such was his almost frightening enthusiasm that they were obliged to let him participate. Which he did, loudly. Having tasted fame, we've had to physically hold him back on several occasions since. Utterly without inhibitions, he's quick to show emotion and will often sing or break into a dance in public. I hope his teenage years don't change him.

Finally there is Agatha, who is a miniature version of her mother: smart, observant and calculating. By the age of eight she had established an art club at school, complete with a colour-coded project list, timetable and register. By ten she could have managed a small business. The first possession I can remember her coveting was a mermaid's tail. After a week of meticulous research, she presented her mother with a list of the best candidates along with a price breakdown. She bought it with her own money and waited nearly six months before we went on holiday to a place where she could actually use it. At the pool, it made her the centre of attention and she soon had a crowd of admirers, which is exactly what she had planned. I have no doubt she will go far in life.

Christmases are loud and messy in the Boardman household and holidays are like full-scale troop manoeuvres. We have plenty of family gatherings and with the older children we often occupy a table at the local pub quiz. My mum and dad regularly attend these and I love to see them all together, although I'm not sure having a team of eight goes down too well with the other contestants.

As an athlete I rode the emotional rollercoaster. With highs and lows surrounding every training session and competition, my psychological responses were usually way out of proportion to the magnitude of the events themselves. Without being able to come home to an ever-expanding house full of the ultimate perspective-givers, who didn't give a toss whether I won or lost, I'd have drowned in self-pity long before the Olympics in 1992, never mind my pro years.

I have perhaps painted a rosy picture of parenthood here, but it hasn't all been perfect and I have plenty of regrets. During the kids' formative years I was so wrapped up in my own passions that I didn't pay nearly enough attention to theirs. I've not been the dad that I hoped I would be. Luckily for them, they have an amazing mother who has spent more than two decades running around gathering up all the slack I left.

Whenever anyone asks us for advice on bringing up kids, we usually just say we have none to give, you'll have to make it up as you go. But if I had to offer an observation it would be this: you get what you give. Everything else is stuff that happens along the way.

Thanks

This is the spot in the book where I get to thank all the people that helped me get to the finish line. It was a task that petrified me because I knew with cold certainty that I would leave one of them out. So, rather than risk a hurtful omission, I've decided to offend everyone equally and leave all of them out. Yes, I am a coward.

There is one individual though that absolutely has to be acknowledged or I couldn't live with myself; Gary Imlach, the editor of this book and my mentor for the painful 2.5 years it took to finish. Incapable of doing anything 'a bit', Gary put his heart and soul into the project, holding me to account for fudging facts (it was not uncommon to get an annotated draft back with the words 'you lying bastard' in the margins), helping me discover a unified writing style and steering me away from rambling jokes that only I thought were funny. It wasn't an easy working relationship but I've never been in a worthwhile partnership that was. I'm deeply grateful for his guidance. Ta La.

Photo credits